Wok & Stir-Fry Cooking
AT • THE • ACADEMY

JOYCE JUE
Writer

BARBARA FELLER-ROTH
Editor

KEITH OVREGAARD
Photographer

STEPHANIE GREENLEIGH
Food Stylist

AMY GLENN
Photographic Stylist

CALIFORNIA CULINARY ACADEMY

Joyce Jue is a culinary instructor and an authority on Asian cuisines. A native San Franciscan, she has studied cooking in France, Spain, Hong Kong, Thailand, and Singapore. Jue designs and leads her own cooking tours of Asia, produces special culinary events, and consults to cookware manufacturers and food corporations. She has been a guest food editor for the San Francisco Examiner and has written numerous food articles in national publications. As a culinary personality, she has been featured in newspapers in the United States, Hong Kong, and Thailand and has made appearances on U.S. and Hong Kong television. She was consultant to the prestigious Thai Cooking School at the Oriental Hotel in Bangkok, Thailand. She is a member of the American Institute of Wine & Food, the San Francisco Professional Food Society, the International Association of Cooking Professionals, and the United States–China Educational Institute.

The California Culinary Academy In the forefront of American institutions leading the culinary renaissance in this country, the California Culinary Academy in San Francisco has gained a reputation as one of the most outstanding professional chef training schools in the world. With a teaching staff recruited from the best restaurants of Western Europe, the Academy educates students from around the globe in the preparation of classical cuisine. The recipes in this book were created in consultation with the chefs of the Academy. For information about the Academy, write the Office of the Dean, California Culinary Academy, 625 Polk St., San Francisco, CA 94102.

Front Cover
Ants Climbing a Tree, a traditional Szechuan dish, uses bits of pork and translucent bean thread noodles (page 100).

Title page
East meets West in an unexpected combination of cooking techniques in Pasta With Tea-Smoked Duck, Grilled Mushrooms, and Arugula (recipe page 88/photo page 89).

Back Cover
Upper: Dry-frying prawns in the shell imparts a crunchy texture and intense flavor (page 80).
Lower: Serve Dry-Fried Spicy Shredded Beef as a first course to stimulate the palate. Its jerky-like texture and twig-like appearance are intriguing and its slightly sweet, peppery flavor is tantalizing (page 101).

Special thanks to The Art Co-op; Diane Blacker; Brad Borel; Virgina Breier; Beth Corwin; Cottonwood; Sally Dinwoodie; Peggy Fallon; Fauxcus; Fillamento; Ward Finer; The Gardener; Annie Glass; Bea and Marty Glenn; Nancy Glenn; J. Goldsmith Antiques; Leigh Hughes; Randall Kay; Sue Fisher King; James Nassikas; Doug Ohm; Erikas Paper; Jeff Paris; Paula Ross; Francesca Roveda; Glenys Hunt Rowan; RushCutters; Jan Schacter; Natalie Sellers; Sally Smith; Patricia Stapley; John Swindle; the Thai Cooking School at the Oriental Hotel, Bankok, Thailand; Chris Tong; Vee Tuteur; Jerome White; Martin Yan; Zosaku.

Contributors

Calligraphers
Keith Carlson, Chuck Wertman

Illustrator
Edith Allgood

Additional Photographers
Alan Copeland, Academy photography
Kit Morris, author
Richard Tauber, pages 7, 20, 22, 40, 86, and 119

Additional Food Stylists
Will Guazzaloca, Randy Mon, Patricia Stapley, Clay Wollard

Photographic Design Consulting and Painted Backgrounds
Debbie Dicker

Copy Chief
Melinda E. Levine

Copyeditor
Ellen O. Setteducati

Editorial Assistant
Karen K. Johnson

Indexer
Elinor Lindheimer

Proofreader
Tova F. Fliegel

Series Format Design
Linda Hinrichs, Carol Kramer

Production
Lezlly Freier

Lithographed in the USA.

The California Culinary Academy Series is published by the staff of The Cole Group.

Publisher
Brete C. Harrison

Associate Publisher
James Connolly

Director of Operations
Linda Hauck

Director of Production
Steve Lux

Production Assistant
Dotti Hydue

Copyright © 1989, 1993 The Cole Group
All rights reserved under international and Pan American copyright conventions.

A B C D E F G H
3 4 5 6 7 8 9 0

ISBN 1-56426-044-5
CIP 92-44850

Address all inquiries to
The Cole Group
4415 Sonoma Highway/ PO Box 4089
Santa Rosa, CA 95402-4089
(707) 538-0492 FAX (707) 538-0497

Distributed to the book trade by
Publishers Group West

Wok & Stir-Fry Cooking

PLEASURES OF THE WOK   **5**
Stir-frying in a Wok   6
Types of Woks   6
Glossary of Ingredients   8
The Asian Pantry   13

APPETIZERS   **15**
Dim Sum   16
Deep-frying in a Wok   16
Boning Chicken Wings   22
Sauces, Dips, and Other
     Sundries   24
International Cocktail Party   28

BREAKFAST, LUNCH
    & SNACKS   **35**
Rice, Noodle, and
     Wonton Dishes   36
Making Perfect Rice   37
Making Barbecued
     Pork Buns   40
Classic Chinese Lunch   51

SALADS, SOUPS &
    VEGETABLES   **55**
Vegetables   56
Salads and Soups   65
A Refreshing Summer
     Brunch   69

SEAFOOD & POULTRY
    ENTRÉES   **73**
Fish and Shellfish   74
Poultry   83
Steaming in a Wok   86
Light Sunday Buffet   91

MEAT ENTRÉES   **95**
Pork   96
Beef and Lamb   101
Light Theater Supper
     For Six   107

FESTIVE FOODS   **111**
Entertainment Dishes   112
Making Stuffings in a Wok   114
Boning a Whole Chicken   119
An Elegant Dinner   120

Index   124
Metric Chart   128

Using a bamboo steaming basket in a wok makes this versatile pan an ideal vessel for steaming as well as for stir-frying.

Pleasures of the Wok

Versatility is one of the great features of the wok. In addition to stir-frying, which is explored in detail throughout this book, the wok is well suited to deep-frying, steaming, and even indoor smoking. Ideas and simple tricks to perfect these techniques are illustrated with easy stir-fried dishes such as Snow Peas, Pine Nuts, and Chinese Sausage (see page 57); classic dishes such as Steamed Whole Fish (see page 78) and Tea-Smoked Duck (see page 86); novel adaptations such as Pasta With Tea-Smoked Duck, Grilled Mushrooms, and Arugula (see page 88); and international recipes such as Tamales con Mole Verde de Pepitas (see page 30). Enjoy!

STIR-FRYING IN A WOK

Food trends come and go, with only a few weathering the high attrition rate. Stir-frying in a wok is one culinary tradition that has thrived for centuries in Asia. In the last decade it has become widely known throughout the world for its fuel and time efficiency and for its minimal use of oil.

THE WOK

Woks are available in various sizes, are made of any of several materials, and now come with such adaptations as flat bottoms, electric heat controls, and nonstick finishes. Yet the ancient round-bottomed prototype has remained essentially the same. After all is said and done, what one should look for in a wok are the bare necessities: the fewer trappings the better.

Types of Woks

The best woks are made of light iron manufactured in Asia, but they are becoming increasingly difficult to find. High-quality spun carbon steel woks (look for the fine rings visible on the sides of the wok) are perfectly acceptable and have been adapted by the Asian community in the United States. They conduct heat evenly and efficiently, respond immediately to stovetop temperature adjustments, and develop a seasoned finish that will not rust if the wok is properly cared for.

Woks made of stainless steel or cast aluminum and those with nonstick finishes are ideal for steaming, braising, and deep-frying. They are not recommended for stir-frying, because timing is crucial to the success of stir-frying and these metals do not respond as rapidly as carbon steel to stovetop temperature changes.

Round-bottomed woks, which come with a ring stand, are designed to be used on gas stoves. Remove the metal burner support on the stove and replace it with the ring stand placed wide edge up.

Flat-bottomed woks are designed to be used on electric stoves and should be set directly on the electric element without the ring stand.

A 14-inch wok is best suited for most needs in the home kitchen. Larger woks are cumbersome and can overwhelm an entire stove; a 12-inch wok, although it works well for apartment kitchens and small meals for two, is not as practical for general use, such as tossing noodle dishes, steaming, and smoking. The recipes in this book are written for a 14-inch flat-bottomed spun carbon steel wok, which works well on both gas and electric stoves.

Caring for a Wok

To season a new carbon steel wok, scrub it thoroughly inside and out with hot water, mild soap, and a steel wool scouring pad to remove the manufacturer's protective coating. Rinse thoroughly with hot water and dry with paper towels. Set the wok over medium heat and heat it until a few drops of water sprinkled in the wok dance across the surface. Pour 2 tablespoons vegetable oil into the wok and with paper towels wipe the oil over the entire inside surface. Reduce the heat to low and let the lightly oiled wok sit over the heat 15 minutes. Remove the wok from the burner and allow it to cool. Rinse with hot water and repeat the entire process without scouring. (Most non-carbon steel woks do not need to be seasoned. For their care follow the manufacturer's recommendations.)

With use, carbon steel woks take on a seasoned finish or patina that should never be scoured clean. Think of a seasoned wok as grandma's cherished cast-iron skillet. Rinse only with hot water and scrub gently with a dishwashing brush, not a scouring pad, to remove cooked-on food. If food is burnt on, dry the wok and add 2 to 3 tablespoons salt. Scour with paper towels, using the salt as an abrasive; rinse with hot water; and dry. If you absolutely must, use a very mild dishwashing soap to remove built-up grease. Dry wok with paper towels or set it over high heat to dry completely. Never put a wok in a dishwasher. If the wok becomes rusty, clean and scour only enough to remove the rust area; then dry the wok, wipe the dried surface with oil, and season again.

A well-seasoned wok exudes a special fragrance and flavor that the Chinese call *wok hay*. It is not unlike the special flavor produced by a well-tended cast-iron skillet or by an old coffee shop hamburger grill. As you become more accomplished with a wok, you will discover that wonderful flavor. There is no substitute or shortcut for wok hay; it comes from use.

Wok Accessories

A long-handled Chinese spatula or shovel, a ladle, a strainer, and a dome lid are essential accessories for a wok. The spatula has a slightly curved edge so that it slides smoothly over the rounded inside of the wok. The ladle facilitates the tossing of food, transfers liquids to the wok, and removes finished food from the wok.

Bamboo wire strainers come in sizes ranging from a 2-inch-wide cup-shaped strainer used to retrieve foods from a Mongolian fire pot to a 14-inch or wider strainer used to scoop wontons or noodles from a wok or to lower a whole chicken or duck into a wok for deep-frying. The strainers are indispensable and worth having in several sizes.

THE SECRET OF PERFECT STIR-FRYING

The keys to successful stir-frying are timing, preparation, and organization. Because most stir-fried dishes cook in only 3 to 5 minutes, sauces should be mixed ahead of time and seasonings arranged in small dishes within close reach of the stove. Meats and vegetables should be cut into suitably sized pieces before you begin cooking. Hard vegetables with long cooking times, such as cauliflower, broccoli, and carrots, should be cut into bite-sized pieces and either steamed (leaving them slightly underdone) or blanched in boiling water that has been "greased" with 1 tablespoon vegetable oil. Cook them 1 to 2 minutes short of being done, drain, rinse with cold water, and pat dry.

Moisten is a more appropriate term than *marinate* to describe what is actually done to cut-up meat, fish, and poultry before stir-frying. Stir-fried meat needs only to be moistened with a small amount of liquid rather than submerged. Moistening enhances the natural flavor of the food, suppresses unpleasant flavors and odors, and provides some protection from the hot oil.

The amount of moistening time is usually very short—from a few minutes to about 30 minutes. Remember, a marinade should enhance the flavor of the meat to be stir-fried, not mask it. Before adding marinated meat to a hot wok, check for too much liquid in the marinating bowl. Should there be a pool of liquid in the bottom of the bowl, pour out the excess and add just enough cornstarch to dry the meat.

The marinade for stir-fried meat, fish, or poultry is usually composed of five basic ingredients: wine, soy sauce, sugar, cornstarch, and oil. When adding each ingredient, keep in mind that the eye is a better gauge than a measuring spoon.

The fermented alcohol in the wine counteracts any unpleasant flavors and odors of the uncooked food. Add just enough wine to moisten the meat; too much prevents the meat from being seared when stir-fried. Soy sauce adds flavor and coloring. Add just enough to moisten the meat and give it a slight tint.

The Chinese believe that a healthy pinch of sugar acts much like salt; it enhances the natural flavor of ingredients. Unless the dish is meant to taste sweet, that pinch should not be detected. If it is forgotten, however, finely tuned palates can detect its absence.

Cornstarch absorbs excess marinating liquid, such as wine and soy sauce, and dries the meat for stir-frying. It serves the same purpose as a batter that traps meat juices. Use it sparingly, or you risk duplicating the gooey sauces that are frequently served in bad Chinese restaurants.

Finally, a little oil (preferably Asian sesame oil for its nutty aroma and flavor) lubricates the moistened meats for ease in stir-frying. Add just enough oil to give the meat a slight sheen.

In the recipes in this book, the marinades are mixed separately to facilitate advance preparation. After preparing a few stir-fried dishes, it will become second nature to you, as it is for the Chinese, to simply sprinkle the food—during both marinating and stir-frying—with some wine, soy sauce, sugar, cornstarch, and oil. Use just enough liquid to moisten the food and give it a slight sheen and tint. The likelihood of error decreases the more you depend on your eye and nose rather than measuring spoons.

The term *stir-frying* is not an accurate description of the process, since stirring can damage soft ingredients such as tofu. The actual motion is a rapid, gentle lifting and tossing of the food with a shovel-like action, so that all sides are evenly seared. To avoid confusion this book uses the term *stir-frying* except when the actual motion is critical to a recipe's success, such as for tofu, when tossing is advised.

As a general rule, seasonings, condiments, meats, and vegetables are cooked in the wok separately, in batches, in the order of required cooking times. Each is tossed with the hot seasoned oil in the wok to accentuate its individual flavor. Depending

Tips

. . . ON PERFECT STIR-FRYING

☐ Before stir-frying, thoroughly blot dry all ingredients.

☐ Preheat wok until hot before pouring in oil. Wok is hot when a few drops of water sprinkled in it dance across the surface.

☐ Add oil to hot wok; then tilt wok to coat sides with oil.

☐ Crush ginger, garlic, and green onion against sides of wok with the back of a spatula (see above) so that their juices season the oil.

☐ Always wait until oil and wok are hot before adding additional food.

☐ Unless recipe states otherwise, add food in batches to center of wok, pushing cooked foods up sides of wok to make room.

☐ When stir-frying minced meat, press and poke meat with edge of spatula to break up clumps for even cooking.

☐ When adding wine or stock, splash against sides of hot wok. The liquids should sizzle, intensifying their flavors.

☐ If too much liquid accumulates in wok, push food up sides and reduce liquid in center of wok over high heat; then proceed.

on the recipe, it can then be either left in place, pushed up the sides of the wok, or removed while the next batch is cooked. Then all the foods are stir-fried together.

Preheating a wok is so vital that it is indicated in every recipe. This step conditions the surface of the wok and creates the first barrier against sticking. If an ungreased, well-seasoned wok is hot enough, any uncooked food added to it will simply sear on the edges and practically deflect from the pan rather than stick to it.

Preheat a wok over medium-high heat about 2 minutes (depending on your stove). The wok is hot enough to accept oil when a few drops of water splashed into it dance across the surface. Avoid preheating a wok over high heat: Oil that is added may heat too quickly, burn, and smoke, and you will then have to start over.

When adding oil, pour it down from the rim of the wok so that it warms as it flows down the sides. Then tilt the wok to swirl the oil and coat the entire surface of the pan.

Remember that seasoned oil not only cooks food but seasons it as well. Adopt the habit of adding a slice of bruised ginger to the heating oil before adding meats or vegetables. Ginger suppresses the oily smell with an appetizing, fresh scent.

Oil flavoring agents include garlic, green onion (or leek), and salt. Introduce them to warm oil—not hot. With the back of a Chinese spatula, squeeze the ginger, garlic, and green onion against the sides of the wok to extract their juices, and cook gently for about 30 seconds. Adding salt to the oil as it heats creates a roasted flavor and distributes the salt evenly throughout the stir-fried mixture, thereby necessitating less salt overall.

Fragrance indicates that the oil is ready for stir-frying. The ginger, garlic, and green onion may be removed and discarded at this point; however, that is solely a matter of preference and aesthetics.

Now turn the heat to high (unless the recipe specifies otherwise). When the oil is very hot but not smoking, add the meat in batches of approximately 1 cup each, seconds apart. It should sizzle on contact.

When the first batch of meat is cooked, push it up the sides of the wok to make room in the center for the second batch. When all the meat is cooked, remove it and set it aside to be returned to the wok at the end of cooking. (Note that in some recipes the meat stays in the wok while the vegetables cook.)

The spices of Asian cuisines and the bases of Asian sauces are condiments such as salted black beans, bean sauce, and chile paste and reconstituted dried ingredients such as Chinese black mushrooms, lily buds, and shrimp. To activate their flavors, add the condiments to the hot seasoned oil in a separate stage (having pushed cooked foods up the sides of the wok to make room in the center) and fry a few seconds. Reconstituted dried ingredients follow; stir-fry each in the center of the wok for a few seconds before adding the next.

Never add vegetables (or any food, for that matter) to the wok all at once. The temperature of the wok will drop instantly, canceling the searing effect that traps the juices inside the food, resulting in watery vegetables.

Add vegetables in batches of approximately 1 cup, starting with longer-cooking vegetables such as carrots and broccoli. When the oil is hot enough, add the next batch.

White pepper, sugar, and other dry seasonings are added individually after all vegetables are stir-fried; they are tossed with vegetables a few moments to activate their flavors. Liquid seasonings such as soy sauce and wine are added next by splashing them against the sides of the hot wok; the resulting sizzle burns off the alcohol in the wine, intensifying the wine flavor. Stock is added in the same manner to deglaze the pan and incorporate any browned bits of foods on the sides of the wok.

Thickening the sauce is a matter of individual preference. Often the cornstarch in the marinated meat is enough to thicken a thin sauce. Traditionally, cornstarch blended with water is added during stir-frying to the boiling liquid in the center of the wok and then stirred to thicken it into a smooth sauce.

GLOSSARY OF INGREDIENTS

Here is a list of ingredients used in this book, including oils, dried seasonings, mushrooms, and prepared condiments and sauces. For a glossary of vegetables, see page 56.

Oils

Oils play a prominent role in stir-frying and deep-frying in a wok, so the use of high-quality oils is essential. Listed below are oils suitable for Asian cooking and seasoning; they are all readily available in American supermarkets.

Chile oil, Asian hot Used as a dipping sauce and seasoning oil, this oil is made from heating vegetable oil with chiles until the oil is infused with their spicy, hot flavor. Commercially prepared chile oil varies in hotness according to brand.

Coconut milk and cream An essential ingredient of Southeast Asian cuisines, coconut milk is made from the grated white flesh of the coconut, which is steeped in hot water, then strained and pressed through cheesecloth. Although coconut milk is available both fresh and frozen, canned unsweetened coconut milk is used in these recipes for convenience. Open the can and pour the contents into a tall glass container. The thick white substance that rises to the top is the coconut cream, and the thinner liquid that settles to the bottom is the coconut milk.

Ghee This Indian cooking oil is made by simmering clarified butter until all the moisture is cooked off and milk solids are separated from the clear butterfat. It keeps refrigerated up to 6 months.

Peanut oil This oil is preferred for cooking because of its high smoke point and neutral flavor.

Sesame oil, Asian Used primarily as a seasoning and seldom for cooking, this oil is pressed from seeds that are toasted, which gives it a strong nutty flavor and aroma.

The crisp textures, bright colors, and lightness of Snow Peas, Pine Nuts, and Chinese Sausage (see page 57) epitomize the art of stir-frying.

Condiments

Many flavors in Asian dishes come from condiments and sauces, which usually have a preserved-bean base and are available bottled and canned. After opening, transfer the contents to a jar and store refrigerated; they will keep indefinitely.

Bean sauce, brown　This commercially prepared product is actually a paste and is marketed as brown bean sauce (the whole-bean version) and ground brown bean sauce (a purée). The base of the sauce is fermented soybeans, wheat flour, and oil. Used to impart a distinctive savory flavor, it comes in jars and cans. To store indefinitely, transfer to a well-sealed jar and refrigerate.

Bean sauce, hot　This popular Szechuan cooking condiment is made from brown bean sauce and crushed chiles. It keeps indefinitely in a well-sealed jar in the refrigerator.

Black beans, salted　These small, soft, wrinkled beans, speckled with salt crystals, are sold packed in plastic bags. They are used sparingly as a cooking condiment with most meat, fish, poultry, and strongly flavored vegetables. Before using, cover the beans with water, drain, and mash with 1 or 2 cloves garlic. Occasionally 1 teaspoon minced ginger per tablespoon of salted black beans is also added.

Chile paste with garlic　Made from crushed fresh chiles, soybeans, and salt, chile paste is similar to hot bean sauce (see above) but much hotter. It is used sparingly as a cooking condiment. For the best flavor, sauté chile paste in oil a few seconds before mixing in other ingredients. Chile paste keeps indefinitely in the refrigerator.

Chile sauce, Sriracha　Made from chiles, sugar, and vinegar, this Southeast Asian–style prepared chile sauce is used for cooking and as a table condiment for dipping.

Fish sauce, Thai　*Nam pla*, as it is called in Thai, is Southeast Asia's equivalent of soy sauce. It is salty, translucent, and dark brown, with a very thin consistency. Its pungent odor dissipates during cooking.

Hoisin sauce　This popular table and cooking condiment is best known as a dipping sauce for Peking duck and mu shu pork. One of the many variations of bean sauce, hoisin sauce contains the basic bean sauce with garlic, chiles, vinegar, and sugar. It is often incorrectly referred to as duck sauce.

Oyster sauce　This dipping sauce and cooking condiment is made from oyster extract reduced to a thick, rich concentrate, with a savory but not unpleasantly fishy flavor. It should be used sparingly. It will keep indefinitely if refrigerated.

Sesame paste, Chinese　This butter made from roasted sesame seed is used as a base for salad dressings in cold salads. It keeps indefinitely in the refrigerator.

Soy sauce　Chinese soy sauce comes in many varieties and grades, and it differs greatly from Japanese soy sauce. The two grades used in this book are light and dark soy sauce. Light (sometimes referred to as thin) soy sauce is light-colored and delicate but a bit saltier in flavor than dark soy sauce. It is usually used as a table dipping sauce and for cooking delicate dishes. Dark soy sauce is an all-purpose cooking soy with a sweeter flavor, darker color, and thicker consistency than light soy sauce. Blend the two sauces in cooking to create a well-balanced flavor. Naturally fermented soy sauce has a superior flavor to that made from chemically derived protein extracts. It stores indefinitely in a cupboard.

Tofu, fermented　This popular Chinese cooking condiment adds a slightly bitter, alcohol-like flavor to stir-fried spinach, watercress, and other vegetables and to braised meats. It is made from fresh bean curd inoculated with a yeast culture and then packed and aged in a brine of salt and alcohol. It looks like a small cake of soft, very ripe cheese. Adding a pinch of sugar to the finished food balances the flavor of the tofu.

Asian Ingredients, Dried Seasonings, and Herbs

A well-stocked Asian pantry should contain the following ingredients, many of which may already be in your cupboard. Most have a long shelf life. All are regularly stocked by Asian food stores, and many can be found in well-stocked supermarkets and specialty food stores or through mail-order sources. Store dried ingredients in lock-top plastic bags in a cupboard. After opening canned and bottled condiments and sauces, transfer them to airtight containers and keep in the refrigerator.

Agar-agar　This dried white seaweed comes in both fine shreds and 1-inch-thick rectangular strips. Rehydrate it in cold water to use as a noodle or in hot water to use as gelatin.

Basil　In Thailand many varieties of basil are used, including anise- and lemon-flavored basil. Basil is stir-fried or cooked as though it were a leafy vegetable rather than a fresh herb. The fresh large-leafed basil available in American supermarkets is a good substitute.

Chiles, dried red These hot, thin, 3- to 4-inch-long dried chiles are packaged as hot red chiles or · *chiles japoneses* (Japanese chiles) in American markets. To seed chiles, crack the brittle skin and shake out the seeds. Soak chiles in warm water to soften before using.

Chiles serranos These hot smooth-skinned fresh green chiles, about 2 inches long and up to ½ inch in diameter, are used extensively in Southeast Asian cooking. They can be found in Asian and many standard markets. A similar variety is available dried. Fresh chiles will keep for several weeks in the refrigerator.

Coriander The fresh plant is also known as cilantro and Chinese parsley. Choose bunches that still have their hairlike roots, which are used in wet spice paste in Southeast Asian cooking. If roots aren't present, use an equal amount of the stem. The pungent leaves are used as a seasoning and garnish, and the dried seeds are toasted and ground to be used in spice paste.

Five-spice powder This is a pungent blend of five spices (more or less, depending on the manufacturer): cinnamon, cloves, Szechuan peppercorns, star anise, and fennel. It is used for grilled and braised meats and poultry.

Galangal Also known as *kha* and Siamese ginger, this rhizome, a member of the ginger family, is used primarily to flavor food but also for medicinal purposes. It is available fresh and dried in Asian specialty stores. If dried galangal is used, soak in water until soft and pliable. There is no substitute.

Ginger See page 56.

Kaffir lime Indigenous to Southeast Asia, fresh Kaffir limes and leaves are occasionally available in North America in Southeast Asian markets. The golf ball–sized fruit has a lumpy green skin and leaves that yield an oil, flavor, and perfumelike aroma that are very desirable in Thai cooking. The rind and the leaves, fresh or dried, are used as flavoring. Domestic limes are good substitutes for lime juice and leaves, but do try to locate the Kaffir lime rind.

Lemongrass Available almost the year around in Asian markets, fresh lemongrass is used for its lemony flavor in soups, stews, and spice pastes. Peel away the dried tough outer stalks and cut up the fresh tender middle stalks for salads and stir-frying. The zest of half a lemon can be substituted for one stalk fresh lemongrass.

Lily buds, dried Also known as golden needles and tiger lily, these buds are sold by weight and packed in cellophane bags. Look for a light gold color. They must be soaked in water about 30 minutes to become soft and pliable. Stored in a well-sealed container in a cupboard, the dried buds will keep several months.

Mustard greens, Szechuan preserved Often called Szechuan preserved vegetables, this specialty of Szechuan province is vaguely related to mustard cabbage. It is preserved in salt, pickled with ground chiles, and canned. Rinse before using. Because of its salty, spicy taste and crunchy texture, it is a good seasoning vegetable; it can be shredded, sliced, or minced for stir-fried, steamed, and braised dishes. Stored in a well-sealed container in the refrigerator, it will keep indefinitely.

Noodles See page 36.

Oysters, dried Oysters are preserved by sun-drying, which intensifies their flavor. To be reconstituted they often need overnight soaking; when soft they should be rinsed well to remove sand. They may be braised whole, cooked in soup, and cut up or minced for stir-fried dishes. They are sold in bulk or small packages; if dried oysters are unavailable, tinned unflavored smoked oysters packed in oil are an acceptable substitute.

Palm sugar Also known as jaggery and coconut sugar, this unrefined coarse brown sugar is made from sap drained from the palmyra palm. Available as a paste or as hard blocks that must be grated, it is used extensively in Indian and Southeast Asian cooking. If it is unavailable, dark brown sugar can be substituted.

Peppercorns, Szechuan These tiny reddish brown peppercorns have a flavor and aroma that are distinctive and lasting. Not at all spicy, the brittle toasted husks impart an unusual numbing sensation to the mouth. Look for packages of seeded peppercorns, since the husk is the desired part. Before using, toast in a dry wok over low heat until fragrant (about 5 minutes), stirring occasionally. Crush or grind to a fine powder in a mortar. The powder will keep several weeks in a well-sealed container. Untoasted whole peppercorns, whether seeded or unseeded, will keep indefinitely.

Radishes, preserved These come in a plastic bag sometimes marked "brine-cured radishes." Salting and sun-drying gives them a dark tan color. Rinse with water before using. They store indefinitely in the refrigerator. There is no substitute.

Shrimp, dried Sun-drying intensifies the flavor of the shrimp. Available in various sizes—the small ones are called rice-sized shrimp—they are used as a seasoning agent for stir-fried, braised, and simmered dishes and for soups. They should be soaked in warm water 30 minutes, drained, and patted dry. They may be found in the ethnic food section of large supermarkets and keep indefinitely in a well-sealed container.

Shrimp paste An essential ingredient in Asian cooking, this extremely pungent cooking condiment is made from fermented shrimp. Also known as *kapi, blachan,* and *trasi,* it comes in many forms: wet, pinkish gray in color, and packed in jars; purple-brown solid blocks; and brownish black and sun-dried in solid cakes. A good substitute is anchovy paste.

Star anise This eight-pointed star-shaped spice seedpod comes from a Chinese tree that belongs to the magnolia family. Its pungent anise flavor complements braised and simmered meat and poultry dishes. Store as you would other spices.

Tamarind Tamarind is known for its fruity, sweet-and-sour flavor. In some dishes the preserved pulp or the entire fresh pod, which looks like a lumpy, brown string bean, is used; in other dishes the pulp is diluted with hot water and pressed through a strainer to make Tamarind Water (see page 24). Avoid using tamarind concentrate, which is diluted with hot water; its flavor is satisfactory only in a pinch.

Tangerine peel, dried The aromatic oil of the dried peel of the sour tangerine, indigenous to southern China, has a pleasant, bitter flavor. It comes in 1-inch-square pieces; rehydrate in warm water until soft.

Tientsin cabbage, preserved This preserved vegetable comes from the city of Tientsin and is made from what is known in the American market as napa cabbage, a thick, dense, leafy cabbage. It is chopped, preserved in salt, garlic, and spices, and packed in an earthenware container. Preserved cabbage should be rinsed with cold water and used sparingly as a seasoning vegetable.

Tofu, fresh and fried See page 57.

Mushrooms

Dried mushrooms are used as both a vegetable and a seasoning ingredient in Asian cooking. Dried mushrooms are available in Asian markets and the ethnic food section of many American supermarkets. To rehydrate, soak them in water for the time specified in the recipe. You can save the soaking water to use in place of tap water in soups and stews.

Black mushrooms, Chinese dried Marketed as dried *shiitake* mushrooms in American supermarkets, this Asian staple comes in several varieties ranging in color from light tan to black. The mushrooms are packaged in cellophane bags. The best grades are whole and perfectly shaped caps, light tan with a speckled, flowerlike pattern. They must be soaked in water, rinsed, drained, squeezed dry, and have their hard stems removed before using. The soaking water is sometimes strained and used to flavor stocks or sauces. Store the dried mushrooms in an airtight container.

Cloud ears This small black fungus is a member of the black jelly fungus family and is a smaller version of the wood ear (see below). Cloud ears are about ½ inch across. They are more delicate and have a finer texture than wood ears. When reconstituted in water, the wrinkled black fungi triple in size; they may be cooked whole or torn apart.

Straw mushrooms Currently available only dried or canned (not fresh) in American markets, straw mushrooms are used in stir-frying or general cooking. Reconstitute the dried mushrooms in water before using them.

Wood ears Also known as *mukyee* and *mo-er,* this black fungus (1½ to 2 inches across) with a tan underside is a larger version of the cloud ear (see above). Wood ears have a faint flavor, if any, and are prized for their crunchy yet chewy texture and their ability to absorb other flavors. They should be used in recipes calling for black fungus to be julienned. Stored in an airtight container in a cupboard, they will keep indefinitely.

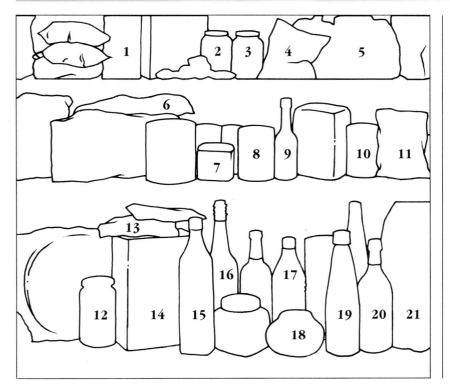

Preserved Asian seasonings, ingredients, and condiments, many of which are available in well-stocked supermarkets countrywide, include (1) sizzling rice cakes, (2) chile paste with garlic, (3) sesame seed paste, (4) pine nuts, (5) mung bean noodles, (6) dried wood ear mushrooms, (7) salted plums, (8) straw mushrooms, (9) Asian sesame oil, (10) coconut milk, (11) dried red chiles, (12) brown bean sauce, (13) dried shrimp, (14) peanut oil, (15) Shaoxing rice wine, (16) light soy sauce, (17) Thai fish sauce, (18) preserved Tientsin cabbage, (19) oyster sauce, (20) soy sauce, and (21) agar-agar.

13

Among the ingredients used to make the delicious appetizers in this chapter are gingerroot, dried shrimp, Chinese dried black mushrooms, and dried rice cakes.

Appetizers

In this chapter are make-ahead and freezable classics such as Classic Shrimp Toast (see page 19), Kuo Teh or potstickers (see page 26), and Crisp Fried Wontons (see page 33). Because all good dumplings and pastries take time, make big batches and freeze them. They reheat beautifully. Also in this chapter are fun dishes that work extremely well in the wok. Add an exotic element to your next dim sum or tapas party with such intriguing recipes as Indonesian Potato and Beef Fritters (see page 33), Thai Egg Net Pillows (see page 20), and Gambas al Ajillo, a Spanish garlic-shrimp tapa (see page 29).

APPETIZERS FROM THE WOK

Asian foods were compact even before they became known as appetizers. Originally designed for light meals, many just naturally fit the specifications for the perfect cocktail-party appetizer—neat, tidy, and finger food–sized. Sticky and soft foods are stuffed in bread dough to make barbecued pork buns (see page 40), wrapped in a fresh pasta sheet and steamed into a *siu mai* dumpling (see page 32), or deep-fried into a crisp Vietnamese-style spring roll called *cha gio* (see page 69).

DIM SUM

Preparing dim sum dumplings is a highly developed style of cooking, perhaps one of the most noted and recognized specialties of China's vast cuisine. Dim sum translates as "touch of the heart" or "heart's delight." A dim sum meal may be consumed anytime from early morning to late afternoon as a social or business luncheon, a family meal, or a casual snack. It can also be a formal affair.

Dim sum appetizers are steamed, deep-fried, baked, roasted, barbecued, or poached. In an authentic Chinese teahouse, many varieties of dumplings are individually prepared by hand in the early morning by a human assembly line. Because of the immense amount of work involved, an entire dim sum luncheon is seldom prepared at home. However, one or two types of dim sum dumplings can be prepared and offered as appetizers for special home meals to signify the importance of the guests.

DEEP-FRYING IN A WOK

The technique of deep-frying has long been practiced throughout the Asian world. Unfortunately, deep-frying has a negative connotation in the West from the standpoint of health. However, if the oil temperature is correct (375° F for most foods), deep-fried foods are crisp without being greasy and they retain far less oil than panfried or sautéed foods. For successful deep-frying, high-quality oil is essential. The Chinese favor peanut or soy oil because of the high smoke points of these oils, but corn and other vegetable oils are also suitable.

DEEP-FRIED MUSHROOMS WITH ANCHOVY-CAPER RÉMOULADE

Bernice Hagen, an Italian cook and owner of La Bernice Cooking School in Sacramento, California, loves using a wok for deep-frying foods such as her favorite mushroom appetizer.

>   40 *medium-sized fresh mushrooms*
>   ½ *cup flour seasoned with 1 teaspoon salt*
>   2 *eggs, beaten with 1 teaspoon each water and oil*
>   1½ *cups fine dried bread crumbs*
>   2 *cups peanut or corn oil, for deep-frying*

Anchovy-Caper Rémoulade

>   1½ *cups mayonnaise*
>   1 *tin (2 oz) anchovy fillets, drained and minced*
>   1 *hard-cooked egg, finely chopped*
>   2 *tablespoons finely chopped parsley*
>   2 *tablespoons capers, minced*
>   2 *teaspoons fresh lemon juice*
>   1 *teaspoon minced onion*
>   1 *teaspoon finely chopped chives*
>   1 *teaspoon Dijon mustard*
>   ½ *teaspoon dried tarragon, crumbled*

1. Trim and discard stems from mushrooms. Dredge mushrooms in seasoned flour; then dip in and thoroughly coat with egg mixture. Roll in bread crumbs. Set aside.

2. Preheat wok over medium-high heat until hot. Pour in oil and heat to 375° F. Add mushrooms, in batches, and deep-fry until mushrooms are golden brown (2 to 3 minutes). Drain on paper towels. Serve hot with Anchovy-Caper Rémoulade.

Serves 10 with other dishes.

Anchovy-Caper Rémoulade In a medium bowl combine all ingredients and blend well.

Makes about 2 cups.

TAMARIND SHRIMP DIP WITH SIZZLING RICE CAKES
Kao tang nar thang

In this fascinating Thai version of chips and dip, the tamarind and spicy flavors are mellowed with coconut cream. The dip is served on the Sizzling Rice Cakes, which do not sizzle in this dish but make a great dipping chip.

>   1 *can (14 oz) unsweetened coconut milk Vegetable oil, for deep frying*
>   1 *recipe Sizzling Rice Cakes (see page 68) or 12 squares packaged dried rice cakes (1½-in. squares)*
>   1 *teaspoon black peppercorns*
>   1 *whole large clove garlic, plus 2 cloves garlic, sliced*
>   1 *tablespoon fresh coriander root (see page 11)*
>   4 *shallots, sliced*
>   ½ *cup chopped roasted peanuts*
>   ½ *pound ground chicken*
>   6 *ounces shrimp, shelled, deveined, and coarsely chopped*
>   1 *red chile, chopped, plus 1 red chile, slivered, for garnish*
>   2 *tablespoons palm sugar or firmly packed brown sugar*
>   2 *tablespoons Thai fish sauce*
>   3 *tablespoons Tamarind Water (see page 24) Fresh coriander leaves, for garnish*

1. Without shaking can, pour coconut milk into a tall glass container and set aside until coconut cream rises to top (1 to 2 hours). Skim off ½ cup cream, place in a small bowl, and set aside. Reserve milk in glass.

2. Preheat wok over medium-high heat until hot. Pour in oil to a depth of 2 inches and heat to 375° F. Add rice cakes in batches and fry until golden (about 1 minute), turning once. Remove and drain on paper towel. Repeat with remaining cakes. Pour oil from wok and wipe dry.

3. *To prepare in an electric mini-chopper:* Chop peppercorns, whole garlic clove, and coriander root. Set aside. *To prepare in a mortar:* Pound peppercorns, garlic clove, and coriander root to a paste. Set aside.

4. Place reserved coconut cream in wok; replace wok over medium-high heat and cook cream until it is thick and oily (about 2 minutes), stirring continuously. Add reserved peppercorn mixture and fry until oil is fragrant (about 30 seconds). Add shallot, garlic slices, and peanuts; stir-fry until shallot is lightly browned (about 1 minute). Add chicken, shrimp, and chopped red chile; stir-fry until shrimp turns pink (2 to 3 minutes). Add sugar, fish sauce, and Tamarind Water; cook together 1 minute. Add reserved coconut milk and cook, stirring constantly, until liquid is reduced to the consistency of light cream and is caramel colored. Transfer to a saucer. Garnish with coriander leaves and chile slivers. Arrange rice cakes around dip. To serve, spoon a little sauce onto rice cake and eat with your fingers.

Makes 1½ cups, serves 6 as an appetizer dip.

Begin a meal with this delightful peanut-flavored tamarind dip studded with morsels of chicken and shrimp. Sizzling rice cakes are an excellent alternative to crackers or chips. This appetizer dip is also delicious served with crisp, chilled fresh vegetables.

This piquant New Orleans barbecued shrimp dish illustrates how shrimp cooked in their shells impart a stronger flavor than shelled shrimp.

SHRIMP MOUSSE–STUFFED ROASTED PEPPERS

In this recipe shrimp are finely puréed, then made moist, light, and fluffy with chicken stock, egg white, and pork fat. The bell peppers are roasted and stuffed with the shrimp filling and then braised in Chinese garlic-black bean sauce. Roasted bell pepper is a delicious departure from Chinese tradition.

1 teaspoon salted black beans
1 clove garlic, minced
1 teaspoon minced fresh ginger
2 teaspoons sugar
2 tablespoons rice wine or dry vermouth
¾ cup chicken stock, or more as needed
2 teaspoons oyster sauce
1 teaspoon Asian sesame oil
3 medium red or green bell peppers
1 teaspoon cornstarch mixed with 1 tablespoon water, plus more cornstarch for dusting
2 tablespoons peanut or corn oil
Fresh coriander, for garnish

Basic Shrimp Mousse Filling

8 Chinese water chestnuts, preferably fresh, peeled
1 large green onion, white part only
1 ounce fresh pork fat (optional)
1 pound shrimp, shelled and deveined
1 tablespoon dry vermouth or rice wine
1 piece (½ in.) fresh ginger, pressed through a garlic press, juice reserved
1 teaspoon salt
¼ teaspoon sugar
2 tablespoons cornstarch
3 tablespoons chicken stock
1 large egg white, beaten until fluffy but not stiff

1. Soak beans in water until soft (about 5 minutes). Rinse with cold water and strain. Place beans in a small bowl; add garlic and ginger and pound into a coarse paste. In another small bowl combine sugar, wine, stock, oyster sauce, and sesame oil. Set both bowls aside.

2. Over a gas flame or on an electric burner over medium-high heat, roast whole peppers until they are charred and blistered (about 5 minutes), turning peppers frequently. Place in a plastic bag, seal, and let stand 10 minutes. Remove peppers and peel and discard charred skin. Cut flesh into 1½-inch squares and dust insides with cornstarch. With a knife dipped in water, spread about 1 heaping tablespoon Basic Shrimp Mousse Filling on each square. Smooth filling into a ½-inch-thick mound.

3. Preheat wok over medium heat until hot. Pour in oil. When hot add as many stuffed peppers as will fit in one layer, shrimp side down. Fry until peppers are golden brown and shrimp feels firm (about 2 minutes per side). Remove, arrange on a platter, and keep warm. Repeat with remaining peppers. Pour off all but a thin film of oil from wok.

4. Add reserved black bean mixture to wok and stir-fry until fragrant (about 15 seconds). Add reserved stock mixture, increase heat to high, and bring to a boil. Add cornstarch mixture and stir until sauce thickens. Spoon sauce over peppers. Garnish with coriander. Serve hot.

Serves 8 as an appetizer.

Basic Shrimp Mousse Filling
To prepare in a food processor: Place water chestnuts in the work bowl of a food processor fitted with a steel blade. Process to a fine mince (about 10 seconds) and remove to a small bowl. Place green onion in work bowl; process to a fine mince, scraping down sides between pulses. Add to minced water chestnuts. Process pork fat, if used, to a smooth purée (about 10 seconds); add to water chestnut mixture. Place shrimp in work bowl; process to a smooth purée (about 15 seconds). Return reserved water chestnut mixture to work bowl and add vermouth, ginger

juice, salt, sugar, and cornstarch. Pulse several times until mixture is thoroughly blended. With processor running pour stock down feed tube. Process until mixture is light and fluffy. Add egg white and pulse until blended. Transfer mixture to a large bowl, cover, and refrigerate 1 hour. *To prepare by hand:* With a cleaver finely mince, separately, water chestnuts and green onion; transfer to a large bowl and set aside. If pork fat is used, finely chop it to a smooth paste with a cleaver; then finely chop shrimp with fat and add to water chestnut mixture. Add vermouth, ginger juice, salt, sugar, and cornstarch; blend thoroughly. Beat in stock. Fold in egg white. Cover mixture and refrigerate 1 hour.

Makes 2 cups filling.

CLASSIC SHRIMP TOAST
The basic shrimp mousse at left is an indispensable element in many classic Chinese appetizers. One of the most popular dim sum dishes is shrimp toast. The shrimp mousse is mounded on sliced bread; the coated bread is then deep-fried until crisp on the outside and juicy and succulent on the inside. Shrimp toast tastes best when served right out of the fryer.

    30 slices stale white or
         French bread
     1 recipe Basic Shrimp Mousse
         Filling (at left), well chilled
         Fresh coriander or black
         sesame seed, for garnish
         Peanut or corn oil, for
         deep-frying

1. Trim crust from bread and cut bread into 2-inch rounds or other attractive shapes. Spread a ½-inch-thick layer of shrimp mousse evenly over bread. Garnish with coriander and set on a tray.

2. Preheat wok over medium-high heat until hot. Pour in oil to a depth of 2 inches and heat to 350° F. Add bread rounds, shrimp side down, and fry 3 minutes. Turn over and fry 1 minute longer. Remove and drain. Serve hot.

Makes 30 pieces.

NATALIE'S NEW ORLEANS BARBECUED SHRIMP
Natalie Sellers, who owned the former Truffles Cooking School in Reno, says making barbecued shrimp is easier in a wok; the deep-sided, concave shape of a wok is ideal for tossing and stirring the large quantity of shrimp needed for her version of this New Orleans specialty. Serve this dish with chunks of French bread and a crisp green salad.

     2 cloves garlic, minced
     1 tablespoon minced parsley
     2 tablespoons lemon juice
     ¼ cup chile sauce
     3 tablespoons Worcestershire
         sauce
     ½ teaspoon hot-pepper sauce
     1 tablespoon liquid smoke
         flavoring
     1 teaspoon paprika
     1 teaspoon dried oregano
    1½ teaspoons cayenne pepper
         Freshly ground black pepper
     2 lemons, thinly sliced
     ½ cup olive oil
     ½ cup butter or margarine
    2½ pounds large shrimp, shells
         on, rinsed and patted dry

1. In a medium bowl combine garlic, parsley, lemon juice, chile sauce, Worcestershire sauce, hot-pepper sauce, liquid smoke, paprika, oregano, cayenne, a few twists black pepper, and lemon slices.

2. Preheat wok over medium heat until hot. Pour in olive oil, then add butter. When hot add seasoning mixture, reduce heat to low, and simmer to blend flavors (8 to 10 minutes). Increase heat to high and add shrimp. Cook, stirring, until shrimp turn pink (5 to 8 minutes). Serve hot.

Serves 12 as an appetizer.

MAKING EGG NETS

Thai cooking is known for its colorful and meticulous presentations. Egg nets are a perfect example. These popular decorative jackets, made of beaten egg, make delicate food wrappers or lacy garnishes. Their preparation requires smooth waves of the hand and wrist: The beaten egg is dripped in streams into a lightly oiled 7- to 8-inch skillet or wok to form spaghettini-thin threads. The technique, illustrated here, takes a little practice to master, but the pretty and dainty bundle is well worth the effort.

The beaten egg may also be dripped into hot cooking oil, fried until golden brown and crunchy, and torn into pieces to be used for garnishing.

An easier and faster method of preparing egg nets (not illustrated) is used by cooks who want a more solid wrapper. A small amount of beaten egg is poured into an ungreased wok, which is swirled in order to coat the sides with a thin, crêpelike layer of egg. The egg is then cooked briefly until set.

2. *Spread fingers and, holding them 2 inches above skillet, wave your hand back and forth across full width of skillet, letting egg drip from fingertips in fine threads. Repeat until bottom of skillet is covered with egg threads.*

3. *With same motion wave fingers back and forth across skillet at right angle to first threads, repeating several times to form a fine netting.*

1. *Flatten your hand and dip your fingers and palm into beaten egg mixture (see recipe for Egg Net Pillows at right).*

4. *Cook until egg is set and light yellow. With the edge of a spatula, carefully lift edges of net and remove from skillet. The entire process for each net takes 2 to 3 minutes. Cut, fill, and roll nets according to recipe directions.*

EGG NET PILLOWS
Rhoom

Although some Thai cooks make thin omelets in place of the traditional lacy egg nets for convenience and to save time, the egg nets are particularly attractive. These wrappings with a minced pork filling make tasty "pillow" surprise packages.

    2   cloves garlic
    1   teaspoon whole black
          peppercorns
    1   tablespoon minced fresh
          coriander root (see page 11)
    2   tablespoons peanut or corn oil
    2   shallots, minced
    ¾   pound pork butt, minced
    1½ tablespoons Thai fish sauce
    2   teaspoons palm sugar or
          firmly packed brown sugar
    2   tablespoons chopped roasted
          peanuts
    6   eggs
    3   tablespoons water
    3   cloves Thai pickled garlic, cut
          into thin slices (optional)
    16 leaves fresh coriander, plus
          more for garnish
    3   red chiles serranos, seeded
          and slivered
          Thai Sweet Garlic Dipping
          Sauce (see page 24), for
          accompaniment

1. *To prepare in an electric mini-chopper:* Chop garlic, peppercorns, and coriander root. *To prepare in a mortar:* Pound garlic, peppercorns, and coriander root to a paste.

2. Preheat wok over medium-high heat until hot. Pour in 1 tablespoon of the oil; then add garlic mixture and shallot and stir-fry until oil is fragrant (about 30 seconds). Add pork and stir-fry until browned (about 2 minutes). Add fish sauce and sugar; cook until liquid is completely reduced. Mix in peanuts. Remove to a bowl and set aside.

3. Beat eggs and water and pour into a shallow plate; set aside. Preheat a 7- to 8-inch nonstick skillet over medium heat until hot. Pour in the remaining 1 tablespoon oil. With several rolled-up paper towels, spread oil throughout skillet and wipe up excess; set towels aside. Make egg nets following Step-by-Step on page 20, removing each net to a work surface as it is cooked, wiping skillet with oiled towels, and repeating with remaining egg mixture to make 8 nets.

4. Cut each egg net in half. In center of each half place 1 slice pickled garlic (if used), 1 coriander leaf, and a chile sliver. Top with 1 tablespoon pork mixture. Fold up bottom of turn in sides, and roll into a small pillow. Place fold side down on a serving plate. Garnish pillow with more chile slivers and coriander leaves and serve with dipping sauce.

Makes about 16 pillows.

Egg Net Pillows always steal the show. At your next cocktail party, dazzle guests with these prized little bundles. They are delicious at room temperature, so make them in advance and have plenty on hand for appetizers or a first course with Thai Sweet Garlic Dipping Sauce (see page 24).

BONING CHICKEN WINGS

Purchase chicken wings that have all three wing sections intact. Plan on spending about 30 minutes to bone the six wings necessary for Thai Angel Wings (see recipe at right). If this is your first attempt at boning chicken wings, buy extra to practice your skills. Most important is a sharp paring knife.

1. *Gently bend both wing joints backward to crack joints and tendons.*

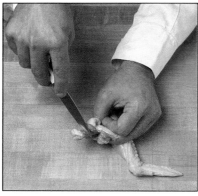

2. *With a very sharp knife cut and scrape around knuckle and underside of large exposed joint (the one originally joined to body). Rotate joint to help free the meat.*

3. *With edge of knife against bone, scrape downward toward middle joint, pulling meat and skin inside out to expose middle joint. Scrape lightly around joint; when joint is totally exposed, bend it backward to snap off large bone.*

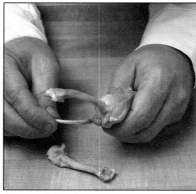

4. *Carefully loosen meat on sides and underside of middle joint, working around and between the two little bones in middle wing section. As meat and skin are freed, turn inside out and pull down toward wing tips. Slip knife tip between the two smaller bones and cut them apart. Bend each bone backward at that joint, twisting to detach bones. You now have a boned chicken wing with tip attached and, preferably, without skin punctures.*

THAI ANGEL WINGS

How can six chicken wings serve six people? Stuff them and cut each into five or six finger food–sized pieces. Thai Angel Wings have a delicious, crisp, and unusual coating. In Western cooking deep-fried foods are usually first dipped in beaten egg and then dusted with flour. In Thai cooking the process is reversed: The ingredient is dusted with flour, then coated with beaten egg. When deep-fried, the egg coating bursts and swells into an intricate gold filigree-like wrap that calls to mind an angel's wings.

  6 *whole chicken wings, including tips*
  2 *ounces bean thread noodles*
  1 *tablespoon minced fresh coriander root (see page 11)*
  2 *teaspoons whole black peppercorns or 1 tablespoon freshly ground pepper*
  6 *cloves garlic, finely minced*
  ¾ *pound ground pork butt*
  1 *tablespoon Thai fish sauce*
  1 *teaspoon salt*
  2 *green onions, minced*
  1 *teaspoon shrimp powder with chile (optional)*
     Peanut oil, for deep-frying
  ¼ *cup rice flour or all-purpose flour*
  2 *large eggs, lightly beaten with a pinch salt*
     Thai Sweet-and-Sour Cucumber Relish (see page 25) or Sriracha chile sauce, for accompaniment

1. Bone chicken wings, following Step-by-Step at left. Set aside.

2. In a small bowl soak noodles in water until soft. Drain and cut into 2-inch lengths. Set aside.

3. *To prepare in an electric minichopper:* Chop coriander root, peppercorns, and garlic. *To prepare in a mortar:* Pound coriander root, peppercorns, and garlic to a paste.

4. In a medium bowl combine garlic mixture, pork, fish sauce, salt, green onion, shrimp powder (if used), and reserved bean thread noodles.

5. Divide pork mixture into 6 portions. Stuff 1 portion into each boned wing with your thumb and index fingers or with a pastry bag fitted with a plain tip. Do not overfill, or stuffing will not fully cook.

6. Preheat wok over medium-high heat until hot. Fill wok half full with peanut oil and heat to 375° F. Meanwhile, in each of 2 shallow plates place flour and egg mixture. Lightly coat each wing with flour and dip in egg to completely cover. Holding wing by tip, add to wok. Add only as many wings at one time as will fit without crowding or reducing the temperature. Egg coating should sizzle and become lacy. Deep-fry about 8 minutes, turning occasionally. Remove wings, drain, and let cool. Repeat with remaining wings.

7. Cut wings crosswise into 5 or 6 pieces. Serve hot or at room temperature with cucumber relish.

Serves 6 with other dishes.

These deep-fried Thai Angel Wings have a crisp, lacy skin. Serve this enchanting appetizer with Thai Sweet-and-Sour Cucumber Relish (see page 25). When stuffing the wings, be careful to not overfill them.

SAUCES, DIPS, AND OTHER SUNDRIES

Many of the sauces and dips included in this chapter are interchangeable among recipes. For example, try the Indian Raita (opposite page) with Indonesian Corn-Shrimp Fritters (see page 26), or sprinkle the Crisp Fried Garlic or Shallot Flakes (at right) over a fruit salad—a common Thai practice. The sweet-and-sour sauces—some light and refreshing and others spicy hot—lend themselves well to deep-fried foods.

THAI SWEET GARLIC DIPPING SAUCE
Nam jim kra tiam

Serve this Thai-style sweet-and-sour dipping sauce with deep-fried foods. It is based on the Chinese classic sweet-and-sour sauce but is hot. It can be prepared in advance and kept for several weeks in a covered jar in the refrigerator.

  ½ cup water
  ½ cup sugar
  ¾ cup red wine vinegar
  1 tablespoon Thai fish sauce
  1 teaspoon tomato paste (optional)
  2 dried red chiles, coarsely chopped
  4 cloves garlic, bruised
  1 small carrot, cut into julienne (⅛ inch or less), for garnish
  ¼ cup chopped peanuts

In a small stainless steel saucepan, combine the water, sugar, vinegar, fish sauce, tomato paste (if used), chiles, and garlic. Bring to a boil, reduce heat, and boil slowly until sauce is consistency of thin syrup (about 10 minutes). Strain and cool. Blend in carrot and peanuts.

Makes 1 cup.

OIL-SEARED GINGER SAUCE

Although this Cantonese dipping sauce sounds oily, everyone who has tried it says, "Please pass the sauce." It is exceptionally good with Basic Chinese Steamed Chicken (see page 90) and steamed or poached fish.

  6 green onions, white portion only, cut into 2-inch-long shreds
  8 thin slices fresh ginger, very finely shredded
  1 tablespoon salt
  ½ cup peanut oil
  Fresh coriander, for garnish

1. Scatter green onion in a heat-resistant shallow saucer. Scatter ginger over green onion and sprinkle salt on top.

2. Add oil to wok and heat over medium-high heat. When oil is hot but not smoking, pour it over mixture; mixture should sizzle. Stir to mix in salt. Garnish with coriander.

Makes ½ cup.

TAMARIND WATER

In Southeast Asia tamarind is used to impart a sour citrus flavor. Make this preparation in batches; it will keep refrigerated for 10 days or frozen for about 2 months.

  1 piece (8 oz) tamarind pulp, cut into 4 pieces
  2 cups boiling water

1. Place tamarind in a medium bowl and pour the boiling water over it. Let stand 30 minutes, breaking up fibers and seeds with a fork.

2. Pour mixture through a sieve positioned over a bowl, mashing pulp to squeeze out juices. Scrap off and reserve pulp on underside of sieve. Transfer pulp and liquid to a jar and refrigerate, or pour mixture into an ice cube tray and freeze. When frozen, remove to a lock-top freezer bag and store in freezer.

Makes about 1½ cups.

HOISIN SAUCE DIP

This dip is traditionally served with Peking duck, Tea-Smoked Duck (see page 86), or mu shu pork (see page 115).

  6 tablespoons hoisin sauce
  3 tablespoons water
  1 teaspoon sugar, or to taste
  1 teaspoon Asian sesame oil

In a small saucepan combine hoisin sauce, the water, and sugar; bring to a boil over medium-high heat. Fold in oil. Let cool. Serve in a saucer.

Makes about ½ cup.

CRISP FRIED GARLIC OR SHALLOT FLAKES

Southeast Asian dishes often call for fried garlic or shallot flakes to garnish noodles, soups, salads, and entrées. It is difficult to imagine, but they are delicious with sweet dessert dishes, too. To ensure even cooking, the garlic or shallot slices must be of equal thickness. It is a good idea to make this condiment in batches; if the slices are fried until completely dry, they will keep several weeks.

  12 cloves garlic or 8 shallots
  2 cups peanut or corn oil
  Salt, to taste

1. Peel garlic or shallots and cut crosswise into slices that are uniformly paper-thin.

2. Preheat wok over medium heat until hot. Pour in oil and heat to 300° F. Add garlic or shallot slices and fry until slices are completely dry, golden brown, and crisp (at least 3 to 5 minutes). Remove, drain on paper towel, and let cool. Sprinkle with salt. Store in an airtight container.

Makes about ½ cup flakes.

THAI HOT SAUCE
Nam prik

Try this hot dipping sauce with grilled or fried foods.

> 2 tablespoons hot water
> 2 tablespoons Thai fish sauce
> 4 tablespoons lime juice
> 1½ tablespoons sugar
> 2 teaspoons finely minced garlic
> 2 teaspoons finely minced green onion

In a small bowl combine the water, fish sauce, lime juice, sugar, and garlic. Let cool, then add green onion. Serve in a shallow dipping bowl.

Makes ½ cup.

INDIAN RAITA

Indian yogurt salads, known as *raita*, are cool, refreshing accompaniments to the highly seasoned dishes of Indian cuisine. They are made with an assortment of cooked or raw vegetables, as well as fruit and nuts. *Rai* means *black mustard seed*, which is essential in certain types of Indian cooking; if it is not readily available, however, this recipe is also delicious without it.

> 1 English cucumber or 2 small regular cucumbers, seeded
> 1 cup plain yogurt
> ¼ cup sour cream
> 1½ tablespoons chopped fresh mint
> 1 tablespoon chopped fresh coriander
> ½ teaspoon ground cumin
> ⅛ teaspoon cayenne pepper
> 1 small Bermuda onion, thinly sliced
> 1 teaspoon black mustard seed (optional)
> 1 tablespoon vegetable oil (optional)
> ½ teaspoon salt

1. Peel, halve, and thinly slice cucumber. In a medium bowl combine yogurt, sour cream, mint, coriander, cumin, and cayenne. Stir in cucumber and onion.

2. If using black mustard seed, heat wok or small skillet over medium heat. Pour in oil. When oil is hot add mustard seed and fry until seeds turn gray and stop sputtering. Add toasted seed to yogurt mixture and stir until blended. Refrigerate. When ready to serve, stir in salt.

Makes about 3½ cups.

THAI SWEET-AND-SOUR CUCUMBER RELISH

This relish is an excellent accompaniment to deep-fried foods.

> 1 English cucumber or 2 small regular cucumbers, seeded
> 1 small Bermuda onion
> ½ teaspoon shrimp powder with chile, toasted in an ungreased wok until aromatic (optional)
> 3 fresh red chiles, finely chopped
> 1 tablespoon coarsely chopped fresh coriander, plus more for garnish
> 1 teaspoon salt
> ⅓ cup sugar
> ½ cup water
> ½ cup white vinegar
> 1 tablespoon Thai fish sauce

1. Peel cucumber, leaving a few lengthwise strips of green skin for color. Cut in half lengthwise; then cut crosswise into ⅛-inch-thick slices. Transfer to a medium bowl. Cut onion in half, peel, and cut crosswise into ⅛-inch-thick slices. Toss with cucumbers. Add shrimp powder (if used), chiles, and the 1 tablespoon coriander.

2. In a small saucepan over low heat, combine salt, sugar, and the water. Stir until dissolved. Remove from heat and stir in vinegar and fish sauce. Pour over cucumber mixture. Garnish with coriander. Serve chilled or at room temperature.

Makes 3 cups.

HAWAIIAN RICE STICK PRAWNS

The rice stick noodle coating makes these prawns look like porcupines. Peggy Fallon, former owner of San Francisco Bay Area Haute Stuff Catering, shared her tropical salsa recipe to accompany this unusual dish.

> 1 ounce rice stick noodles
> Peanut or corn oil, for deep-frying
> 1 pound large prawns, shelled except for tails, deveined, and patted dry
> Salt, to taste
> Flour, for coating
> 2 eggs, slightly beaten

Peggy's Pineapple Salsa

> 1 cup chopped fresh pineapple
> ½ cup chopped red onion
> ¼ cup chopped fresh coriander
> 1 small chopped red chile
> Dash salt

1. In a large brown paper bag, break up rice stick noodles into ¼-inch-long pieces. Pour into a small bowl.

2. Preheat wok over medium-high heat until hot. Pour in oil to a depth of 2 inches and heat to 375° F. Season each prawn with salt, lightly dust with flour, roll in beaten egg, and then roll in rice stick noodle crumbs. Add prawns in batches to hot oil and deep-fry until prawns are golden brown and crisp (about 2 minutes). Remove and drain on paper towel. Repeat with remaining prawns. Serve hot with a bowl of Peggy's Pineapple Salsa.

Serves 8 as an appetizer.

Peggy's Pineapple Salsa In a medium bowl thoroughly blend all ingredients.

Makes about 1¾ cups.

INDONESIAN CORN-SHRIMP FRITTERS
Perkedel djagung

Wherever you wander in Indonesia, you never seem to escape the tantalizing and seductive aroma of frying fritters. This corn fritter with shrimp and Indonesian spices makes an exciting appetizer.

> 3 large ears corn, scraped and coarsely chopped (about 2 cups), or 1 package (10 oz) frozen corn, defrosted
> ½ pound shrimp, shelled, deveined, and cut into ½-inch pieces
> ½ teaspoon chopped garlic
> 4 green onions, chopped (about ½ cup)
> 2 stalks celery, finely chopped (about ½ cup)
> 1 teaspoon ground coriander
> ½ teaspoon ground cumin
> 2 tablespoons chopped fresh coriander
> 3 tablespoons flour
> 1 teaspoon salt
> 2 eggs, beaten
> Peanut or vegetable oil, for deep-frying
> Sriracha chile sauce or other hot sauce, for dipping

1. In a large bowl combine corn, shrimp, garlic, green onion, celery, ground coriander, cumin, fresh coriander, flour, salt, and eggs. Mix thoroughly.

2. Preheat wok over medium-high heat until hot. Pour in oil to a depth of 1 inch; heat oil to 375° F. Add corn mixture in ¼-cup batches, leaving ½ inch space between fritters. Fry until fritters are golden brown and crisp (about 2 minutes per side). Remove, drain on paper towels, and keep warm while frying remaining mixture. Serve hot or at room temperature with chile sauce.

Makes twelve 2½-inch fritters, serves 6 as an appetizer.

KUO TEH

These plump, piquant, juicy dumplings are the northern Chinese specialty many know as potstickers. Commercial wrappers lack the elastic, chewy texture of homemade, and they rarely cook to a good crusty bottom, so it is worth the time and effort to make homemade wrappers. Potstickers freeze well, so make a big batch (see Note).

> 8 leaves napa cabbage, cut into 1-inch chunks (about 2½ cups)
> 1 piece (about ¼ in.) peeled fresh ginger
> 2 green onions, cut into 1-inch lengths
> 2 tablespoons chopped fresh coriander
> ½ teaspoon salt
> ¼ teaspoon white pepper
> ¼ teaspoon sugar
> 1 tablespoon light soy sauce
> 1 tablespoon rice wine or dry vermouth
> 2 teaspoons cornstarch
> 1 tablespoon Asian sesame oil
> ½ pound pork butt, cut into 1½-inch cubes
> 2 tablespoons peanut oil, or as needed
> ½ cup chicken stock mixed with 1½ cups water

Potsticker Wrappers

> 2 cups flour, plus more for kneading
> 1 cup boiling water

Soy Vinegar Chile Dip

> 4 tablespoons white vinegar
> 2 tablespoons light soy sauce
> Few drops Asian hot chile oil
> 1 teaspoon minced fresh coriander

1. *To prepare in a food processor:* Place half the cabbage in the work bowl of a food processor fitted with a steel blade. Pulse 4 or 5 times or until coarsely minced. Remove to a medium bowl. Repeat with remaining cabbage. Wrap minced cabbage in a towel and thoroughly squeeze out excess liquid. You should now have about 1¼ cups cabbage. Set aside. With processor running, drop ginger

down feed tube and process until finely minced (about 10 seconds); then add green onion and coriander and process until finely minced (about 15 seconds more). Scrape down sides. Add salt, pepper, sugar, soy sauce, rice wine, cornstarch, and sesame oil. Pulse twice to mix; then add pork and process until finely ground (about 20 seconds). Add half the reserved cabbage and pulse 3 times. Scrape down sides. Add remaining cabbage and pulse 3 times or until mixed. Do not purée. Remove to a medium bowl, cover, and refrigerate. *To prepare by hand:* Coarsely chop cabbage and wrap in a tea towel. Squeeze out excess liquid. Place cabbage in a medium bowl. Finely chop ginger, green onion, coriander, and pork; add to cabbage mixture. Add salt, pepper, sugar, soy sauce, rice wine, cornstarch, and sesame oil; mix well. Cover and refrigerate.

2. To make potstickers place 1 tablespoon filling in center of each wrapper. Lift opposite sides up to meet over filling and pinch at center. On curved rim of near side, make 3 small pleats to left of center. To right of center, make 3 pleats in opposite direction.

3. Pinch pleated side of wrapper together with unpleated side, making a ½-inch pinched border on top. Set potsticker on a flat surface with pleated side away from you. Place both thumbs on smooth side and push filling forward while pulling ends back toward you to make a pouch. Then gently flatten bottom of potsticker to form a platform. Place on a baking sheet, and refrigerate or freeze until ready to cook.

4. Preheat wok over medium heat until hot. Pour in peanut oil. When hot add 8 to 10 potstickers platform side down; fry until bottoms are browned and crusty (about 1 minute). Add enough stock mixture to come halfway up sides of potstickers. Increase heat to high and bring to a boil. Reduce heat to low, cover, and simmer until liquid has been completely reduced (about 7 minutes),

shaking wok occasionally and adding water if needed. Wok should not be dry before cooking time is up. Remove cover and nudge potstickers with a spatula to loosen. Fry until bottoms are crisp (about 30 seconds). Remove and keep warm. Repeat with remaining potstickers. Serve hot with Soy Vinegar Chile Dip.

Makes about 24 potstickers.

Potsticker Wrappers

1. *To prepare in a food processor:* Place the 2 cups flour in the work bowl of a food processor fitted with a steel blade. With processor running pour the boiling water down feed tube in a steady stream (make sure the water is boiling). Process until dough forms a ball and pulls away from sides (about 30 seconds; do not overprocess). Transfer dough to floured work surface. *To prepare by hand:* Place the 2 cups flour in a large mixing bowl. Add the boiling water and mix with a wooden spoon

into a crumbly dough. Mold into a ball and transfer to a floured work surface. Knead, dusting with flour if necessary, until dough is smooth and no longer sticky (about 2 minutes).

2. Cover dough with a damp towel. Let rest 30 minutes.

3. Dust dough with flour and knead until smooth (2 to 3 minutes). Roll dough into ⅛-inch-thick sheet. Cut out 4-inch-diameter wrappers; cover with a damp towel until ready to use.

Makes about 24 wrappers.

Soy Vinegar Chile Dip   In a small bowl combine all ingredients.

Makes about ½ cup.

<u>Note</u>   To make ahead complete through step 3. Place baking sheet of potstickers in freezer. When potstickers are frozen solid, transfer them to a freezer bag and keep frozen. To cook, proceed with step 4, placing frozen potstickers directly into hot oil in wok; simmer in stock mixture about 9 minutes.

These Indonesian deep-fried fritters—more corn, shrimp, and green onion than batter—are excellent appetizers. Serve them with bottled Sriracha chile sauce, available in Asian specialty food stores, or your choice of hot sauce.

THAI CURRY PASTES

Making your own curry pastes may seem complicated, but only on paper. With an electric minichopper or food processor, the entire procedure takes less than 15 minutes. Hand pounding the paste in a mortar, as the Thais do, produces the best results; if you choose this method, however, plan on taking a good hour and then nursing a "pestle elbow." A critical step is simmering the curry paste in coconut cream, which marries the spice mixture while developing its complex flavors and mellowing its pungency. This is accomplished in an Asian-style wok or, better yet, an Indian-style wok known as a *kadhai*. Its wide, rounded bottom makes it ideal for preparing curries.

THAI RED CURRY PASTE

Thai curry pastes vary according to color and combination of ingredients. Red curry paste is made from dried red chiles and is fiery hot, but it is not as hot as green curry paste. Make a large batch of curry paste. It keeps several weeks in the refrigerator, or it can be frozen in tablespoon amounts in an ice cube tray and the cubes kept in lock-top freezer bags in the freezer.

>　1　can (14 oz) unsweetened coconut milk
>　14　large dried red chiles, stems removed
>　3　strips dried Kaffir lime rind or *zest of 1 lime*
>　3　quarter-sized slices dried galangal (see page 11)
>　1　stalk fresh lemongrass
>　1　teaspoon caraway seed
>　1　tablespoon cumin seed
>　1　tablespoon coriander seed
>　1　teaspoon black peppercorns
>　1　teaspoon salt
>　1　tablespoon paprika
>　7　cloves garlic
>　1　shallot, chopped
>　3　tablespoons minced fresh coriander root (see page 11)
>　1　teaspoon shrimp paste or anchovy paste
>　2　tablespoons vegetable oil, or more if needed

1. Without shaking can pour coconut milk into tall glass container and let stand until coconut cream rises to top (1 to 2 hours). Skim off ½ cup cream; reserve in a small bowl. Set aside remaining coconut milk.

2. In separate small bowls cover chiles, lime rind, and galangal with hot water until soft and pliable (at least 30 minutes). Trim and discard green tops from lemongrass.

3. Heat an ungreased wok over low heat. Toast caraway, cumin, coriander seed, peppercorns, and salt until fragrant (about 5 minutes). Let cool. Transfer to an electric minichopper; add paprika and process to a very fine powder. Remove and set aside.

4. Drain chiles, lime rind, and galangal. In an electric minichopper individually grind drained chiles, lime rind, galangal, and lemongrass to a very fine mince (about 1 minute for each). Transfer minced spices to the work bowl of a food processor fitted with a steel blade. Add garlic, shallot, coriander root, shrimp paste, and reserved toasted spice mixture. With processor running, slowly pour oil down feed tube; process to a finely ground paste (5 to 8 minutes), scraping down sides of bowl every few minutes and adding more oil if needed. Set paste aside.

5. Heat an ungreased wok or kadhai over medium-high heat. Pour in reserved coconut cream and cook until cream is thick and oil separates (2 to 3 minutes), stirring constantly. Add reserved paste and fry 5 minutes, stirring frequently. Add 1 cup of the remaining coconut milk (reserving rest for another use), reduce heat to medium-low, and simmer 20 minutes, stirring often. Paste should be thick and oily. Let cool.

Makes about 1 cup.

INTERNATIONAL COCKTAIL PARTY

Thai Galloping Horses

Gambas al Ajillo

Suppli al Telefono

Tamales con Mole Verde de Pepitas

Brad Borel's Cajun Popcorn

Steamed Siu Mai

Indonesian Potato and Beef Fritters

Crisp Fried Wontons

Beaujolais and White Zinfandel

Here is a chance to show off your culinary skills with an international menu of cocktail foods, including a Spanish tapa, a refreshing citrus appetizer from Thailand, a festive tamale from Mexico, an Indonesian fritter, prosciutto and rice balls from Italy, the jazzy "popcorn" of New Orleans, and, of course, the sweet-and-sour tastes of China. The menu, which easily serves 12 people, is sensational, and the dishes are all made ahead in one pan—a wok.

THAI GALLOPING HORSES
Ma-ho

Eating a Thai meal in Bangkok is like feasting on a banquet of children's portions. The main entrées are quite dainty but plentiful in number and served communally. The Thais take their meals as they do most other things in life—leisurely and with pleasure. They also place great emphasis on presentation. This dish is an excellent example of their flair for color and lightness.

> 3 large navel oranges (see Note)
> 1 teaspoon black peppercorns
> 2 tablespoons minced fresh coriander root (see page 11)
> 4 cloves garlic, chopped
> 2 tablespoons vegetable oil
> 2 shallots, chopped
> 1 fresh chile serrano, chopped
> ¾ pound pork butt, finely chopped
> 1½ tablespoons Thai fish sauce
> 3 tablespoons palm sugar or firmly packed brown sugar
> 4 tablespoons coarsely chopped roasted peanuts
> 2 tablespoons coarsely chopped fresh coriander leaves
> 6 fresh mint leaves, coarsely chopped, plus 24 whole leaves for garnish
> 3 fresh red chiles, slivered, for garnish

1. Hand peel oranges and separate into segments. With a vegetable peeler or sharp paring knife, remove pith on outer curved edge of each segment. Butterfly each segment by cutting lengthwise two-thirds down through the outer curved edge, opening up and flattening into a circle. Repeat with remaining segments. Arrange on a serving dish, skin side down. Cover and refrigerate.

2. *To prepare in an electric mini-chopper:* Chop peppercorns, coriander root, and garlic. *To prepare in a mortar:* Pound together to a paste.

3. Preheat wok over medium-high heat until hot. Pour in oil; then add peppercorn mixture, shallot, and chile and stir-fry until oil is fragrant (about 30 seconds). Increase heat to high and add pork in batches, seconds apart; stir-fry until pork is dry and browned (3 to 4 minutes). Add fish sauce and sugar; stir-fry until mixture becomes dry, dark brown, and sticky (about 1 minute more). Stir in peanuts. Remove from heat and let cool. Mix in chopped coriander and mint.

4. Spoon a heaping teaspoonful of pork mixture on top of each reserved orange circle. Top with whole mint leaf and red chile sliver. Cover and chill until ready to serve.

Makes about 24 pieces.

Note   Sliced pineapple may be used in place of oranges. The filling can also be stuffed into seeded fresh rambutan or lichee nuts.

GAMBAS AL AJILLO

In Spain *tapas* bars are popular retreats for a glass of wine and little snacks called tapas. This dish—shrimp sautéed in the shell with garlic, salt, and olive oil—is a standard at tapas bars. Soak up the delicious leftover sauce with chunks of bread.

> 1 pound shrimp (30 to 35 per lb), shells and tails on, deveined and patted dry
> 6 tablespoons olive oil
> 3 teaspoons coarsely chopped garlic (about 6 large cloves)
> ⅛ teaspoon sugar
> 1 small fresh Anaheim chile, seeded and chopped
> 1½ teaspoons salt

1. In a large bowl combine shrimp, 2 tablespoons of the oil, 1 teaspoon of the garlic, and sugar. Cover and marinate several hours or overnight.

2. Preheat wok over high heat until hot. Pour in remaining 4 tablespoons oil; then add remaining 2 teaspoons garlic, chile, and salt. Cook until garlic turns golden brown. Add shrimp with marinade. Immediately remove wok from heat, add salt, and stir until shrimp turn pink (45 seconds to 1 minute).

Makes 30 to 35 pieces.

SUPPLI AL TELEFONO

The first bite of these prosciutto and rice balls is luscious as the hot melted cheese escapes and stretches into thin threads like telephone lines. This recipe comes from Lonnie Gandara, a culinary professional whose expertise includes Italian cooking.

> 2 cups cold cooked Arborio rice or white short-grain rice
> ½ cup grated Parmesan cheese
> 3 eggs
> 1 teaspoon salt
> ⅛ teaspoon freshly ground pepper
> ¼ teaspoon ground nutmeg
> 1 tablespoon finely chopped parsley
> 2 ounces prosciutto, finely chopped
> 1 tablespoon water
> ½ cup flour, plus more for dusting
> ½ cup dried bread crumbs
> 2 ounces mozzarella cheese, cut into ¼- by 1-inch strips
> Peanut oil, for deep-frying

1. In a large bowl combine rice, Parmesan, 1 beaten egg, salt, pepper, nutmeg, parsley, and prosciutto. In a small bowl beat remaining 2 eggs with the water. Place flour and bread crumbs in 2 separate shallow dishes.

2. Flour your hands and take a heaping tablespoon of rice mixture in palm of your hand. Place a few strips mozzarella in center. Pack another heaping tablespoon of rice mixture over cheese and form into a compact ball about 1½ inches in diameter. Roll ball in flour and shake off excess. Roll ball in beaten egg, coat with bread crumbs, and set on baking sheet. Repeat with remaining ingredients. Chill 2 hours.

3. Preheat wok over medium-high heat until hot. Pour in oil to a depth of 3 inches and heat to 375° F. Add balls in batches and deep-fry until golden brown (about 3 minutes), turning occasionally. Remove and drain on paper towels. Keep warm while frying remaining balls.

Makes 12 balls.

TAMALES CON MOLE VERDE DE PEPITAS

A wok with a bamboo steaming basket works beautifully for these tamales. The sauce is a festive green mole made with pumpkin seed.

- 1 package (8 oz) dried corn husks or twenty 7- by 9-inch rectangles of aluminum foil
- ½ pound lard or shortening
- 1 teaspoon salt
- 2 cups masa harina (½ lb)
- 1 teaspoon baking powder
- 1½ cups cooled chicken stock
- 1 cup cooked chicken, preferably grilled, cut into ¼-inch-thick strips
- 1 can (14 oz) peeled roasted green chiles, cut into ½-inch-wide strips
- ¼ pound Monterey jack cheese, cut into twenty ½- by 2-inch strips

Mole Verde de Pepitas

- ½ cup hulled unsalted pumpkin seed
- 4 canned tomatillos
- 2 cloves garlic
- 6 sprigs fresh coriander
- 1 small poblano chile, roasted and peeled
- 1 teaspoon salt
- ½ teaspoon sugar
- 1½ tablespoons olive oil
  Freshly ground pepper, to taste
- ¼ cup chicken stock

1. Soak husks in hot water until softened (several hours or overnight). Drain upright. Pat dry and set aside.

2. *To prepare in a food processor:* Place lard in work bowl of a food processor fitted with a steel blade; process until fluffy (about 1 minute). In a small bowl mix together salt, masa, and baking powder; add to lard and process until blended. With processor running pour stock down feed tube; process into stiff, smooth dough (about 3 minutes). Remove to a large bowl. *To prepare by hand:* In a large bowl beat lard until fluffy. In a small bowl mix together salt, masa, and baking powder; alternately add masa mixture and stock to lard and beat well (about 5 minutes).

3. On a work surface flatten 2 husks, overlapping broad ends by about 1½ inches. Spread 2 or 3 tablespoons dough along middle of husks, leaving 2-inch borders at each end. Smooth dough into layer ⅛ inch thick by 3 inches wide by 4 inches long. In center of dough place 1 strip each chicken, chile, and cheese and 1½ teaspoons Mole Verde de Pepitas. Fold sides of husks over firmly to enclose filling. Fold over pointed ends toward center, overlapping ends. Repeat with remaining ingredients. Tear another husk along the grain into ties; tie tamales crosswise to secure top flap in place.

4. Prepare wok for steaming (see page 86). Arrange tamales in bamboo steaming baskets seam side down and overlapping slightly. Cover and steam over medium-high heat until dough can be peeled away cleanly from husks (about 1 hour), adding water if needed. Serve hot with remaining Mole Verde de Pepitas.

Makes about 20 appetizer-sized tamales.

Mole Verde de Pepitas

1. Preheat ungreased wok over medium heat until hot. Lightly toast pumpkin seeds until golden brown (about 30 seconds), stirring constantly. Remove from wok and let cool; then grind in an electric minichopper. Set aside.

2. Place tomatillos in the work bowl of a food processor or blender. Add garlic, coriander, chile, salt, and sugar; process or blend to a purée.

3. Preheat wok or skillet over medium-high heat. Pour in oil. When hot add tomatillo mixture and cook until liquid is reduced (about 2 minutes). Reduce heat to low and stir in reserved pumpkin seed and pepper. Gradually add stock; simmer mixture 2 minutes.

Makes 1 cup.

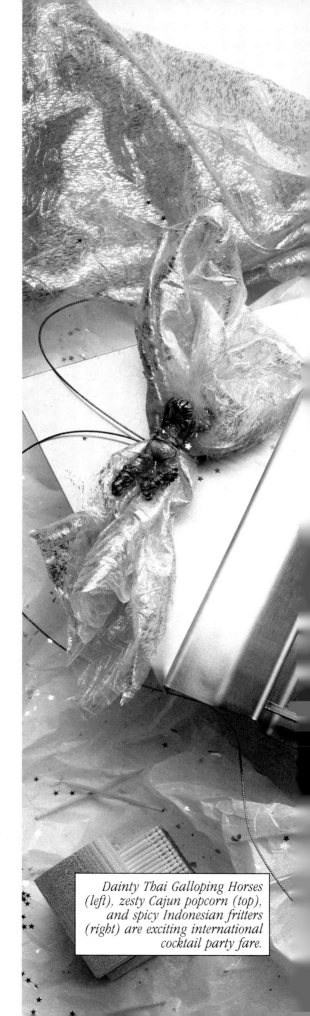

Dainty Thai Galloping Horses (left), zesty Cajun popcorn (top), and spicy Indonesian fritters (right) are exciting international cocktail party fare.

BRAD BOREL'S CAJUN POPCORN

Chef Brad Borel's "popcorn" is one of the most popular dishes on the menu at his restaurant in San Francisco, and for good reason—the flavors are complex and the popcornlike texture is delightful. Chef Borel's method of coating and recoating the crayfish tails with corn flour produces a light crispness—a technique he says he learned from his mom.

> *Peanut oil, for deep-frying*
> 1 *pound cooked crayfish tails* *(see Note)*
> 1 *teaspoon salt*
> ⅛ *teaspoon white pepper*
> 1 *teaspoon cayenne pepper*
> ½ *teaspoon garlic powder*
> 4 *tablespoons water*
> *Tartar sauce or cocktail sauce, for accompaniment (optional)*

Seasoned Corn Flour Coating

> 3 *cups corn flour (see Note)*
> 2 *teaspoons salt*
> ¼ *teaspoon white pepper*
> ½ *teaspoon cayenne pepper*

1. Preheat wok over medium-high heat until hot. Pour in oil to a depth of 2 inches and heat to 375° F.

2. In a large bowl combine crayfish, salt, white pepper, cayenne, and garlic powder. Add 2 tablespoons of the water and blend well. Divide crayfish mixture between 2 bowls.

3. Add 2 tablespoons of the Seasoned Corn Flour Coating to 1 bowl of the crayfish mixture; blend well. Pour entire mixture into large bowl of corn flour coating and toss together gently. With a large skimmer scoop out crayfish, shaking excess coating back into bowl. Add coated crayfish to hot oil in batches, seconds apart, and deep-fry until crayfish are brown and crisp (about 2 minutes). Remove and keep warm. Repeat with remaining crayfish mixture. Serve hot with tartar sauce, if desired.

Serves 8 as an appetizer.

Seasoned Corn Flour Coating

In a large bowl thoroughly blend all ingredients.

Makes about 3 cups.

<u>Note</u> Chef Borel suggests shrimp as a substitute for crayfish tails. If corn flour is not available, substitute a blend of 2 cups cornmeal and 1 cup all-purpose flour.

STEAMED SIU MAI

This delicately seasoned mixture of chopped pork and shrimp in a thin pasta wrapper is standard dim sum fare in all Cantonese teahouses. It can be made at home days in advance and reheated (see Note). Siu mai makes an excellent hors d'oeuvre.

> 1 *pound pork butt, fairly fatty, cut into 1-inch cubes*
> 1 *teaspoon salt*
> ⅛ *teaspoon white pepper*
> 2 *teaspoons sugar*
> 2 *tablespoons light soy sauce, plus more for dipping (optional)*
> 1 *tablespoon dry vermouth or rice wine*
> 1 *piece (½-inch) fresh ginger, pressed through garlic press, juice reserved*
> 1 *tablespoon cornstarch*
> 1 *tablespoon Asian sesame oil*
> ½ *pound shrimp, shelled, deveined, patted dry, and cut into ¼-inch pieces*
> 1 *package (1 lb) siu mai wrappers or wonton wrappers (see Note)*
> *Vegetable oil, for brushing*

1. *To prepare in a food processor:* Place pork in the work bowl of a food processor fitted with a steel blade; coarsely chop 10 seconds. Change to plastic blade. Add salt, pepper, sugar, soy sauce, vermouth, ginger juice, cornstarch, and sesame oil; process 2 minutes. Add shrimp and pulse 2 or 3 times to combine thoroughly. Remove mixture to a large bowl, cover, and refrigerate 2 hours. *To prepare by hand:* Chop pork finely. In a large bowl combine pork, salt, pepper, sugar, soy sauce, vermouth, ginger juice, cornstarch, and sesame oil; beat together until smooth and thoroughly combined (2 or 3 minutes). Fold in shrimp. Cover bowl and refrigerate 2 hours.

2. Place 1 tablespoon filling in middle of each wrapper. Pinch sides into tiny pleats around filling. With your index finger and thumb, cup sides to form a cylinder like a small, straight-edged cupcake. Smooth top with a spoon dipped in water. Tap bottom of dumpling against a flat surface to create a platform. Arrange dumplings ½ inch apart on oiled latticework of bamboo steaming basket or on oiled flat heat-resistant plate. Cover and refrigerate until ready to steam. Repeat with remaining filling.

3. Prepare wok for steaming (see page 86). Cover and steam dumplings over medium-high heat 10 minutes. Serve dumplings hot directly from steaming basket with soy sauce, if desired.

Makes 4 dozen dumplings.

<u>Note</u> Steam already-cooked dumplings 5 minutes to reheat them. If round siu mai wrappers are not available, trim the corners of square wonton wrappers with kitchen shears to make circles.

INDONESIAN POTATO AND BEEF FRITTERS

These potato croquettes are balls of mashed potatoes stuffed with a spiced beef mixture. The first bite explodes with the seductive aromas and intriguing flavors of Indonesia.

    2 pounds baking potatoes,
       boiled and mashed
    2 large eggs
    1½ teaspoons salt, plus more
       to taste
    ½ teaspoon freshly ground
       pepper, or to taste
    ⅛ teaspoon ground nutmeg
    1 tablespoon oil, plus more
       for deep-frying
    4 shallots, finely chopped
    ½ teaspoon finely grated
       fresh ginger
    2 cloves garlic, minced
    2 fresh green chiles, seeded
       and chopped
    2 teaspoons ground coriander
    1 teaspoon ground cumin
    ½ pound lean ground beef
    2 tablespoons chopped fresh
       coriander
    ½ cup very fine dried bread
       crumbs
       Flour, for dusting
       Indian-style chutney, Indian
       Raita (see page 25), or chile
       sauce, for accompaniment

1. In a large bowl combine potatoes, 1 beaten egg, 1 teaspoon of the salt, pepper, and nutmeg.

2. Preheat wok over medium heat until hot. Pour in the 1 tablespoon oil; then add shallot, ginger, garlic, chiles, ground coriander, and cumin. Sauté 1 minute. Increase heat to medium-high, add beef, and cook until browned (about 2 minutes). Add remaining salt and pepper. If liquids accumulate on bottom of wok, cook mixture over high heat to reduce. Transfer mixture to a large bowl and wipe wok dry with paper towels. When mixture is cooled stir in fresh coriander.

3. In a small bowl beat remaining egg. Place bread crumbs in a shallow dish. Flour your hands and place a heaping tablespoon potato mixture in palm of your hand. Place 2 teaspoons meat mixture in center and cover meat with another tablespoon potato mixture. Mold into a ball, enclosing meat filling. Roll ball in beaten egg, coat with bread crumbs, and set on a baking sheet. Repeat with remaining ingredients. Refrigerate balls if not frying immediately.

4. Preheat wok over medium-high heat until hot. Pour in peanut oil to a depth of 3 inches and heat to 375° F. Add balls in batches and deep-fry until golden brown (about 3 minutes), turning occasionally. Remove, drain on paper towels, and keep warm while frying remaining balls. Serve with chutney.

Makes 16 fritters.

CRISP FRIED WONTONS

The sweet-and-sour sauce accompanying these wontons is more salsalike than typical wonton dipping sauces, and the fresh fruit juices hint of the tropics. Note that the basic wonton recipe makes 5 dozen wontons, only 30 of which are needed here, so you will have 30 wontons left over. Keep them in the freezer for future use, or refer to the recipe for Basic Wontons for other suggestions.

    30 deep-fried Basic Wontons
       (see page 42)

Shaved Pineapple Sweet-and-Sour Sauce

    ½ cup fresh orange juice
    ½ cup pineapple juice,
       preferably fresh
    ½ cup red wine vinegar or
       raspberry vinegar
    1 or 2 sticks Chinese brown slab
       sugar or ½ cup firmly packed
       regular brown sugar
    2 tablespoons granulated sugar
    2 tablespoons tomato paste
    ½ teaspoon grated fresh ginger
    1 teaspoon soy sauce
    ½ teaspoon salt
    1 tablespoon cornstarch
    3 tablespoons water
    2 tablespoons each diced green
       and red bell pepper
    ½ cup shaved or grated fresh
       pineapple
    2 teaspoons grated fresh
       lemon zest

Arrange deep-fried wontons on a platter. Serve with Shaved Pineapple Sweet-and-Sour Sauce.

Makes 30 wontons.

Shaved Pineapple Sweet-and-Sour Sauce In a small saucepan over medium heat, combine orange and pineapple juices, vinegar, brown sugar, granulated sugar, tomato paste, ginger, soy sauce, and salt. Bring mixture to a boil, reduce heat, and simmer 5 minutes. Combine cornstarch and the water. Return juice mixture to a boil over medium heat and add cornstarch mixture; cook until sauce is thick, stirring continuously. Add green and red bell pepper, pineapple, and zest. Transfer sauce to a dipping bowl; keep warm.

Makes 1½ cups.

The basics of rice and noodle dishes include glutinous rice, flat rice noodles, rice stick noodles, fresh Chinese egg noodles, and bean thread noodles.

Breakfast, Lunch & Snacks

One-dish meals such as noodles and countless variations of fried rice are popular throughout Asia for lunch and brunch and even a midnight snack. On a hot summer day try Chilled Noodles in Peking Meat Sauce (see page 51) or Singapore Curry Rice Stick Noodles (see page 38). For a casual lunch serve Wonton Noodles With Orange-Coriander Chile Sauce (see page 51). Quickly stir-fry Shrimp and Barbecued Pork Fried Rice (see page 43) as a snack, accompany it with a few dim sum appetizers for brunch, or serve it for breakfast as the Chinese do. Some of the dishes in this chapter are traditionally cooked in a wok and some are not, but all are easy to make, fun to eat, and complete meals in themselves.

RICE, NOODLE, AND WONTON DISHES

Noodle and wonton dishes are popular lunch and snack fare. A noodle dish such as Chilled Noodles in Peking Meat Sauce (see page 51) is usually sufficient as a light lunch for one. A lunch menu for more than one person might include Watercress Wonton Soup (see page 52)—a bowl of wonton dumplings steeped in soup stock and garnished with barbecued pork, strips of roast duck, or crisp stalks of bok choy—as well as Barbecued Pork Buns (see page 40), a fried rice dish, and one or two dim sum appetizers, such as Classic Shrimp Toast (see page 19) and Steamed Siu Mai (see page 32).

In Asia fried eggs and egg dishes are not necessarily thought of just as breakfast food. It is not uncommon to find such lunch or dinner dishes as Coin Purse Eggs With Oyster Sauce (see page 46), Barbecued Pork and Shrimp Egg Fu Yung (see page 45), or Savory Steamed Shrimp Egg Custards (see page 64). Included in this chapter are egg dishes perfectly suited for a Western breakfast or brunch or a side dish for lunch or dinner.

Noodle Basics

Noodles have been so popular with Asians for centuries that one chapter can scarcely address the subject. Until recently, they were denigrated as peasant food in Asia. However, they are now widely accepted and any reputable Hong Kong restaurant has a special noodle chef trained in the art of hand-thrown noodles.

The Chinese savor noodles with gusto. Uttering slurping sounds as every last strand is enjoyed is considered a compliment to the chef. Noodles symbolize longevity, and especially long noodles are served at birthdays, much as a cake is served in the West.

Chinese noodles are easy to store. Dried noodles store indefinitely in an airtight plastic bag in a dry cupboard. Fresh noodles store refrigerated for up to a week and frozen for up to three months. (Fresh rice noodles cannot be frozen but will keep refrigerated for almost a week.) Frozen noodles need not be defrosted; simply add them to boiling salted water and stir continuously with chopsticks until the strands separate.

Fresh Chinese egg noodles

Medium-wide fresh Chinese egg noodles, the most common Chinese noodles, are the spaghetti of this cuisine. They may be found in almost all American supermarkets. Made from wheat flour, egg, and water (the same ingredients as Italian pasta), they may be used for stir-frying, deep-frying, or soup or served slightly chilled. Their diameter makes them substantial enough for crusty Shallow-Fried Noodle Cakes (see page 47) and dense enough to absorb the seasonings of *lo mein*. Use these noodles if other varieties are not available.

Thin fresh egg noodles are best for soups or noodle dishes served at room temperature. They contain more egg than medium-wide noodles, so their texture is a bit more substantial and they hold up better in soups. They also work well with strong seasonings. Thin noodles can be stir-fried or shallow-fried; sauces tend to cling to the noodles rather than be absorbed into them, but sometimes this is desirable.

Keep in mind that fresh egg noodles need preliminary boiling (unless they will be deep-fried) and must be drained and rinsed thoroughly before stir-frying and saucing. For 1 pound of noodles, in a wok or large stockpot over high heat, bring 4 quarts salted water to a boil. Gently pull apart ball of noodles to separate strands. Add noodles to boiling water; with long chopsticks stir to separate strands until water reaches a second boil. Add 1 cup cold water. Continue cooking until water returns to a boil.

Immediately pour noodles into a colander and rinse with cold water. (The Chinese, unlike the Italians, do not rinse pasta with hot water.) Drain noodles thoroughly. Transfer to a large bowl and toss with Asian sesame oil.

Dried Chinese egg noodles

These noodles come packaged in coiled bundles (both flavored and unflavored) or as thin straight noodles. Dried noodles need a slightly longer preliminary boiling than the fresh variety.

Dried noodles often have other ingredients, such as scallops, fish, or shrimp, mixed into the dough. American pasta producers are adapting this popular Chinese technique, using interesting and colorful ingredients, such as tomatoes, chiles, spinach, bell peppers, and even chocolate.

Scallop noodles—ramen-style noodles made with scallops—are coiled in individual servings and packed in bags of ten coils. The coils need a relatively short preliminary boiling, from 2 to 3 minutes.

Bean thread noodles

Also known as transparent, cellophane, glass, mirror, pea starch, and mung bean noodles, bean thread noodles are made from puréed mung bean that is strained and dried. The noodles are packaged as thin, brittle threads and are white in color. Look for individually wrapped 1- or 2-ounce bundles, unless you require more, because they are extremely difficult to cut in their dried state. Store them as you would any other dried noodles—in an airtight plastic bag in a dry cupboard.

Bean thread noodles must be soaked in water before simmering. Soaking makes them pliable; simmering makes them plump, gelatinous, transparent, and smooth. Place the required amount of dried noodles in a bowl. Cover with warm water and soak until noodles are soft and pliable (20 to 30 minutes). Drain. They are then ready to be stir-fried, simmered, or added to soups. They absorb other flavors marvelously and may be simmered without becoming mushy for longer periods than other noodles; they also taste as good reheated as they do freshly cooked.

Rice stick noodles and flat rice noodles   Made from rice flour, both of these noodles are popular in eastern and southern regions of China, as well as throughout Southeast Asia. Rice noodles are enjoyed for their noncompetitive, bland flavor and their ability to soak up even the lightest flavors in a sauce. Dried noodles do not require preliminary boiling, but they must be softened in water and drained. They may then be stir-fried with meat and vegetables or cooked in soups or curry sauces, such as Singapore Curry Rice Stick Noodles (see page 38). Rice stick noodles, which are almost always found dried, can also be deep-fried. They puff up immediately into crispy white noodles. Crushed gently, they form a delicious bed for stir-fried meat and vegetables.

Flat rice noodles come both dried and fresh; they are interchangeable in most recipes. After being softened in water, dried flat rice noodles are popular for stir-frying. Their size and shape are perfect for the assertive flavors of Thai Stir-fried Flat Rice Noodles (see page 48). Fresh flat rice noodles are pure white with a soft and silky smooth texture unlike that of any other noodle. They are made with rice powder prepared in a milk-like batter and steamed in flat trays. Available in Asian grocery stores and noodle shops, these fresh noodles shouldn't be boiled before stir-frying and should be used within five days.

Rice paper wrappers   These dried round wrappers made from rice, salt, and water are tissue thin and very brittle and bear the imprint of a crisscross bamboo pattern on each sheet. To soften, brush with water or quickly slide through a pan of water before using.

Wonton wrappers   High-quality wonton wrappers are available in American supermarkets in 1-pound packages of varying thicknesses (80 to 100 wrappers per pound). Thin ones are best for soups and medium-thick ones for deep-frying, although thin ones can be used for both, including making Steamed Siu Mai (see page 32). Well sealed in plastic wrap and stored in the freezer, the wrappers will keep for a few months.

Making Perfect Rice

Contrary to popular belief, rice has not traditionally been the mainstay of all China. Rice was enjoyed primarily in southern China, where the climate and terrain were suitable for its cultivation. It was regarded as a luxury by the northern Chinese, who consumed millet, sorghum, and corn, and noodles and breads made from wheat as their daily starch.

Perfectly cooked rice is just sticky enough for the grains to adhere to each other yet still part easily with a light nudge of a spoon or chopstick. The size of the pan used to cook the rice is important. The washed uncooked rice should take up no less than a third and no more than half of the pan.

The most common error in preparing rice is serving it immediately after it is done. Rice should stand at least 10 minutes, covered and undisturbed. Before serving, it should be fluffed up with a wooden spoon dipped in water. Cooked rice can be kept warm for up to 45 minutes by removing the pan from the burner and leaving the lid on.

PERFECT RICE

For about 3 cups cooked white long-grain rice, use 1 cup rice and 1¼ cups water; for 4 or 5 cups cooked rice, use 2 cups rice and 2¼ cups water; for 7 or 8 cups cooked rice, use 3 cups rice and 3½ cups water. The same amount of chicken or beef stock can be substituted for the water. Note that the amount of water does not increase proportionately as the amount of rice increases. For this reason the Chinese method of measuring the water by adding enough to cover the rice in a saucepan by one knuckle's worth (or approximately ¾ inch above the rice surface) has been used, successfully, for several centuries.

White long-grain rice
Cold water

1. Rinse rice under cold running water, gently stirring and rubbing grains between fingers to loosen excess starch. Repeat until water runs clear. Drain thoroughly. Pour rice into pan. Add the water and allow to sit at least 30 minutes.

2. With lid ajar bring rice to a boil over high heat, stirring occasionally with chopsticks to loosen grains. Reduce heat to medium-high and continue to boil with lid ajar until all surface water has been absorbed (5 to 8 minutes). Rice surface should appear pitted. Cover pan, reduce heat to low, and simmer undisturbed 20 minutes (see Note).

3. Remove pan from heat and allow to stand, covered, at least 10 minutes before serving. Then with a wet wooden spoon, fluff rice and serve.

Note   Crust that forms on bottom of pan may be saved and used to make Sizzling Rice Cakes (see page 68), Tamarind Shrimp Dip With Sizzling Rice Cakes (see page 16), and Sizzling Rice Soup (see page 68).

SINGAPORE CURRY RICE STICK NOODLES

For this popular teahouse specialty, rice stick noodles are rehydrated in water and then stir-fried like other noodles. The curry seasoning in this dish is borrowed from Indian and Malay cooking. Both cuisines are indigenous to Singapore, hence the recipe's name.

    ½ pound thin rice stick noodles
    6 Chinese dried black
       mushrooms
    3 tablespoons peanut or corn oil
    4 slices fresh ginger
    2 green onions, cut into
       1½-inch lengths
    ½ teaspoon salt
    1 small whole chicken breast,
       boned, skinned, and shredded
    ¼ pound medium shrimp,
       shelled and deveined
    ½ pound Chinese barbecued
       pork or sugar-cured baked
       ham, julienned
    1 small onion, thinly sliced
    1 stalk celery, cut diagonally
       into thin slices
    4 ounces fresh snow peas,
       strings and stems removed,
       julienned diagonally
       (about ½ cup)
    ½ green bell pepper, thinly sliced
    ½ teaspoon sugar
    1 tablespoon curry powder,
       preferably Indian style,
       or to taste
    1 tablespoon light soy sauce,
       or more if needed
    1 tablespoon dark soy sauce
    4 tablespoons chicken stock,
       or as needed

1. In 2 separate medium-sized bowls filled with warm water, soak noodles and mushrooms until they are soft and pliable (about 20 minutes). Drain well. Cover noodles to prevent drying. Squeeze excess water from mushrooms, cut off and discard stems, and shred caps. Set noodles and mushrooms aside.

2. Preheat wok over high heat until hot. Pour in 2 tablespoons of the oil; add 2 slices of the ginger, green onion, and ¼ teaspoon of the salt

and cook until oil is fragrant (about 30 seconds). Add chicken, stir-fry, and seconds later toss in shrimp and pork. Stir-fry just until shrimp and chicken feel firm to the touch (about 1 minute). Remove and set aside. Pick out and discard ginger.

3. To hot wok add remaining 1 tablespoon oil, 2 slices ginger, and ¼ teaspoon salt. Add onion, celery, snow peas, reserved mushrooms, and bell pepper, individually and seconds apart, and stir-fry until vegetables are tender and crisp (1 to 2 minutes). Blend in sugar, curry powder, soy sauces, and 2 tablespoons of the stock. Add reserved noodles, coat evenly with sauce, and stir-fry until noodles are moist but not wet (about 1 minute) and begin to cling to each other, adding more stock if noodles seem too dry. Add reserved meat mixture and toss, adjusting seasoning if necessary. Remove to a serving platter and serve hot.

Serves 4 as a light lunch or snack or 8 with other dishes.

DEEP-FRIED RICE STICK NOODLES

The trick to successfully preparing these noodles is deep-frying them in small amounts and using adequately hot oil.

       Rice stick noodles
    2 cups peanut oil, for
       deep-frying

In a large brown bag pull apart noodles. Preheat wok over medium-high heat until hot. Pour in oil and heat to 375° F (a noodle dropped into oil should puff up within 5 seconds). When oil is hot add noodles a small handful at a time. As soon as they puff, turn noodles over and fry other side for 3 seconds. Immediately remove and drain on paper towel. Repeat with remaining noodles. Rice stick noodles may be fried a few days in advance. Store cooked noodles in an airtight container in a cupboard.

LO MEIN NOODLES WITH BARBECUED PORK AND BEAN SPROUTS

Lo mein refers to a style of noodle preparation in which the noodle is lightly tossed and coated with a sauce. The texture of the noodle is smooth, as opposed to the crisp edges of Shallow-Fried Noodle Cakes (see page 47). To enhance the basic lo mein, various meats and vegetables are added—a perfect means of using leftover bits of barbecued pork or steamed chicken and small portions of sliced cabbage, lettuce, bok choy, or mushrooms.

    1½ tablespoons oyster sauce
    1 tablespoon light soy sauce
    2 tablespoons dark soy sauce
    2 teaspoons Asian sesame oil
    2 teaspoons sugar
    ½ teaspoon white pepper
    4 tablespoons peanut oil
    2 slices fresh ginger, bruised
    2 cloves garlic, bruised
    1 teaspoon salt
    ½ pound Chinese barbecued
       pork or sugar-cured baked
       ham, julienned
    1 cup coarsely chopped Chinese
       garlic chives or green onion
    ½ pound fresh bean sprouts,
       patted dry and tails removed
       (see Note)
    1 pound medium-wide fresh
       Chinese egg noodles (see page
       36), cooked, rinsed, and
       drained

1. In a medium bowl combine oyster sauce, soy sauces, sesame oil, sugar, and pepper; set aside.

2. Preheat wok over medium-high heat until hot. Pour in 2 tablespoons of the peanut oil; then add 1 slice of the ginger, 1 clove of the garlic, and ½ teaspoon of the salt. Cook until oil is fragrant (about 30 seconds). Add pork and chives; stir-fry until chives begin to wilt (about 15 seconds). Increase heat to high and add sprouts in batches, seconds apart; stir-fry each batch until sprouts are limp (about 30 seconds total). Remove to a plate. Remove and discard ginger and garlic. If wok is wet or sticky, rinse with hot water and dry.

3. Replace wok over medium-high heat. When wok is hot add remaining 2 tablespoons oil, 1 slice ginger, 1 clove garlic, ½ teaspoon salt, and reserved sauce mixture; stir until oil is fragrant (about 15 seconds). Add noodles; toss to coat evenly with sauce (1 to 2 minutes). Add reserved pork mixture; toss together to heat through.

Serves 4 as a light lunch or snack or 6 as a side dish.

<u>Note</u> Shredded bok choy or cabbage can be used in place of bean sprouts.

MANDARIN FRIED RICE

The Chinese have long preferred simple boiled rice with dinner; it soaks up the flavors of a dish and its neutral, unassertive taste does not compete with sauces. This Mandarin-style fried rice, delicately seasoned with a hint of ginger and roasted salt, is more colorful and dressy than plain boiled rice and nicely complements many entrées.

> 3 *large eggs*
> 1¼ *teaspoon salt*
> 4 *tablespoons peanut or corn oil*
> 1 *slice peeled fresh ginger, bruised*
> 4 *or 5 cups cold cooked white long-grain rice (see page 37)*
> 2 *green onions, chopped*
> 6 *ounces cooked small bay shrimp*
> ½ *cup cooked peas*

1. In a small bowl lightly beat eggs with ¼ teaspoon of the salt; set aside.

2. Preheat wok over medium-high heat until hot. Pour in 2 tablespoons of the oil. When hot add reserved egg mixture. Scramble and stir-fry egg until egg is set but not dry (about 1 minute), tilting wok and pushing cooked egg up sides to allow

uncooked egg to flow to center. Remove from heat and transfer egg to a medium bowl. With a spatula chop egg into small pieces and set aside.

3. Replace wok over medium-high heat and add remaining 2 tablespoons oil, remaining 1 teaspoon salt, and ginger. Cook until oil is fragrant (about 30 seconds). Add rice. With a spatula press, poke, and toss until grains separate but do not brown (2 to 3 minutes). Add green onion, shrimp, and peas; toss together. Add reserved egg pieces and combine. Serve hot.

Serves 6 with other dishes.

Curried rice stick noodles are standard fare in teahouses. When stir-fried, rice stick noodles absorb other flavors; in this dish they absorb the delicate, light curry flavor of the stir-fried chicken, shrimp, and barbecued pork mixture.

MAKING BARBECUED PORK BUNS

Barbecued pork buns are eaten for breakfast, lunch, and snacks. They are one of numerous dim sum specialties of Cantonese teahouses and a favorite food of Asians and Westerners. In this version (recipe at right), the bread dough is Chinese Sweet Yeast Bread Dough (see page 47), and the barbecued pork for the filling is purchased at a Chinese delicatessen.

The buns can be steamed or baked, depending on your preference. The steamed buns, shaped in a spiral with a steam hole at the top, are more traditional. During steaming, the buns retain their opaque white color but become light and fluffy.

The baked version, which is becoming as popular as the steamed one, is rounded and has a golden brown crust. Baking is a good way to rescue imperfectly shaped buns: Simply pinch the opening closed, set the sealed end on parchment paper, and bake.

1. *Divide dough in half and form each half into a 12-inch-long log. Cut each log into 10 pieces; flour each piece, then roll each into a 4-inch circle about ¼ inch thick. With end of rolling pin, flatten 1-inch perimeter of each circle into ⅛-inch-thick edge.*

2. *Place heaping tablespoon pork mixture in middle of each circle. Hold dough in one hand with thumb resting on pork filling. With your other hand gather an edge and gently pull it up and over pork to create a thin pleat.*

3. *Rotate bun, continuing to make thin pleats all around edge until filling is enclosed.*

4. *Pinch top folds of pleats into spiral tip, then twist to seal. Cook as directed on opposite page.*

BARBECUED PORK BUNS
Cha sui bao

Barbecued pork buns have helped put Chinese cuisine on the culinary map. Pork buns are terrific for breakfast, lunch, or as a snack. There are never enough, so make extra and freeze them (see Note). You can purchase the barbecued pork at a Chinese delicatessen. Unlike other recipes in this book in which ham can be substituted for barbecued pork, this recipe depends on barbecued pork for its unique flavor.

¾ cup water
1 tablespoon each *oyster sauce, hoisin sauce, and dark soy sauce*
2 tablespoons sugar
1 tablespoon peanut or corn oil
1 pound Chinese barbecued pork, cut into ¼-inch cubes (about 3 cups)
1 tablespoon cornstarch mixed with 1 tablespoon water
1 teaspoon Asian sesame oil
1 recipe Chinese Sweet Yeast Bread Dough (see page 47)
20 pieces (3 in. square) parchment paper

1. In a small bowl combine the water, oyster sauce, hoisin sauce, soy sauce, and sugar; set aside.

2. Preheat wok over medium-high heat until hot. Pour in peanut oil. When hot add pork and stir-fry 30 seconds. Add sauce mixture and bring to a boil. Add cornstarch mixture; stir continuously until sauce thickens (about 15 seconds). Fold in sesame oil. Remove to a medium bowl and refrigerate.

3. Make pork buns following Step-by-Step at left.

4. Place each bun pleated side up on a 3-inch square of parchment. Arrange buns about 1 inch apart in bamboo steaming baskets. Cover and let stand until doubled in size (at least 30 minutes).

5. Prepare wok for steaming (see page 86). Cover buns and steam over medium-high heat until buns are puffy (about 20 minutes). Serve hot.

Makes about 20 buns.

Variation   To bake buns rather than steam them, place each filled bun pleated side down on parchment square. Arrange buns 1 inch apart on a baking sheet. Cover and let stand until doubled in size (at least 30 minutes). In a small bowl beat 1 egg yolk, 1 tablespoon water, and ½ teaspoon sugar; brush tops of risen buns with egg wash. Bake in a 325° F oven 20 minutes.

<u>Note</u>   Cooked buns will keep refrigerated 3 to 5 days or frozen several weeks. Reheat refrigerated buns by steaming 10 minutes in a steamer or baking 10 minutes in a 350° F oven. To reheat frozen buns, cook them 5 minutes longer.

For a fabulous breakfast, lunch, or snack, find the Chinese delicatessen with the tastiest barbecued pork and make these delicious stuffed buns. They can be steamed, as shown here, or baked. Make a big batch and freeze extras.

Creamy rice pilaf with pancetta is complemented by crisp fried garlic flakes, a garnish often used in Southeast Asian cooking. This dish is a good accompaniment for grilled meats.

BASIC WONTONS

The Chinese give poetic names to their favorite foods—*wonton* means *cioud swallow.* Use Basic Wontons in soup (see pages 52 and 68), or to make Crisp Fried Wontons (see page 33) or Wonton Noodles With Orange-Coriander Chile Sauce (see page 51). Wontons freeze well. Freeze uncooked wontons on baking sheets; when they are frozen solid, pack in containers. Wontons do not need to be thawed before cooking.

> 1 package (1 lb) wonton skins
> 1 egg, lightly beaten
> 3 quarts water, if boiling, or *peanut oil, as needed, if deep-frying*

Basic Wonton Filling

> ¾ pound shrimp, shelled and deveined
> 2 pinches plus 1 teaspoon salt
> ½ pound pork butt, finely chopped

> 1 teaspoon grated fresh ginger
> 1 teaspoon sugar
>   Pinch white pepper
> 1 tablespoon soy sauce
> 1 tablespoon dry sherry or rice wine
> 2 teaspoons Asian sesame oil
> 2 teaspoons cornstarch
> 2 green onions, white part only, minced
> 6 Chinese water chestnuts, preferably fresh, peeled and minced

1. To wrap wontons lay 1 wonton skin flat in your open hand with one corner pointing at you. Place 1 teaspoon Basic Wonton Filling in top third corner of wonton. Fold over top corner toward you, tucking in filling. Roll filling over again, using only half the skin, forming a triangle. Pinch edges around filling.

2. Pull 2 opposite corners up and around filling, away from exposed corner, and overlap slightly at top edge of filling. Pinch together, moistening edge with beaten egg to seal. Set on baking sheet. Repeat with remaining filling and wonton skins.

3. *To boil:* In a flat-bottomed wok or large stockpot over high heat, bring the water to a boil. Reduce heat to medium-high; add wontons in batches and boil uncovered until wontons float (about 2 minutes). Remove and drain. *To deep-fry:* Preheat wok over medium-high heat until hot. Pour in oil to a depth of 3 inches and heat to 350° F. Add wontons in batches and deep-fry until they are golden brown (about 2 minutes), turning occasionally. Remove and drain.

Makes about 5 dozen wontons.

Basic Wonton Filling   Coarsely chop shrimp. In a medium bowl combine shrimp and the 2 pinches salt. Add pork, ginger, sugar, pepper, soy sauce, sherry, sesame oil, cornstarch, and remaining 1 teaspoon salt. Mix together into a smooth paste. Fold in green onion and water chestnuts. Set aside 30 minutes.

Makes enough filling for 5 dozen wontons.

RICE PILAF WITH PARMESAN CREAM

Leftover rice pilaf is tranformed into an exciting side dish when sautéed with dried *porcini* mushrooms and *pancetta* (thick-sliced Italian bacon) and simmered with heavy cream.

    ¼   cup dried porcini mushrooms
    2   ounces pancetta, diced
    3   tablespoons unsalted butter
    2   shallots, chopped
    ½   cup shelled fresh peas,
        parboiled 2 minutes and
        drained
    ½   cup heavy cream
    ½   cup freshly grated Parmesan
        cheese
        Pinch freshly grated nutmeg
        Freshly ground black pepper,
        to taste
    2½ cups rice pilaf (see Note)
        Fried garlic flakes (see Crisp
        Fried Garlic or Shallot Flakes,
        page 24), for garnish

1. In a small bowl cover mushrooms with warm water and soak until soft (about 3 hours). Strain mushrooms, reserving ¼ cup liquid; coarsely chop mushrooms and set aside.

2. Preheat wok over medium heat until hot. Sauté pancetta until brown. Spoon off and discard all but 1 tablespoon fat. Add butter and heat until it begins to sizzle. Add shallot, reserved mushrooms, and peas; sauté 5 minutes. Add reserved mushroom liquid, cream, cheese, nutmeg, and pepper. Carefully stir in rice and simmer, stirring occasionally, until rice is warm (5 to 8 minutes). Garnish with garlic flakes and more pepper and serve.

Serves 4 with other dishes.

Note   If you have no leftover rice pilaf, make it by sautéing 1 cup uncooked rice in 3 tablespoons unsalted butter 3 to 5 minutes over medium heat, stirring frequently. Add 1¼ cups beef or chicken stock and follow cooking directions for Perfect Rice (see page 37). Or use plain cooked rice instead of rice pilaf.

THAI CHILE-PORK OMELET

The chile-pork omelet served in the coffee shop of the Bangkok Oriental Hotel inspired this recipe. Like many other Asian-style omelets, it is cooked and presented more like a pancake than an omelet.

    4   tablespoons peanut or
        vegetable oil, or more if
        needed
    2   shallots, finely chopped
    2   cloves garlic, finely chopped
    1   green chile serrano, coarsely
        chopped, plus more to taste,
        for dipping
    4   large eggs
    ½   pound chopped pork butt,
        shoulder, or chops
    1   small tomato, seeded and
        coarsely chopped
    1   tablespoon coarsely chopped
        fresh coriander
    3   teaspoons Thai fish sauce, plus
        more for dipping
        Freshly ground pepper, to taste
        Fried shallot flakes (see Crisp
        Fried Garlic or Shallot Flakes,
        page 24), for garnish
        Sliced mango, for garnish
        Hot cooked white long-grain
        rice, for accompaniment

1. Preheat wok over medium heat until hot. Pour in 2 tablespoons of the oil. When hot add shallot, garlic, and chile; stir-fry until vegetables are soft (about 1 minute). Remove from heat.

2. In a medium bowl beat eggs. Add shallot mixture, pork, tomato, coriander, fish sauce, and pepper; mix thoroughly.

3. Reheat wok over medium-high heat. Add remaining 2 tablespoons oil. When hot add ⅓ cup of reserved egg mixture; fry until bottom is golden brown and crisp (about 1 minute), shaking wok occasionally. Turn over and brown other side (30 to 45 seconds). Remove and keep warm. Repeat with remaining egg mixture, adding more oil if needed.

4. Garnish omelets with shallot flakes and mango. Combine the fish sauce and chopped chile to taste, and serve in small dipping bowls. Serve omelets with rice.

Makes eight 4- to 5-inch omelets.

SHRIMP AND BARBECUED PORK FRIED RICE

If you enjoy anchovies, try this fried rice dish with Chinese-style wet shrimp paste. Once you become accustomed to the pungent aroma of this salty preparation, you may find yourself seeking out recipes calling for it.

    3   tablespoons peanut or
        vegetable oil
    ½   teaspoon salt
    1   teaspoon Chinese-style wet
        shrimp paste, or to taste
        (optional)
    3   cups cooked white long-grain
        rice (see page 37), preferably
        cold
    ½   teaspoon sugar
    1½ tablespoons soy sauce
    2   teaspoons oyster sauce
    2   large eggs plus 1 egg yolk,
        lightly beaten
    ½   cup cooked small bay shrimp
    ½   cup diced Chinese barbecued
        pork or sugar-cured baked
        ham (¼-in. cubes)
    ½   cup diced cooked chicken
        (¼-in. cubes)
    ½   cup blanched peas
    1   cup finely shredded romaine
        or iceberg lettuce
    ½   cup chopped green onion

1. Preheat wok over medium-high heat until hot. Pour in oil. When oil is moderately hot, add salt and shrimp paste, if used, and stir until oil is fragrant (about 5 seconds). Immediately add rice and press, poke, and toss until grains are separated but not browned (about 3 minutes). Season with sugar, soy sauce, and oyster sauce; stir-fry until rice is evenly coated (about 1 minute).

2. Push rice up sides of wok and add eggs to center of wok; cook about 1 minute, lightly beating eggs in center of wok only. Then toss together with rice until flecks of egg appear throughout rice. Add shrimp, pork, chicken, peas, lettuce, and green onion; toss and stir until lettuce is wilted (about 2 minutes).

Serves 6 with other dishes.

PEKING BURRITO

Having leftover Peking, tea-smoked, Cantonese roasted, or any other duck seems rather unlikely; however, if you are so fortunate, this is a fun and delicious informal luncheon dish. It is so tasty that it is worth purchasing fresh Cantonese roast duck from a Chinese delicatessen or restaurant. Buy half a duck and have it left unchopped.

- 2 tablespoons peanut oil
- 1 teaspoon finely minced fresh ginger
- 1 teaspoon minced garlic
- 1 tablespoon hot bean sauce
- 1 cup thinly julienned peeled carrot, blanched 1 minute
- 1 cup julienned cabbage
- 1 cup thinly julienned fresh snow peas
- 2 cups shredded cooked duck meat with skin (about half a duck)
- 2 green onions, shredded
- ½ teaspoon sugar
- 1 teaspoon soy sauce, or more to taste
  Asian sesame oil, to taste
  Asian hot chile oil, to taste
  Toasted black sesame seed, for garnish
- 8 warm Mandarin Pancakes (see page 115) or flour tortillas
  Fresh coriander, for garnish
- 4 tablespoons Hoisin Sauce Dip (see page 24)

1. Preheat wok over medium-high heat until hot. Pour in peanut oil; then add ginger and garlic and stir-fry until oil is fragrant (about 10 seconds). Add hot bean sauce and cook 5 seconds longer. Increase heat to high. Add carrot, cabbage, and snow peas; stir-fry until cabbage begins to wilt and snow peas turn bright green (about 30 seconds). Add duck, green onion, sugar, and soy sauce; stir-fry until mixture is heated through (about 30 seconds). Add a few drops each sesame oil and hot chile oil. Remove mixture to a serving platter and garnish with sesame seed.

2. To serve, spread 3 tablespoons filling along center of each pancake, add a few leaves of fresh coriander, and sprinkle on about ½ tablespoon Hoisin Sauce Dip. Fold pancake around filling and eat like a burrito.

Serves 8 with other dishes.

THAI CRISP-FRIED RICE NOODLES
Mee krob

This Thai national dish has as many variations as there are types of noodles. The sweet-and-sour flavor of this version, which comes from the sugar and tamarind, is balanced by fresh lime juice. Pay particular attention to the sauce preparation (step 4). The egg-lace crêpes are optional.

- 6 ounces Deep-fried Rice Stick Noodles (see page 38)
- 4 green onions, cut into 1½-inch lengths
- 2 tablespoons peanut or corn oil
- ½ pound medium shrimp, shelled and deveined
- 1 whole boned chicken breast, cut into ⅛-inch-wide slices
- 4 shallots or 1 small onion, minced
- 1 tablespoon minced garlic
- 2 small red chiles serranos, finely minced, plus 2 slivered chiles, for garnish
  Zest of 1 lime
- 3½ tablespoons tomato paste
- 4 tablespoons sugar
- ½ cup Tamarind Water (see page 24)
- ¼ cup Thai fish sauce
- 3 tablespoons lime juice (about 2 limes), or to taste
- 3 tablespoons chopped fresh coriander
- ½ pound bean sprouts, tails removed, for garnish

Crispy Egg-Lace Crêpes

- Peanut or corn oil, for deep-frying
- 2 eggs
- ¼ teaspoon salt

1. Prepare rice stick noodles and Crispy Egg-Lace Crêpes (if used). Blanch green onion 5 seconds in boiling water. Drain and set aside.

2. Preheat wok over medium-high heat until hot. Pour in oil. When hot add shrimp and chicken; stir-fry until shrimp are pink and chicken is white (about 1 minute). Remove from wok and set aside.

3. To hot wok add shallot, garlic, minced chile, and half the lime zest; stir-fry until vegetables are soft but not browned (about 1 minute).

4. Increase heat to high and add tomato paste and sugar. Cook, stirring constantly, until sugar mixture becomes a sticky, dark red sauce that pulls away from sides of wok, just short of caramelizing (3 to 4 minutes). Be careful not to burn sugar mixture or you will have to start again. Immediately add Tamarind Water and fish sauce, reduce heat to low, and simmer 1 minute. Add lime juice and adjust seasonings. Add reserved chicken-shrimp mixture and remaining lime zest; toss just to heat through. Remove from heat.

5. Add a third of the reserved noodles to sauce, gently crush noodles, and toss to coat. Repeat with another third of the noodles. Add last third of noodles only if there is enough sauce to coat evenly. Fold in reserved green onion and coriander. Mound noodles on a platter and garnish with slivered chiles, Crispy Egg-Lace Crêpes broken into small pieces (if used), and bean sprouts. Serve at room temperature.

Serves 6 with other dishes.

Crispy Egg-Lace Crêpes   Preheat wok over medium-high heat until hot. Pour in oil to a depth of 2 inches and heat to 375° F. Meanwhile, in a small bowl beat eggs and salt. Pour a third of egg mixture through a medium-fine mesh skimmer into hot oil; deep-fry until egg is light brown and crisp (about 30 seconds). Egg should have an irregular lacy shape. Turn over and fry other side 10 seconds. Remove, drain on paper towels, and keep warm. Repeat with remaining egg mixture.

Makes 3 crêpes.

BARBECUED PORK AND SHRIMP EGG FU YUNG

Unlike Westerners, Asians rarely eat eggs for breakfast; they are more likely to serve eggs at lunch or dinner, with rice. Egg fu yung—a winning preparation—is a Chinese-American adaptation of a classic soufflélike egg dish of China. If you prefer, the omelets can be served with a sprinkling of soy sauce instead of Egg Fu Yung Sauce.

> 5 large eggs
> ½ teaspoon salt
> 4 tablespoons peanut or corn oil, or as needed
> 3 shallots, thinly sliced
> 2 cloves garlic, finely minced
> ¼ pound small bay shrimp
> ½ pound Chinese barbecued pork or sugar-cured baked ham, diced
> ⅛ pound fresh snow peas, cut diagonally into thin slices
> 1 cup bean sprouts with tails removed, blanched and drained
> 1 tablespoon finely minced Smithfield ham or prosciutto
> 1 tablespoon chopped fresh coriander
> Watercress, for garnish

Egg Fu Yung Sauce

> ¾ cup chicken stock
> 1 tablespoon oyster sauce
> ¼ teaspoon sugar
> Pinch freshly ground white pepper
> 2 teaspoons cornstarch mixed with 1 tablespoon water
> Few drops Asian sesame oil

1. In a medium bowl lightly beat eggs with salt; set aside.

2. Preheat wok over medium-high heat until hot. Pour in 2 tablespoons of the oil. When hot add shallot and garlic; stir-fry 30 seconds. Add shrimp and pork and stir-fry 1 minute. Increase heat to high; add snow peas and bean sprouts seconds apart and stir-fry until vegetables are crisp-tender (about 1 minute). Remove mixture from wok and let cool; then add to reserved egg mixture. Rinse wok and wipe dry.

3. Reheat wok over medium-high heat until hot. Pour in remaining 2 tablespoons oil. When hot add ⅓ cup of the egg mixture and fry until bottom is golden brown and crisp (30 to 45 seconds). Turn omelet over and brown other side (about 30 seconds). Remove and keep warm. Repeat with remaining egg mixture, pouring in more oil if needed. Arrange omelets on a serving platter and spoon warm Egg Fu Yung Sauce over them. Top with ham and coriander. Garnish with watercress.

Serves 8 with other dishes or 4 for breakfast.

Egg Fu Yung Sauce   After frying omelets set wok over high heat. Pour in stock; then add oyster sauce, sugar, and pepper and bring to a boil. Lower heat and add cornstarch mixture, stirring continuously until sauce thickens (about 30 seconds). Blend in sesame oil.

Makes 1 cup.

Serve this novel Peking-style burrito as casual weekend fare. For convenience, purchase a roast duck from a local Chinese delicatessen or restaurant and stir-fry the filling mixture in advance. Then quickly reheat it and let guests make their own burritos.

The secret to making perfect Coin Purse Eggs is to use very hot oil and very fresh eggs so that the edges will crisp. Serve these over rice for breakfast, as a snack, or as one course in a Chinese dinner.

COIN PURSE EGGS WITH OYSTER SAUCE

A crusty fried egg with a splash of oyster sauce may seem odd, but in fact this dish could easily become one of your favorite ways of eating eggs. The name refers to the way the eggs are cooked and presented; they are folded over like a pocket purse with a gold coin—the yolk—in the center.

> 6　large eggs
> 6½　tablespoons peanut oil
> 　　Salt, to taste
> 　　Hot cooked white long-grain rice, for accompaniment
> 6　teaspoons oyster sauce, for garnish
> 　　Fresh coriander, for garnish

1. Break one of the eggs into a small saucer; set aside.

2. Preheat wok over high heat until hot. Pour in 1½ tablespoons of the oil and add a pinch of salt. When oil is hot but not smoking, carefully slide in reserved egg; it should sizzle. Cook until egg forms a crusty brown bottom and white begins to set around edges but is still wet in center (20 to 30 seconds). Tilting wok toward you, slide a spatula under half the egg and fold it over to form a half-circle. Fry 20 seconds, gently pressing edges of egg with spatula to seal and hold egg in purse shape. The yolk should be soft, the white moist, and the outside edges crunchy. Remove and serve on top of a small plate of hot cooked rice (see Note). Repeat with remaining 5 eggs, adding 1 tablespoon oil and a pinch of salt for each egg.

3. Dribble 1 teaspoon oyster sauce over each egg and garnish with coriander.

Serves 6.

<u>Note</u>　For a multicourse Chinese dinner, transfer each fried egg to a serving platter and keep warm.

CHINESE SWEET YEAST BREAD DOUGH

Archaeological investigations have revealed that Chinese bread making originated as far back as the Han dynasty (206 B.C. to A.D. 220) but that it was most probably borrowed from another culture. Chinese bread dough is quite sweet in comparison to Western bread dough and most often is steamed rather than baked, which is why it appears white and uncooked.

> 1 package (1 tablespoon) active dry yeast
> ¼ cup warm (100° to 110° F) water
> 1 tablespoon plus ⅓ cup sugar
> 3½ cups flour, plus flour for dusting and kneading
> 1 cup warm (100° to 110° F) milk
> 2 teaspoons baking powder

1. In a small bowl sprinkle yeast over the water. Add the 1 tablespoon sugar. Let stand until yeast bubbles (about 5 minutes).

2. *To prepare in a food processor:* In the work bowl of a food processor fitted with a steel blade, combine the 3½ cups flour and the ⅓ cup sugar. Process 2 seconds. Add yeast mixture and process 3 seconds. With machine running pour milk down feed tube in a steady stream. Process until dough forms a rough ball. If ball is sticky and wet, dust with a little more flour and process until dough pulls away from bowl. *To prepare by hand:* In a large bowl combine the 3½ cups flour and the ⅓ cup sugar. Add yeast mixture and stir to blend. Add milk and mix until dough forms a rough ball, adding more flour until dough pulls away from bowl.

3. Remove dough to a lightly floured board. Knead until dough is smooth and elastic (about 2 minutes), dusting with flour to prevent dough from being sticky.

4. Place dough in a large oiled bowl, cover with plastic wrap, and let rise in a warm place until doubled in size (about 1 hour).

5. Punch down dough and place on a lightly floured surface. Flatten dough and add baking powder in center.

Fold over edges to enclose baking powder and knead until baking powder is thoroughly incorporated into dough and dough is a smooth ball. Cover dough and let rest 10 minutes. Dough is now ready to form into rolls, buns, or loaves.

Makes enough dough for 24 Sweet Silver-Thread Rolls or 20 Barbecued Pork Buns.

SWEET SILVER-THREAD ROLLS

Steamed hot sweet breads, rolls, or buns are eaten in place of rice in northern China. Their subtle, sweet flavor nicely balances spicy and savory dishes and is particularly cooling for fiery hot sauces. These silver rolls have specks of minced ham and green onion. They can be prepared ahead and reheated (see Note).

> 1 recipe Chinese Sweet Yeast Bread Dough (at left)
> ⅓ cup melted lard or shortening
> ⅓ cup sugar
> 24 pieces (2 in. square) parchment paper
> ¼ cup minced ham, preferably Smithfield, or proscuitto
> 1 green onion, minced

1. While dough is rising, in a small saucepan melt lard. Remove pan from heat, add sugar, and stir into a paste. Chill until solid.

2. Turn dough onto a floured board. Cut dough in half and roll out half into a 10- by 14-inch rectangle about ⅛ inch thick. Working quickly spread half of the lard paste over rectangle, leaving outer half inch free of paste. Starting with the long end, roll up jelly-roll fashion. Pinch edges to seal ends. With seam side down lightly flatten roll with palms of your hands, forming it into a 4-inch-wide by 10-inch-long rectangle. Cut crosswise into about ¼-inch-thick strands; separate strands into 12 groups. Let stand 15 minutes.

3. Gather up 1 group of strands and grasp ends in each hand; gently stretch until strands are 6 or 7 inches long. Grasp one end between index

and middle finger and wrap stretched strands around your fingers into a cone shape, tucking ends into bottom. Remove roll from fingers and set on square of parchment paper. Repeat with remaining groups of strands. Top each roll with a pinch of ham and green onion and gently press them in. Arrange rolls 1 or 2 inches apart in bamboo steaming baskets or trays. Cover and let rise 15 minutes. Repeat with remaining half of dough, lard paste, and ham and green onion.

4. Prepare wok for steaming (see page 86). Set steaming baskets in wok, cover, and steam over medium-high heat 15 minutes. Serve hot in baskets.

Makes 24 rolls, serves 8.

<u>Note</u> To reheat, steam buns 5 minutes over medium-high heat.

SHALLOW-FRIED NOODLE CAKES

"Two faces brown," the Chinese description of this recipe, refers to the panfrying of both sides of the coiled noodle cakes until they are crunchy and golden brown. The inside of the cakes remains soft and moist. This—not the deep-fried crunchy noodles that come in a can—is the authentic chow mein.

> 1 pound medium-wide fresh Chinese egg noodles (see page 36), cooked, rinsed, and drained
> 1 tablespoon dark soy sauce
> ½ teaspoon salt
> 4 tablespoons peanut or corn oil

1. In a large bowl combine noodles, soy sauce, and salt.

2. Preheat wok over medium heat until hot. Pour in 2 tablespoons of the oil. When hot add a quarter of the noodles, coiling them into wok. Pat down noodles, including edges, to form a round cake. Reduce heat to low and cook until noodle cake is browned and crusty (3 to 5 minutes per side). Remove and keep warm. Repeat with remaining noodles, a quarter at a time, adding more oil as needed.

Makes 4 noodle cakes.

THAI STIR-FRIED FLAT RICE NOODLES
Pad thai

Many Asians favor noodles made from rice flour rather than wheat flour. This recipe uses flat ¼-inch-wide fettuccine-like rice noodles. In Bangkok, *pad thai* is popular street vendor food and is eaten for lunch, as a midday or late-night snack, or as part of a dinner menu. It can be served hot or at room temperature.

½ pound dried flat rice noodles
4 to 6 tablespoons vegetable oil
¼ pound medium shrimp, shelled and deveined
½ whole chicken breast, boned, skinned, and sliced
   Salt, to taste
3 cloves garlic, minced
3 tablespoons brown bean sauce
3 tablespoons tomato paste
2 tablespoons Thai fish sauce
1 tablespoon vinegar
2 tablespoons sugar
3 eggs
2 cups bean sprouts, tails removed
2 tablespoons preserved radish (see page 12), soaked in warm water 10 minutes, drained, and chopped (optional)
1 tablespoon small dried shrimp, soaked in warm water 30 minutes and drained
4 cubes fried tofu (see page 57), each about 1½ inches square, halved, and cut into ¼-inch-thick slices
2 to 4 tablespoons chicken stock or water, as needed
4 green onions, cut into 2-inch lengths
2 tablespoons roasted unsalted peanuts, coarsely chopped, for garnish
   Large pinch hot-pepper flakes, or to taste
2 tablespoons coarsely chopped fresh coriander, for garnish
2 limes, cut into wedges, for garnish

1. In a large bowl cover noodles with warm water and soak until noodles are soft and pliable (about 15 minutes). Drain well and set aside.

2. Preheat wok over medium-high heat until hot. Pour in 2 tablespoons of the oil. When hot add shrimp and chicken; stir-fry until shrimp turns pink and chicken becomes opaque (about 30 seconds). Season with salt. Remove shrimp mixture and set aside.

3. Reduce heat under wok to medium and add 2 more tablespoons oil and garlic; cook until garlic is browned (about 20 seconds). Increase heat to medium-high and add brown bean sauce, tomato paste, fish sauce, vinegar, and sugar; stir until sugar dissolves (about 1 minute).

4. Increase heat to high; break one of the eggs into sauce and beat 3 or 4 times. Let egg cook with sauce until slightly set but still moist (about 20 seconds). Repeat with remaining 2 eggs. Toss until flecks of egg show through.

5. Add 1 cup of the sprouts, radish (if used), and reconstituted shrimp; stir-fry until sprouts are limp (about 15 seconds). Add tofu and reserved noodles a handful at a time; toss until noodles are tender and evenly incorporated (3 to 4 minutes). If noodles seem too dry, add stock 2 tablespoons at a time and toss until noodles are evenly coated with sauce and begin to cling to each other. Add green onion and reserved shrimp mixture; toss 30 seconds to reheat. Transfer to a platter.

6. Sprinkle with peanuts, hot-pepper flakes, and coriander. Arrange remaining 1 cup sprouts and lime wedges around noodles (lime should be squeezed over noodles before they are eaten). Serve hot or at room temperature.

Serves 6 with other dishes.

CAJUN DIRTY RICE

New Orleans native Natalie Sellers, who owned the former Truffles Cooking School in Reno, uses green pepper, onion, and celery—a hallmark combination in Louisana-style cooking—as magic seasonings in her Cajun rice dish. A wok is an ideal cooking vessel for tossing and stirring the large quantity of rice used in this delicious recipe.

3 tablespoons vegetable oil or chicken fat
3 tablespoons flour
1 cup finely chopped onion
1 cup finely chopped celery
½ cup finely chopped bell pepper
2 teaspoons minced garlic
2 bay leaves
½ pound pork, ground
½ pound each *chicken gizzards and livers*, ground
1 teaspoon salt
¼ teaspoon cayenne pepper
   Freshly ground black pepper and white pepper, to taste
¼ teaspoon dried oregano
¼ teaspoon dried thyme
   Dash hot-pepper sauce
1 cup chicken stock
4 or 5 cups cooked white long-grain rice, preferably boiled in chicken stock
3 green onions, coarsely chopped, for garnish

1. Preheat wok over medium-high heat until hot. Add oil and heat until hot but not smoking. Add flour and stir immediately. Reduce heat to medium and continue stirring until roux becomes dark brown (3 to 5 minutes). Add onion, celery, bell pepper, garlic, and bay leaves; stir and cook until wilted (about 3 minutes).

2. Increase heat to medium-high. Add pork and giblets, tossing and stirring until brown (5 to 8 minutes). Season with salt, cayenne, black and white pepper, oregano, thyme, and hot-pepper sauce. Stir in stock, scraping loose any food stuck to bottom of wok. Stir in rice. Pick out and discard bay leaves. Garnish with green onion.

Serves 4 as an entrée or 8 as a side dish.

A twist of fresh lime adds zest to the complex flavors of the sauce, chicken, and shrimp in Thai Stir-fried Flat Rice Noodles.

This light lunch serving for two of wonton noodles with Orange-Coriander Chile Sauce is a Western approach to a traditional Asian dish.

WONTON NOODLES WITH ORANGE-CORIANDER CHILE SAUCE

The zesty, assertive citrus sauce makes this an appealing dish for a summer luncheon. Note that the recipe for Basic Wontons makes 5 dozen wontons, only 20 of which are needed here, so you will have 40 wontons left over. Keep them in the freezer for future use or see the recipe for Basic Wontons for other suggestions.

> ½ pound fresh Chinese egg noodles (see page 36), cooked, rinsed, and drained
> 20 boiled Basic Wontons (see page 42)
> Chopped fresh coriander, for garnish

Orange-Coriander Chile Sauce

> 6 tablespoons dark soy sauce
> 2 teaspoons minced fresh ginger
> 2 teaspoons minced garlic
> ½ teaspoon salt
> 1 tablespoon sugar
> 1 tablespoon raspberry vinegar or red wine vinegar
> 1 tablespoon Asian sesame oil
> 2 teaspoons Asian hot chile oil
> 1 orange, seeded and juiced
> 1 tablespoon orange zest
> 2 tablespoons coarsely chopped fresh coriander

Divide noodles among 4 soup bowls and keep warm. Distribute 5 boiled wontons over each serving of noodles. Pour about 4 tablespoons Orange-Coriander Chile Sauce over contents of each bowl. Garnish with coriander.

Serves 4 with other dishes.

Orange-Coriander Chile Sauce

In a medium bowl whisk together all ingredients.

Makes about 1 cup.

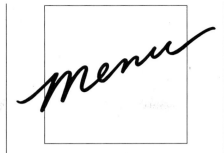

CLASSIC CHINESE LUNCH

Chilled Noodles in Peking Meat Sauce

Crisp Green Onion Pancakes

Watercress Wonton Soup

Sugared Bow Ties

Chrysanthemum Petal or Jasmine Tea

Make your next luncheon a delightful occasion with this classic Chinese menu for six. It works well for entertaining, since much of the food can be prepared in advance and heated at the last minute. To make the tea, purchase dried chrysanthemum petals or jasmine from an Asian grocery. To a warm teapot add 10 to 12 dried chrysanthemum petals or 2 or 3 teaspoons jasmine tea per quart of boiling water and steep for 10 minutes.

CHILLED NOODLES IN PEKING MEAT SAUCE
Cha chiang mein

Tangy Peking meat sauce exudes sweet, savory, and mildly spicy flavors in this simple northern Chinese-style noodle dish; the cucumber has a cooling effect. The sauce may be prepared several days in advance.

> 2 tablespoons peanut or corn oil
> 1½ pounds pork butt, finely chopped
> 2 tablespoons rice wine or dry vermouth
> 2 teaspoons minced fresh ginger
> 2 teaspoons minced garlic
> ⅓ cup hoisin sauce
> ¼ cup hot bean sauce
> 2 tablespoons sugar
> 6 green onions, including some of the green tops, chopped
> ½ cup chicken stock
> 2 tablespoons Asian sesame oil
> 1 pound fresh Chinese egg noodles (see page 36), cooked, rinsed, and drained
> 1 firm large cucumber, peeled and coarsely grated, for garnish
> Toasted black sesame seed, for garnish

1. Preheat wok over medium-high heat until hot. Pour in oil. When oil is hot, add pork in batches and stir-fry until meat is lightly browned (3 to 5 minutes total). Add wine; stir together 1 minute. Push pork up sides of wok and add ginger, garlic, hoisin sauce, hot bean sauce, sugar, and half of the green onion to center of wok. Stir-fry until mixture is fragrant (about 30 seconds); then mix with pork. Add stock and bring to a boil. Reduce heat to low and simmer until sauce thickens (about 10 minutes), stirring frequently. Swirl in 1 tablespoon of the sesame oil. Set aside.

2. Toss cooked noodles with remaining 1 tablespoon sesame oil and rest of green onion. Divide among 6 shallow soup bowls. Spoon reserved sauce on top. Garnish with cucumber and sesame seed. Serve at room temperature.

Serves 6 with other dishes.

CRISP GREEN ONION PANCAKES

These pancakes are a favorite street vendor food. Although they are a bit laborious to make, each crispy bite makes the effort worthwhile, and they can be made ahead and reheated (see Note). Serve them as an appetizer or side dish.

  2 cups flour, plus more for
     dusting and kneading
  ¾ to 1 cup boiling water
     Asian sesame oil, for
     brushing dough
     Salt, to taste
  4 teaspoons minced green onion
     Peanut oil, for frying

1. *To prepare in a food processor:* Place flour in the work bowl of a food processor fitted with a steel blade. With machine running add ¾ cup boiling water in a steady stream through feed tube and process into a rough ball (about 20 seconds), adding more water, 1 tablespoon at a time, as necessary until dough is soft, moist, and smooth. *To make by hand:* Sift flour into a medium bowl. Add 1 cup boiling water and stir mixture into a rough ball.

2. Turn dough out onto a floured board and knead until smooth (about 5 minutes). Place dough in a bowl and cover with a damp cloth for 15 minutes.

3. Return dough to board; knead, dusting with flour, until dough is smooth and no longer sticky. Shape dough into a sausage and cut into 8 pieces.

4. Dust board with flour. Roll 1 piece of dough into a 7- to 8-inch circle. Lightly brush circle with sesame oil. Sprinkle salt and ½ teaspoon of the green onion on top; gently press onion into dough.

5. Roll circle jelly-roll fashion into a sausage. Pinch ends closed to seal in green onion. Gently flatten sausage to a thickness of ½ inch and coil it into a 3- to 4-inch disk. Pinch ends

to seal. With your hands shape and press disk so it does not come apart. With a rolling pin roll disk into a 7- to 8-inch pancake, pressing bits of green onion back into dough. Cover with a dry cloth. Repeat with remaining dough.

6. Preheat flat-bottomed wok or skillet over medium heat until hot. Pour in 4 tablespoons peanut oil. When oil is moderately hot, add 1 pancake. Fry until bottom is browned and crisp (about 1 minute). Cover pan and fry pancake 1 minute more. Remove cover and turn pancake over; cover pan and fry until pancake is crisp and brown (1 or 2 minutes more), shaking pan occasionally. Remove and drain on a paper towel. Keep warm. Repeat with remaining pancakes, keeping about ⅛ inch of oil in pan.

Makes 8 pancakes.

<u>Note</u> Reheat pancakes in a 425° F oven for 3 minutes.

WATERCRESS WONTON SOUP

A bowl of boiled wontons covered with steaming stock and garnished with a favorite topping is Chinese "comfort" food—delicious and satisfying. This recipe makes a wonderful first course for dinner or a complete light lunch. Note that the recipe for Basic Wontons makes about 60 wontons, only 30 of which are called for here. Keep leftover wontons in the freezer for future use, or see the recipe for Basic Wontons (see page 42) for other ideas.

  30 boiled Basic Wontons
  ½ pound Chinese barbecued
     pork or sugar-cured baked
     ham, cut into ¼-inch-thick
     slices, for garnish (optional)
  1 bunch fresh watercress, large
     stems removed, for garnish
  6 cups chicken stock
  1 piece (1 in.) fresh ginger,
     peeled and bruised
     Salt and white pepper, to taste
  1 teaspoon soy sauce, or to taste
  2 teaspoons Asian sesame oil

1. Portion boiled wontons among 6 individual serving bowls, or place all wontons in a large soup tureen. Arrange pork, if used, and watercress on top. Cover to keep warm.

2. Meanwhile, in a 2-quart saucepan bring stock and ginger to a boil. Add salt, pepper, and soy sauce and simmer 5 minutes. Add sesame oil; stir once or twice. Remove ginger. Ladle about 1 cup hot stock over each bowl of wontons or pour all into tureen.

Serves 6 with other dishes.

SUGARED BOW TIES

On Chinese New Year these confections are traditional cookies for children. It is also customary for married adults to give little red good-luck envelopes stuffed with money to children who respectfully wish them *gung hay fat choy*—Happy New Year.

  30 wonton wrappers
     Peanut oil, for deep-frying
  ¼ cup confectioners' sugar, for
     sprinkling

1. Cut each wrapper in half, making a rectangle. Make a lengthwise slit 1¾ inches long down the center and 2 more slits of the same length about ⅝ inch from either side of center slit. Pick up one end of the rectangle and insert it through center slit. Pull it through gently and bring it back to original position to form bow tie.

2. Preheat wok over medium-high heat until hot. Pour in oil to a depth of 2 inches and heat to 375° F. Add bow ties in batches and fry until they are puffed and golden brown (about 1 minute). Remove, drain, and let cool. Sprinkle with confectioners' sugar.

Makes 60 bow ties.

Wonton soup, a noodle entrée, and tea make a classic Chinese lunch. Green onion pancakes and Sugared Bow Ties make it memorable.

Baby bok choy, Asian eggplant, asparagus beans, and bitter melon are among the exotic but commonly used vegetables of Asian cooking.

Salads, Soups & Vegetables

Although this book takes a modern and informal approach to Asian cooking, it observes and applies the gastronomic philosophy of China. In this chapter are a host of Asian and international vegetable, salad, and soup recipes that range from simple to fairly elaborate but are all fun and excitingly new to an adventurous palate. If you are unable to find some of the Asian vegetables, try substituting and experimenting with seasonal greens, melons, and beans carried by the local market. Success comes not from having the right Asian vegetable but from understanding the stir-fry method and applying it to whatever vegetable might be available.

VEGETABLES

The centuries-old Chinese technique of stir-frying gained its popularity by turning out perfectly cooked vegetables—tender and crisp, with brilliant color and natural flavor. Fresh vegetables are extraordinarily tasty when stir-fried in a wok with hot oil and seasoned with fresh ginger, garlic, a good pinch of salt, and green onion.

Preserving also plays a prominent role in Asian cooking; vegetables—as well as meats, poultry, and seafood—are sun-dried, air-dried, fermented, cured in brine, salted, or pickled. These preserving methods intensify the flavors of vegetables, making them delicious seasoning agents.

Bitter melon   Also known as balsam pear, this melon is oblong, tapered at one end and flattened at the base, with a long stem. It ranges from 4 to 10 inches long and from bright to pale green, with smooth, waxy, wartlike bulges. Choose bright green melons that are just turning yellow but are still firm. An orange-yellow color indicates that the melon is overripe, slightly sweet, and too soft. The flesh surrounds a white pulpy pith and seeds, which must be removed. The flavor of the flesh is bitter, not unlike chicory, dandelion, or watercress. For most Westerners it is an acquired taste.

Stir-frying bitter melon with chicken, beef, or shrimp in Chinese black bean sauce is a favorite way of serving it. Stuffing and braising are popular methods as well. Use a bit more sugar than usual to balance the bitter flavor.

Eggplant, Asian   Also known as Chinese eggplants and Japanese eggplants, these are approximately one third the width of domestic eggplants. They are purple and measure from 6 to 10 inches long. Look for eggplants that are small, firm, and uniformly smooth, with unblemished skin. The skin is tender and not bitter, so it does not require peeling. Asian eggplants are available the year around.

Ginger   A basic seasoning of Chinese cooking, ginger is prized for its culinary value as well as medicinal characteristics. In cooking it is used to suppress any unpleasant odors and flavors of uncooked meat, fish, and poultry. Frying a bruised slice of ginger in oil before stir-frying or deep-frying removes the oil's greasy flavor and aroma.

Supermarkets across the country carry this popular knobby rhizome the year around. It has light tan skin, a firm solid feel, and pale gold flesh. Ideally, it is medium spicy and not too fibrous. Stored in a paper bag in the vegetable crisper of the refrigerator, ginger will keep several weeks.

Peeling ginger is not always required, but it is a good habit. When a slice of ginger is called for, cut it across the grain into the size and thickness of a quarter. To bruise the slice, with the side of a cleaver slap the slice just enough to spread open the fibers, which helps release the flavor and aroma of the ginger during cooking. For small pieces of ginger, cut off the small protruding fingers and whack them soundly with the cleaver before using them.

Kale, Chinese   Also known as Chinese broccoli and Chinese mustard greens, Chinese kale has large leaves and dark green, smooth, ungrooved stems ½ to 1 inch in diameter and 8 to 14 inches long. Unlike those of other cabbages, the leaves of Chinese kale branch out halfway up the stalk. Select kale with solid stalks and with buds rather than flowers. The stalks have a delicately bitter flavor and when cooked properly are crunchy, like broccoli, and faintly sweet. They are particularly good stir-fried with rice wine or whiskey and a large pinch of sugar.

Long beans, Chinese   Also known as asparagus beans, long beans sometimes reach 3 feet in length. The best ones are pencil-thin and dark green in color. Long beans are considered tastier and crunchier in texture than other green beans and are sometimes likened to the French green bean *haricot vert*.

Lotus root   A whole lotus root may be 4 feet long, segmented into long links like 2- to 3-inch-long sausages. The outside is a light reddish tan color. The root should be smooth, firm, and unblemished. When cut crosswise, the root displays an intricate lacy pattern of wide and narrow canals around a hollow core.

If not used immediately, cut lotus roots should be covered with acidulated water (1 tablespoon white vinegar in enough water to cover) to prevent discoloration. This rhizome may be stir-fried, cooked into a soup, stuffed, braised, and even candied. When stir-fried, the roots have a peculiar nutty, sweet flavor and a unique crunchy texture. When simmered, braised, or made into soup, they lose their crunchy texture and produce unusual long, fine hairs that stretch like cotton candy when one takes a bite.

Snow peas   Also called edible pea pods, snow peas are flat pods with a sweet flavor and crisp texture. Look for small unblemished pods with tiny peas inside. They may be eaten whole. The best-tasting snow peas are stir-fried in hot seasoned oil. If you plan to stir-fry a large quantity, blanch or steam them 20 seconds before stir-frying to ensure even cooking.

Tofu, fresh   Also known as soybean curd, tofu (its Japanese name) is rather bland by itself but readily absorbs the flavors of accompanying sauces and ingredients. High in protein and lecithin, tofu is made from ground soybeans mixed with water and strained into a milk. A coagulant is added, and the mixture is poured into a cheesecloth-lined mold. The finished product is cut into squares. The two most frequently found varieties are firm and soft tofu. Firm tofu is ideal for braising, stir-frying, and deep-frying, whereas soft tofu is best for delicate soups or served chilled and topped with Oil-Seared Ginger Sauce (see page 24) or a few drops of oyster sauce. Store tofu in the refrigerator, completely covered with cold water, and change the water every third day.

Tofu, fried   A purchased item, this is simply deep-fried squares of fresh tofu sold by weight or per square in Asian grocery stores. The squares are crusty and golden brown in color on the outside and hollow in the center. They act like absorbent sponges in stir-fried, simmered, or braised dishes. They may also be stuffed to make a delicious appetizer.

You can also make your own fried tofu. Cut firm tofu into 1-inch cubes and blot thoroughly with a paper towel. Deep-fry them in peanut oil preheated to 375° F until they puff up and turn golden brown (3 to 5 minutes). Remove and drain on paper towels; store in a plastic bag. Fried tofu will keep 3 to 5 days in the refrigerator.

Water chestnuts, Chinese   These sweet, crisp, meaty tubers, or corms, cultivated in rice paddies, are flat-based with the top coming to a tip. They are ringed with ridges of very thin brown scaly skin. Store the tubers in the refrigerator unpeeled and loosely covered. Peel them as you need them, covering with cold water to prevent discoloration. They may be eaten raw or stir-fried and are delicious in soups as well as desserts.

SNOW PEAS, PINE NUTS, AND CHINESE SAUSAGE

The subtly sweet, light wine flavor of Chinese sausage complements the tastes and textures of pine nuts and stir-fried vegetables.

> 4 *Chinese sausage links*
> 1½ *teaspoon salt*
> 3 *tablespoons peanut or corn oil*
> 1 *pound small fresh snow peas, stems and strings removed*
> 2 *slices peeled fresh ginger, bruised*
> 8 *Chinese water chestnuts, preferably fresh, peeled and sliced*
> 1 *teaspoon Asian sesame oil*
> 3 *tablespoons pine nuts, toasted, for garnish*

1. Prepare wok for steaming (see page 86). Place sausage on a shallow heat-resistant plate, cover, and steam over medium-high heat 10 minutes. Remove sausage and let cool. Cut diagonally into ¼-inch-thick slices; set aside.

2. Add 1 teaspoon of the salt and 1 tablespoon of the peanut oil to a large pot of water. Over high heat bring water to a boil. Plunge snow peas in water until they turn bright green (about 30 seconds). Drain and rinse with cold water; set aside.

3. Preheat wok over medium-high heat until hot. Pour in remaining 2 tablespoons peanut oil; then add remaining ½ teaspoon salt and ginger and cook until oil is fragrant (about 30 seconds). Add water chestnuts; stir-fry 30 seconds. Add reserved snow peas in 3 batches, seconds apart, and stir-fry each batch about 10 seconds. Add reserved sausage and sesame oil; toss together 10 seconds. Remove to a serving plate and garnish with pine nuts.

Serves 6 with other dishes.

CHINESE ASPARAGUS BEANS WITH CHICKEN

The hearty taste and texture of asparagus beans combine beautifully with the assertive flavor of the brown bean sauce in this recipe.

> ½ *pound dark chicken meat, coarsely chopped*
> 2 *tablespoons peanut or corn oil*
> ¼ *teaspoon salt*
> 2 *slices fresh ginger, minced*
> 2 *cloves garlic, minced*
> ½ *cup chopped green onion*
> 2 *teaspoons hot bean sauce*
> 1 *pound Chinese asparagus beans or other green beans, cut into 1½-inch-long pieces*
> ½ *teaspoon sugar*
>   *Pinch white pepper*
> 1 *tablespoon soy sauce*
> ⅓ *cup chicken stock*
> 1 *teaspoon oyster sauce*
> 1 *teaspoon cornstarch mixed with 1 tablespoon water*
> 1 *teaspoon Asian sesame oil*

Basic Chicken Marinade

> 1 *teaspoon dry vermouth*
> 2 *teaspoons soy sauce*
> ¼ *teaspoon sugar*
> 1 *teaspoon cornstarch*
> 1½ *teaspoons Asian sesame oil*

1. In a medium bowl toss chicken with Basic Chicken Marinade and set aside.

2. Preheat wok over medium-high heat until hot. Pour in peanut oil; then add salt, ginger, garlic, and half the green onion. Stir-fry until oil is fragrant (about 30 seconds). Increase heat to high. Add reserved chicken and stir-fry until meat turns white (about 1 minute). Add bean sauce and toss to mix. Add beans, sugar, pepper, and soy sauce. Stir-fry until beans are crisp-tender (2 to 3 minutes). Add stock and oyster sauce; toss to mix. Add cornstarch mixture and stir until thickened (about 10 seconds). Fold in remaining green onion and sesame oil.

Serves 4 with other dishes.

Basic Chicken Marinade   In a small bowl combine all ingredients.

Makes about 2 tablespoons.

DAD'S WHISKEY STIR-FRIED CHINESE KALE

The flavor of this leafy green vegetable is faintly sweet and bitter. Choose narrow stalks of deep green Chinese kale. If you can't find kale, domestic broccoli also works well. Before stir-frying hard vegetables such as kale, broccoli, and cauliflower, steam or blanch them for 2 minutes to facilitate even cooking.

- 1½ pounds Chinese kale or domestic broccoli, rinsed and trimmed
- 2 tablespoons peanut oil, plus 2 teaspoons if blanching kale
- 1 teaspoon salt
- 2 slices peeled fresh ginger, bruised
- 2 cloves garlic, bruised
- ¼ teaspoon sugar
- 2 tablespoons whiskey

Sesame Oyster Sauce

- 3 tablespoons oyster sauce
- 1 tablespoon soy sauce
- 3 tablespoons chicken stock
- 1 teaspoon sugar
- 1 teaspoon Asian sesame oil

1. Cut kale into 3- to 4-inch lengths, including stems and flowers. If stalks are thicker than ½ inch or skin is tough, peel stalks.

2. *To steam kale:* Prepare wok for steaming (see page 86). Place kale in bamboo steaming basket, cover, and steam over medium-high heat about 2 minutes. Stems should still be crunchy. *To blanch kale in water:* Fill wok half full with water and add the 2 teaspoons peanut oil. Bring to a boil over high heat. Add kale and cook until it turns bright green (about 2 minutes). Drain in a colander and rinse with cold water.

3. Preheat wok over medium-high heat until hot. Pour in remaining 2 tablespoons peanut oil. When hot add salt, ginger, and garlic and cook until oil is fragrant (about 30 seconds). Add kale in 4 batches, seconds apart, and stir-fry until kale is crisp-tender (about 45 seconds total). Add sugar; toss. Add whiskey and stir-fry 5 seconds. Remove to a serving platter and top with Sesame Oyster Sauce.

Serves 4 with other dishes.

Sesame Oyster Sauce   In a small saucepan over medium heat, combine oyster sauce, soy sauce, stock, and sugar. Cook until sugar is dissolved and sauce is reduced to a creamy consistency. Allow to cool. Fold in sesame oil.

Makes about ¼ cup.

DEEP-FRIED ASPARAGUS WITH GAZPACHO COULIS

This recipe was inspired by a cook's tour of Spain. Simple deep-fried asparagus is an intriguing and absolutely delicious first course. To ensure even cooking and greaseless results, start with the correct frying temperature and use high-quality oil.

- 2 cups light olive oil
- 1 pound asparagus with ½-inch-wide stalks, trimmed, rinsed, and patted dry
  Coarsely ground salt, to taste

Gazpacho Coulis

- 1 large tomato, coarsely chopped
- 1 small red pepper, seeded and cubed
- 2 cloves garlic, chopped
- ½ cucumber, peeled, seeded, and cubed
- ¼ cup chopped white onion
- 1 tablespoon red wine vinegar
- ⅓ cup olive oil
- 1 teaspoon salt
  Freshly ground pepper, to taste

1. Preheat wok over medium-high heat until hot. Pour in olive oil and heat to 375° F. Add asparagus and deep-fry until it turns bright green (about 2 minutes). Remove asparagus and drain well.

2. Divide and arrange asparagus on 6 salad plates or 1 large oblong platter. Sprinkle with salt. Pour Gazpacho Coulis over top and serve immediately.

Serves 6 as a first course.

Gazpacho Coulis   In a food processor or blender, combine all ingredients. Chill. Adjust seasonings if necessary.

Makes about 1 cup.

MOM'S STIR-FRIED FRESH LOTUS ROOT
Siu chao

Soft, crunchy, and dried preserved vegetables are combined in Mom's home-style dish. Stir-frying the lotus root accentuates its crunchy texture and peculiar sweet flavor.

- 6 ounces fresh pork loin (see Note)
- ½ pound fresh lotus root
- 6 Chinese dried black mushrooms
- 4 brine-cured radishes (optional)
- ¼ cup dried cloud ear mushrooms
- 3 tablespoons peanut oil
- 2 slices fresh ginger, crushed
- 2 cloves fresh garlic, crushed
- 1½ teaspoons salt
- 1 small onion, cut into ¼-inch-thick slices
- 8 Chinese water chestnuts, preferably fresh, peeled and sliced
- ¼ pound snow peas, stems and strings removed
  Large pinch white pepper
- ¼ teaspoon sugar
- 2 teaspoons soy sauce
- ¼ cup chicken stock

Pork Strip Marinade

- 1 teaspoon soy sauce
- 1 teaspoon dry vermouth
  Large pinch sugar
- 1 teaspoon cornstarch
- 1 teaspoon Asian sesame oil

1. Cut pork into strips ¼ inch wide by 2 inches long; toss with Pork Strip Marinade. Set aside.

2. Peel lotus root; cut in half lengthwise and then cut crosswise into ⅛-inch-thick slices; set aside. If lotus root is prepared more than 20 minutes before stir-frying, cover with acidulated water.

3. In three separate small bowls, cover black mushrooms, radishes (if used), and cloud ears with water and soak until soft and pliable (about 30 minutes). Rinse and squeeze out excess water. Remove and discard stems from black mushrooms; cut caps in half. Rinse radishes; cut crosswise into ⅛-inch strips. Pinch off and discard hard center from cloud ears; tear large pieces in half. Reserve ingredients in separate bowls.

4. Preheat wok over medium-high heat until hot. Pour in oil; then add ginger, garlic, and ½ teaspoon of the salt. Cook mixture until oil is fragrant (about 30 seconds). Add reserved pork; stir-fry until it turns white (about 30 seconds). Remove pork and set aside, leaving ginger, garlic, and oil in wok.

5. Increase heat to high and add remaining 1 teaspoon salt. When hot add in separate batches, seconds apart, onion, reserved lotus root, reserved black mushrooms, reserved radishes (if used), reserved cloud ears, water chestnuts, and snow peas. Stir-fry about 2 minutes. Add pepper, sugar, and soy sauce; toss to mix. Deglaze sides of wok with stock. Cover, reduce heat to medium, and cook 2 minutes. Remove cover, increase heat to high, add reserved pork, and toss until sauce is reduced.

Serves 6 with other dishes.

Pork Strip Marinade In a medium bowl combine all ingredients.

Makes about 4 teaspoons.

<u>Note</u> Shrimp, chicken, or beef may be substituted for pork.

Deep-frying asparagus gives it a slightly crisp texture. The Gazpacho Coulis is a refreshing complement.

59

For a vegetable dish that's a hands-down winner, combine fresh corn and charred roasted chiles and bell pepper in a wok, then fold in creamy avocado.

CORN, ROASTED PEPPERS, AND AVOCADO

Chiles and bell peppers are excellent grilled on a barbecue. Sautéing them afterwards with butter in a wok enhances their roasted flavor.

> 2 Poblano or Anaheim chiles, fresh or canned
> 1 red bell pepper
> 3 tablespoons unsalted butter
> 1 small onion, chopped
> 3 ears fresh corn, scraped, or 1 package (10 oz) frozen corn, thawed and drained (about 2 cups kernels)
> Salt and freshly ground pepper, to taste
> Dash hot-pepper sauce
> 1 avocado, cut into ½-inch cubes

1. Blacken fresh chiles and bell pepper on a barbecue grill or over a medium-high gas flame or electric burner. Seal in a plastic bag 10 minutes. Remove chile stems, peel chiles, and cut into ½-inch dice. Seed and devein pepper; cut into ½-inch dice. Set aside.

2. Preheat wok over medium-high heat until moderately hot. Heat butter. When butter foam subsides, sauté onion until soft (about 3 minutes). Add corn; reduce heat to medium and cook 8 minutes (2 minutes for frozen corn), stirring often. Add reserved chiles and bell pepper, salt, ground pepper, and hot-pepper sauce. Fold in avocado. Serve hot.

Serves 6 with other dishes.

STIR-FRIED BRUSSELS SPROUTS, PANCETTA, AND PARMESAN

Try stir-frying Brussels sprouts with an Italian touch in a wok. This could be the dish for those who turn up their noses at this tasty vegetable.

> 1½ pounds small Brussels sprouts
> 2 ounces pancetta, cut into ¼-inch dice
> 1½ tablespoons olive oil
> 1½ tablespoons unsalted butter
> 2 cloves garlic, chopped
>   Salt and freshly ground pepper, to taste
> ¼ cup grated Parmesan cheese

1. Trim sprouts and make a ¼-inch-deep crisscross cut at base of each.

2. Prepare wok for steaming (see page 86). Place sprouts into bamboo steaming basket, cover, and steam over medium-high heat until sprouts are tender (about 10 minutes). Remove basket and set sprouts aside; dry wok and return to heat.

3. Sauté *pancetta* in ungreased wok until soft (about 2 minutes.)

4. Add oil, butter, and garlic; sauté until garlic is lightly browned. Add reserved sprouts and toss 1 minute. Season with salt and pepper, and sprinkle with cheese.

Serves 6 with other dishes.

POMMES DE TERRE SAUTÉES

The next time you cook new potatoes, try sautéing them in a flat-bottomed wok. Notice how the wok's curved sides cradle and evenly brown round-edged foods like potatoes; how easy it is to stir them; and how only 1 tablespoon each of oil and butter is required for cooking.

> 2 pounds new red potatoes (about twelve 2-inch potatoes)
> 1 tablespoon olive oil
> 1 tablespoon unsalted butter, preferably clarified
> 1 teaspoon salt
>   Chopped parsley, for garnish

1. Peel and trim potatoes so they are smooth and round. Avoid rinsing with water; simply pat dry with paper toweling.

2. Preheat wok over medium-high heat until hot. Pour in oil, then add butter. When butter foam subsides, add potatoes and shake wok to evenly oil potatoes. Fry until potatoes are crusty (about 5 minutes), tossing occasionally. Add salt, reduce heat to low, cover wok, and cook 15 minutes, shaking wok occasionally to prevent sticking (potatoes will lose crustiness). Uncover wok, increase heat to medium, and cook until potatoes become crusty again (about 2 minutes longer). Transfer to a serving plate. Garnish with parsley.

Serves 4 to 6 with other dishes.

A wok is a natural for stir-frying round foods, such as Brussels sprouts, and for browning the pancetta in this dish inspired by Italian cuisine. Like Asian cooks, Italian cooks appreciate how small amounts of oil can brighten the colors and enhance the flavors of fresh vegetables and other foods.

The assertive flavors of this Szechuan eggplant dish make it an excellent accompaniment to grilled or barbecued meat or poultry for a Western-style family dinner.

SAUTÉED WILD MUSHROOMS WITH MARSALA

Mushrooms require lots of space for tossing and stirring, both of which are quickly done in a wok with much less oil than a skillet would use. Serve this delicious three-mushroom dish on the side with grilled steaks, chops, or chicken.

- ½ ounce dried porcini mushrooms
- 1 tablespoon olive oil
- 2 tablespoons unsalted butter
- 3 shallots, diced
- 2 cloves garlic, chopped
- 4 ounces fresh chanterelle mushrooms, sliced
- 4 ounces fresh shiitake or oyster mushrooms, sliced
- 1 teaspoon Dijon mustard
  Salt and freshly ground pepper, to taste
- ⅓ cup Marsala or Madeira wine
- ½ cup heavy cream
  Chopped parsley, for garnish

1. Soak *porcini* mushrooms in hot water until they are soft (about 30 minutes). Rinse well, thinly slice, and set aside.

2. Preheat wok over medium-high heat until hot. Pour in olive oil, then add butter. When butter foam subsides, add shallot and garlic, sauté until soft (about 1 minute). Increase heat to high; add reserved porcini mushrooms, then chanterelle and *shiitake* mushrooms, in batches about 30 seconds apart; stir-fry until mushrooms make a squeaky sound when rubbed against sides of wok (2 to 3 minutes total). Stir in mustard, salt, and pepper. If too much liquid forms, push mushrooms up sides of wok and reduce liquid to a light syrup. Deglaze wok with Marsala for about 10 seconds. Add cream; cook until sauce is reduced and coats mushrooms. Garnish with parsley.

Serves 4 with other dishes.

STIR-FRIED SPINACH

The use of dairy products in China disappeared after the T'ang dynasty (A.D. 618 to 906). White fermented tofu—soybean curd inoculated with a yeast culture and aged—is perhaps the Chinese food item most similar to cheese. This pungent cooking condiment, for which there is no substitute, lends itself well to stir-fried spinach, watercress, or other bitter greens.

> 2 Chinese sausage links
>   (see Note)
> 2 bunches fresh spinach
> 3 tablespoons peanut or corn oil
> 1 teaspoon salt
> 2 slices fresh ginger, bruised
> 3 cloves garlic, bruised
> 1 cake (1-in. cube)
>   fermented tofu
> 1 teaspoon sugar

1. Prepare wok for steaming (see page 86). Place sausage on heat-resistant plate, cover, and steam over medium-high heat 10 minutes. Remove sausage and keep warm.

2. Meanwhile, rinse spinach and thoroughly blot dry. Cut large leaves in half; set aside.

3. Wipe wok dry and return to medium heat. Pour oil in hot wok; then add salt, ginger, and garlic. Cook until oil is fragrant (at least 1 minute).

4. Increase heat to high. When hot add reserved spinach in batches, seconds apart, and stir-fry until spinach is wilted (30 to 60 seconds total), moving cooked spinach up sides of wok and reducing or spooning off excess liquid on bottom of wok to leave about 1 tablespoon oil. Add tofu and sugar to hot oil in center of wok. Fry 5 seconds; then toss together with spinach. Remove and discard ginger and garlic. Transfer spinach to serving plate. Dice warm sausage and place on top of spinach.

Serves 6 with other dishes.

<u>Note</u> If you are making a pot of rice, steam the sausage with the rice and eliminate step 1. Place sausage directly on top of rice after water has boiled off, cover, and simmer 20 minutes.

EGGPLANT SZECHUAN STYLE

From the first bite, this unique dish explodes with sweet, spicy, tart, and savory flavors.

> 6 Asian eggplants or 1 large
>   domestic eggplant, peeled
> 2 teaspoons salt
> 1 tablespoon soy sauce
> 1 tablespoon sugar
> ¼ cup chicken stock
> 4 tablespoons peanut or corn
>   oil, or as needed
> 2 teaspoons grated fresh ginger
> 1 tablespoon minced garlic
> ¼ teaspoon hot-pepper flakes
> ¼ cup chopped peeled Chinese
>   water chestnuts, preferably
>   fresh
> 3 green onions, chopped
> 1 tablespoon red wine vinegar
> 1 tablespoon Asian sesame oil
> 1 tablespoon toasted black ses-
>   ame seed, for garnish

1. Cut eggplant into strips ½ inch wide by 2 inches long. In a colander toss eggplant with salt; drain 30 minutes over a bowl. Squeeze out excess water and pat dry; set aside.

2. In a small bowl mix soy sauce, sugar, and stock. Set aside.

3. Preheat wok over high heat until hot. Pour in 3 tablespoons of the peanut oil. When hot add reserved eggplant slices 1 layer at a time; stir-fry until tender and seared (about 3 minutes). Remove to colander and drain over a bowl, reserving juices.

4. Reduce heat to medium-high. Add remaining 1 tablespoon peanut oil, ginger, garlic, and hot-pepper flakes; cook gently but do not brown. Add water chestnuts and half of the green onion; stir-fry 5 seconds. Increase heat to high, add reserved soy sauce mixture and reserved eggplant juices, and bring to a boil. Add reserved cooked eggplant; toss until most of the sauce is absorbed (1 to 2 minutes). Fold in vinegar and sesame oil. Remove to a serving dish and top with remaining green onion and sesame seed. Serve hot or cold.

Serves 4 as a first course or 8 with other dishes.

MA POCKED TOFU

The most popular story about the name of this dish is that the recipe belonged to the wife of a famous restaurateur whose complexion was not flawless. Tofu cooked in an assertive sauce is a good way to try out this ingredient on people who are not familiar with it.

> ½ pound chopped pork butt
> 2 tablespoons dark soy sauce
> 1 tablespoon dry vermouth
>   or rice wine
> 3 teaspoons cornstarch
> 2 teaspoons Asian sesame oil
> 1 tablespoon water
> 2 tablespoons peanut or corn oil
> 2 teaspoons finely minced
>   fresh ginger
> 1 teaspoon minced garlic
> 1 tablespoon hot bean sauce
> 4 green onions, coarsely
>   chopped
> ½ teaspoon sugar
> ¼ teaspoon white pepper
> 1 pound firm fresh tofu, cut into
>   ½-inch cubes, drained, and
>   blotted dry
> ½ cup chicken stock
> ½ cup green peas, blanched
>   Cooked white long-grain rice,
>   for accompaniment

1. In a medium bowl combine pork, 1 tablespoon of the soy sauce, vermouth, 1 teaspoon of the cornstarch, and 1 teaspoon of the sesame oil; set aside. In a small bowl mix the remaining 2 teaspoons cornstarch with the water; set aside.

2. Preheat wok over medium-high heat until hot. Pour in peanut oil; then add ginger, garlic, and hot bean sauce. Stir-fry until oil is fragrant (about 30 seconds). Increase heat to high; add reserved pork mixture and stir-fry until pork turns white (about 1 minute). Add green onion, sugar, and pepper; stir-fry 10 seconds. Add tofu and toss gently 3 minutes. Add remaining 1 tablespoon soy sauce, stock, and peas; stir-fry while bringing to a boil. Add reserved cornstarch mixture and cook until thickened. Fold in 1 remaining teaspoon sesame oil. Serve over rice.

Serves 4 with other dishes.

Dry-frying green beans gives them a delicious, slightly crunchy texture. Canned Szechuan preserved mustard greens, available in Asian grocery stores, are essential to this dish. Store leftover mustard greens in an airtight glass container in the refrigerator; they will keep indefinitely. Dried shrimp are available in well-stocked supermarkets; if they are large, chop them after soaking.

SAVORY STEAMED SHRIMP EGG CUSTARD

Chinese steamed egg dishes are surprisingly soothing, delicate, and flavorful. To ensure a velvety texture, do not overbeat the eggs.

 ¼ cup dried straw mushroom pieces (optional)
 2½ cups chicken stock
 1½ teaspoons soy sauce
  1 teaspoons salt
  ¼ teaspoon sugar
  4 large eggs
  2 ounces spinach, blanched, drained, and cut into 1-inch lengths
 12 medium shrimp, shelled and deveined
  1 green onion, chopped
    Oyster sauce, for sprinkling

1. In a small bowl cover mushrooms (if used) with warm water and soak until they are soft and pliable (about 30 minutes). Rinse, squeeze out excess moisture, and set aside. Brush six 1-cup ramekins lightly with oil.

2. In a 1½-quart saucepan over high heat, bring stock, soy sauce, salt, and sugar to a boil. Let cool completely.

3. In a large mixing bowl, beat eggs. Add cooled stock mixture in a slow, steady stream; stir gently. Strain egg mixture through a fine mesh strainer into a 1-quart measuring cup. Evenly divide reserved mushrooms, if used, and spinach among oiled ramekins and fill each with ¾ cup egg mixture.

4. Prepare wok for steaming (see page 86). Set ramekins in bamboo steaming baskets or on a steaming tray, cover, and steam over medium-high heat 1 minute. Reduce heat to medium and steam gently until custard is firm (about 15 minutes). Top each with 2 shrimp and green onion. Cover and steam until a knife comes out clean (about 5 minutes longer). Top with a few drops of oyster sauce and serve hot.

Serves 6 with other dishes.

SZECHUAN DRY-FRIED GREEN BEANS

In this recipe, which contradicts many basic stir-fry rules, dry-frying, a variation of stir-frying, produces a slightly crunchy and chewy texture and infuses the green beans with an extraordinary rich seasoning.

> 1 tablespoon dried shrimp
> ¼ pound pork butt, finely chopped
> 2 tablespoons dry vermouth or rice wine
> 1 teaspoon cornstarch
> 2 cups peanut oil, for deep-frying
> 1½ pounds green beans, rinsed, patted dry, and cut into 2-inch lengths
> 2 teaspoons minced fresh ginger
> 2 teaspoons minced garlic
> 1 piece (1 in.) Szechuan preserved mustard greens (see page 11), rinsed and finely chopped
> 1 teaspoon sugar
> Pinch white pepper
> 1 tablespoon dark soy sauce
> 2 tablespoons chicken stock
> 1 teaspoon Asian sesame oil

1. In a small bowl cover shrimp with warm water; soak 20 minutes. Drain and finely chop; set aside. In another small bowl combine pork, 1 tablespoon of the vermouth, and cornstarch; set aside.

2. Preheat wok over medium-high heat until hot. Pour in oil and heat to 375° F. Add beans in 3 batches and deep-fry until they blister and turn khaki-colored (about 5 minutes). Remove with a slotted spoon and drain on paper towels. Pour off all but 1 tablespoon oil from wok.

3. Add reserved pork and stir-fry until meat is seared and browned (about 2 minutes). Add ginger, garlic, reserved shrimp, and mustard greens; stir-fry until oil is fragrant (about 30 seconds). Increase heat to high. Add reserved beans and stir-fry until liquid is absorbed and beans are dry

(about 30 seconds). Add sugar and pepper; toss. Deglaze sides of wok with remaining vermouth, followed seconds later by soy sauce and stock. Stir-fry until beans are glazed and liquids are completely reduced. Fold in sesame oil and serve hot.

Serves 6 with other dishes.

SYLVIA'S POTATO LATKES

Sylvia Kay's Jewish-style potato pancakes are mouth-wateringly light, thin, and crispy. A flat-bottomed wok conducts heat so well and evenly that the pancakes turn out even crispier cooked this way than in a skillet. Sylvia serves them as a side dish with applesauce and sour cream.

> 2 eggs
> 1 small onion, finely grated
> 4 tablespoons flour
> 1½ teaspoons salt
> Large pinch white pepper
> 5 medium baking potatoes (about 2 lb), peeled
> Light olive oil or vegetable oil, for frying
> Applesauce, for accompaniment
> Sour cream, for accompaniment
> Italian parsley, for garnish

1. In a large mixing bowl beat eggs. Stir in onion, flour, salt, and pepper; set aside.

2. Coarsely grate potatoes into a colander. Drain, squeezing out excess liquid. Add potatoes to reserved egg mixture and stir to combine.

3. Preheat wok over medium-high heat until hot. Pour in oil to a depth of ¼ inch. When oil is hot add ¼ cup of the drained potato mixture; flatten it lightly with a spatula to a thickness of ⅓ inch. Repeat with remaining mixture, adding as many pancakes as will fit in 1 layer without crowding and adding oil as needed. Fry until pancakes are browned and crisp around edges (about 2 minutes per side). Remove and keep warm. Serve hot with applesauce and sour cream. Garnish with parsley.

Makes about 12 pancakes, serves 6 with other dishes.

SALADS AND SOUPS

Asian salads created in the Western fashion are a recent innovation. Virtually meals in themselves, they are elaborately prepared, with loads of cooked meats, vegetables, fruits, and nuts served on a bed of chilled or crispy noodles. The usual dressing consists of vinegar, soy sauce, and oil; a thick roasted sesame paste seasoned with sugar, chile oil, and soy sauce; or a plum sauce concoction. In Southeast Asia common dressings include such ingredients as lime juice, Thai fish sauce, sugar, and garlic; peanut butter; and coconut milk. Some foods are sauced or dressed while hot, others when cool. Enjoy and experiment, then savor the compliments elicited by your efforts.

In Asia soups play a prominent role in meals. The soups range from light, thin, simple ones of chicken, pork, or beef stock with chopped-up vegetables, appropriate as a first course, to hearty, thickened soups with noodles or wontons, which are one-dish meals enjoyed for lunch or as a snack.

Many soups taste better when started in a wok, such as home-style Hot-and-Sour Soup (see page 121). After the meats and vegetables are stir-fried, stock is added to deglaze the wok; the bits of food clinging to the sides become part of the seasoning of the soup. For Szechuan Garlic-Eggplant Soup With Scallop Noodles (see page 70), all the seasonings are sautéed in the wok before the liquid is added.

BON BON CHICKEN SALAD

In this chilled salad a bed of bean thread noodles is studded with julienned cucumber. The flavor of the toasted sesame paste is tantalizing.

> 2 whole chicken breasts
> 2 green onions, bruised
> 1 piece (1 in.) fresh ginger, bruised
> 2 teaspoons Asian sesame oil
> 3 quarts water
> 2 ounces bean thread noodles, soaked in warm water 20 minutes, then drained
> 1 English cucumber, peeled, cut in 1½-inch-long julienne strips
> 1 tablespoon sesame seed, preferably black, toasted, for garnish

Toasted Sesame Paste Dressing

> 3 tablespoons Chinese sesame paste
> 1 teaspoon finely minced fresh ginger
> 2 cloves garlic, finely minced
> 1 tablespoon peanut oil
> 3 tablespoons soy sauce
> 2 tablespoons wine vinegar
> 1 tablespoon sugar
> 1 teaspoon Asian sesame oil
> 1 teaspoon Asian hot chile oil, or to taste
> 3 tablespoons reserved chicken juices or water, or as needed

1. Prepare wok for steaming (see page 86). Place chicken, green onions, and ginger in a heat-resistant bowl. Cover and steam over medium-high heat 30 minutes. Let cool. Remove chicken, reserving juices for Toasted Sesame Paste Dressing. Tear meat into matchstick shreds, discarding skin and bones. In a medium bowl toss chicken with sesame oil; refrigerate.

2. In a 4-quart saucepan over high heat, bring the water to a boil. Add bean thread noodles, reduce heat to medium, and simmer until noodles are plump (5 minutes). Pour into a colander, rinse with cold water, and drain. Cut into 2-inch lengths, place in a medium bowl, cover with cold water, and refrigerate until chilled (about 1 hour). Drain well.

3. On a serving platter arrange drained bean thread noodles. Layer with cucumber, then reserved chicken. Top with Toasted Sesame Paste Dressing and garnish with sesame seed. Serve chilled.

Serves 8 as a first course salad or 4 as an entrée.

Toasted Sesame Paste Dressing
Place sesame paste in a heat-resistant bowl; place ginger and garlic on top. In a small saucepan over high heat, heat peanut oil until almost smoking; pour over paste and stir thoroughly. Add soy sauce, vinegar, sugar, sesame oil, and hot chile oil; mix well. Add chicken juices until mixture is consistency of thin cream. Chill. Before serving, check consistency of dressing. If too thick add more chicken juices to thin. Adjust seasoning if necessary.

Makes about 1 cup.

HUNAN EGGPLANT SALAD

Try this refreshing salad as part of a light summer luncheon. Steaming the eggplant accentuates its flavor and texture. Serve the salad chilled over a bed of agar-agar, a seaweed with an exotic crunchy texture.

> 4 small Asian eggplants or 1 large domestic eggplant
> 1½ ounces agar-agar strips (see page 10) or shredded lettuce
> 2 tablespoons chopped fresh coriander, for garnish
> 2 tablespoons sesame seed, toasted, for garnish

Hunan Vinaigrette

> 1 teaspoon finely minced fresh ginger
> 1½ teaspoons finely minced garlic
> 2 tablespoons dark soy sauce
> 1 tablespoon white wine vinegar
> 1½ teaspoons Asian hot chile oil, or to taste
> 2 teaspoons Asian sesame oil
> ¼ teaspoon salt
> 2 green onions, finely minced
> 1 tablespoon minced fresh coriander

1. Cut eggplant in half lengthwise, then crosswise into thirds. (If using domestic eggplant cut lengthwise into 1-inch-wide strips, then crosswise into 3-inch lengths.) Arrange on a shallow heat-resistant plate; set aside.

2. Prepare wok for steaming (see page 86). Cover eggplant and steam over medium-high heat until tender (about 20 minutes). Let eggplant cool; then cut into ⅛-inch strips. Cover and refrigerate.

3. In a medium bowl cover agar-agar with cold water (see Note); soak until soft (about 1 minute). Drain and cut strands into 1-inch lengths. Cover and refrigerate until chilled.

4. Arrange chilled agar-agar on a serving platter. Add reserved eggplant to Hunan Vinaigrette and pour over agar-agar. Garnish with chopped coriander and sesame seed. Serve chilled.

Serves 4 with other dishes.

Hunan Vinaigrette   In a medium bowl whisk together all ingredients.

Makes about ½ cup.

<u>Note</u>   Do not soak agar-agar in warm or hot water; it will dissolve into a gelatin.

WILTED ESCAROLE SALAD WITH FRIED POLENTA STICKS

Think of the wok as a salad bowl. It is excellent for preparing a hot or wilted salad such as this unique combination.

> 6 ounces pancetta (thick-sliced Italian bacon) or regular bacon, cut into ½-inch pieces
> ⅓ cup balsamic vinegar
> ¼ cup light olive oil
> Salt and freshly ground pepper, to taste
> 1 bunch escarole, torn into bite-sized pieces
> 2 tomatoes, cut into wedges
> ¼ cup walnuts, toasted
> ¼ pound Gorgonzola cheese, crumbled

Fried Polenta Sticks

- *2 cups water*
- *1 teaspoon salt*
- *½ cup polenta*
- *¼ cup grated Parmesan cheese*
- *¾ cup light olive oil*
- *¼ cup yellow cornmeal*

1. Preheat ungreased wok over medium-high heat until hot. Fry *pancetta* until lightly browned (about 2 minutes). Remove and set aside. Pour off and discard fat. Return wok to medium heat.

2. Add vinegar to wok and bring to a boil (about 30 seconds). Remove wok from heat; stir in olive oil, salt, and pepper. Add escarole, tomatoes, reserved pancetta, and walnuts; toss. Distribute among 6 large salad plates and sprinkle with cheese. Garnish with warm Fried Polenta Sticks.

Serves 6 as a first course.

Fried Polenta Sticks

1. In a medium saucepan over high heat, bring the water and salt to a boil. Reduce heat to medium and stir in polenta in a thin, steady stream. Stirring continuously, cook until polenta is thickened and pulls away from sides of pan (about 20 minutes), keeping water at a steady simmer. Fold in Parmesan cheese. Pour into a 4- by 10-inch baking pan. Smooth top; set aside until completely firm (about 30 minutes).

2. Cut cooled polenta into strips ½ inch wide by 2 inches long. Preheat wok over medium-high heat until hot. Pour in oil and heat until hot. Lightly coat polenta sticks with cornmeal and fry in batches, turning occasionally to brown and crisp all sides (about 5 minutes). Remove. Drain polenta sticks on paper towels and keep warm.

Makes 30 sticks.

Bon Bon Chicken Salad, a substantial entrée or a complete light meal, is dressed with a unique sesame paste dressing. Pouring hot peanut oil over the garlic, ginger, and sesame paste is a subtle but crucial step that the Chinese say "opens the flavor."

SMOKED HAM–CORIANDER FRIED WONTON SOUP
Heung tao ye foo wonton

In this hearty soup the deep-fried wontons are immersed in a broth garnished with egg whites and seasoned with fresh coriander, green onion, and Smithfield ham. Note that the basic wonton recipe makes about 5 dozen wontons, only 3 dozen of which are used here. Freeze the 2 dozen extras, or see the recipe for Basic Wontons for other suggestions.

> 36 deep-fried Basic Wontons (see page 42)
> 8 cups chicken stock
> 2 tablespoons dry vermouth
> 1 tablespoon light soy sauce, or to taste
> ¼ teaspoon white pepper
> ⅓ cup cornstarch mixed with ⅓ cup water
> 1 teaspoon Asian sesame oil
> 2 egg whites, beaten
> 3 tablespoons minced fresh coriander, for garnish
> 2 green onions, finely minced, for garnish
> 2 tablespoons minced Smithfield ham or prosciutto, for garnish

1. Place deep-fried wontons in a 3-quart soup tureen.

2. In a large stockpot over high heat, bring stock, vermouth, soy sauce, and pepper to a boil. Add cornstarch mixture and cook until soup thickens (about 15 seconds), stirring continuously. Fold in sesame oil. Remove from heat and pour egg whites in a steady stream into soup while slowly stirring in a circular motion. Egg whites should set into a lacy pattern within seconds. Pour soup over wontons; garnish with coriander, green onion, and ham. Serve hot.

Makes 8 cups, 6 servings.

SIZZLING RICE SOUP

Who would ever think that the rice crust stuck to the bottom of the cooking pan is worthy of the culinary attention it has received from this dish? Sizzling Rice Cakes make a hearty garnish and give the soup a roasted flavor. Timing is essential, however, for the dramatic sizzling effect. The soup must be hot and ready to serve when the cakes are added. Prepare the rice crust for the cakes at least a day in advance so it can air-dry overnight. The cakes will keep for several months stored in an airtight container. Or, if you prefer, use packaged dried rice cakes available in Asian grocery stores.

> 6 Chinese dried black mushrooms
> 1 tablespoon peanut oil, plus 2 cups for deep-frying
> 1 teaspoons salt, or to taste
> 2 slices peeled fresh ginger, bruised
> ½ cup diced bamboo shoots (¼-in. pieces)
> 4 Chinese water chestnuts, preferably fresh, peeled and cut into ¼-inch dice
> ¼ cup diced red bell pepper
> 2 tablespoons dry vermouth
> 6 cups chicken stock
> 1 tablespoon soy sauce, or to taste
> ¼ teaspoon white pepper
> ½ cup peas
> ¼ cup cornstarch mixed with 3 tablespoons water
> ¼ pound medium shrimp, shelled and deveined
> Asian sesame oil, to taste
> 2 green onions, coarsely chopped, for garnish

Sizzling Rice Cakes

> 1½ cups white long-grain rice, washed and drained
> 2 cups water

1. In a small bowl soak mushrooms in water until soft and pliable (about 30 minutes). Remove and discard stem from base of each; cut cap into ¼-inch dice. Set aside.

2. Preheat oven to 275° F. Preheat wok over medium-high heat until hot. Pour in the 1 tablespoon peanut oil; then add salt and ginger and cook until oil is fragrant (about 30 seconds). Add reserved mushrooms, bamboo shoots, water chestnuts, and bell pepper; stir-fry 1 minute. Add vermouth; toss. Increase heat to high; add stock, soy sauce, white pepper, and peas and bring to a boil. Add cornstarch mixture and stir until soup thickens. Add shrimp and sesame oil; cook 15 seconds. Transfer soup to tureen and garnish with green onion; keep hot. Rinse and dry wok; return to medium-high heat.

3. To hot wok pour in the 2 cups peanut oil and heat to 375° F. Add a batch of Sizzling Rice cakes. They should puff immediately. Fry until they are light golden (about 15 seconds); turn over and fry 10 seconds longer. Remove, drain on paper towel, and transfer to a serving plate; keep hot in warm oven. Repeat with remaining batches.

4. As soon as cakes are done, bring tureen to dining table; pour hot rice cakes into soup. They should sizzle on contact. Serve immediately.

Makes 7 cups, serves 8 with other dishes.

Sizzling Rice Cakes

1. The day before you plan to make soup, place rice and the water in a 9-inch-wide Dutch oven or skillet. Bring to a boil over high heat, stir rice and shake pan, and boil, uncovered, until all water is absorbed. Cover pan, reduce heat to low, and simmer 20 minutes. Let cool.

2. Remove cover and set pan over very low heat; dry-cook until rice shrinks from sides of pan (about 1 hour). Carefully remove rice in one piece and let air-dry overnight. Break into 10 to 12 pieces. If pieces are not bone-dry, place in a 250° F oven at least 2 hours.

Makes 10 to 12 pieces.

A REFRESHING SUMMER BRUNCH

Vietnamese Crab Imperial Rolls

Mandarin-Style Orange-Duck Salad

*Szechuan Garlic-Eggplant Soup
With Scallop Noodles*

Iced Lemongrass Tea

*Summer weather evokes
thoughts of chilled fresh
fruits, iced drinks, and lazy
days of minimal cooking.
If you plan to entertain, try
this simple menu, the focus
of which is a Chinese salad
using a whole roasted duck
available from a Chinese
delicatessen or restaurant.
Such salads are elaborate
entrées of fresh fruits, nuts,
seeds, pickled vegetables,
and shredded cooked meats.
Melon might be substituted
for the mandarin orange
slices, or fried Chinese bread
slices for the rice stick
noodles. Most of the cooking
for this impressive light meal
may be done in advance.*

VIETNAMESE CRAB IMPERIAL ROLLS
Cha gio

Wrapping imperial rolls in rice paper
makes them extra thin and crispy
when fried. Start with warm oil; then
increase the temperature. This keeps
the wrappers smooth and free of
cracks and bubbles. Imperial rolls
may be made in advance and refrigerated or frozen (see Note).

    3 tablespoons small dried cloud
       ear mushrooms
    2 ounces bean thread noodles
    1 pound ground pork butt
    4 cloves garlic, finely minced
    1 tablespoon Thai fish sauce
    ½ teaspoon ground pepper
    1 cup flaked crabmeat
    1 cup grated carrot
    1 cup bean sprouts, tails
       removed
    4 shallots or 1 small onion,
       minced
   16 sheets (12-in. diameter) dried
       rice paper wrappers or Chinese
       spring roll wrappers
    4 eggs, well beaten
       Peanut oil, for deep-frying
       Lettuce leaves, for
       accompaniment
       Fresh mint and fresh
       coriander, for accompaniment

Nuoc Cham Dipping Sauce

    1 clove garlic, squeezed through
       a garlic press, juice reserved
    4 teaspoons sugar
       Juice of 1 lime
    3 tablespoons Thai fish sauce
    2 tablespoons water
    1 fresh or dried red chile, seeded
       and pounded
    2 tablespoons finely grated
       carrot

1. In a small bowl cover mushrooms
with water and soak until they are
soft. Remove and discard hard centers. Coarsely chop caps. In another
small bowl cover noodles with water
until soft. Drain and cut noodles into
2-inch lengths.

2. In a medium bowl combine mushroom caps, drained noodles, pork,
garlic, fish sauce, pepper, crabmeat,
carrot, sprouts, and shallot; set aside.

3. To make imperial rolls, with scissors cut 1 rice paper wrapper into
quarters. Lay wrapper on a work
surface and brush generously with
beaten egg. Let wrapper sit until it
softens and becomes pliable (about
2 minutes). If wrapper does not
soften, dip it into a shallow bowl of
water just long enough to moisten
(about 2 seconds), lay wrapper on
counter, and brush again with egg.

4. With your hands shape 1½ tablespoons reserved pork mixture into a
compact roll 1 inch wide by 3 inches
long. Place roll along curved edge of
wrapper. Roll curved edge over roll;
then fold both outside edges inward,
enclosing ends. Finish rolling to seal.
(Roll must be firmly packed and
uniformly round to cook and brown
evenly.) If wrapper tears, mend it
with softened rice paper remnant. Set
roll on baking sheet and cover. Repeat with remaining wrappers and
filling.

5. Preheat wok over medium-high
heat until hot. Pour in oil to a depth
of 2 inches and heat to 300° F. Add
rolls in batches; fry each batch
10 seconds and then immediately
increase heat to high (375° F) and
fry until rolls are golden brown (6 to
8 minutes), turning occasionally.
Remove and drain on paper towels.

6. To serve, arrange rolls on a
platter. On a separate plate arrange
lettuce, mint, and coriander. To eat,
wrap imperial roll and sprigs of mint
and coriander in a lettuce leaf; dip
into Nuoc Cham Dipping Sauce.

Makes 3 dozen rolls.

Nuoc Cham Dipping Sauce   In
a bowl combine garlic juice, sugar,
lime juice, fish sauce, the water, and
chile. Strain into another bowl; add
carrot. Serve at room temperature.

Makes about ¾ cup.

Note   To make in advance, complete
step 5, then let rolls cool. Wrap in
airtight freezer bags and refrigerate
or freeze. To reheat, thaw if frozen,
place on a baking sheet, and heat,
uncovered, in a 350° F oven 10
minutes.

MANDARIN-STYLE ORANGE-DUCK SALAD

Make this dish with a fully cooked hanging roast duck from your local Chinese delicatessen or restaurant (remember to ask for the aromatic duck juice sealed in its cavity). Homemade Cantonese roast duck simply never seems to equal the marvelous flavor of the purchased variety. This summer salad makes an eye-catching centerpiece for a buffet table as well as a wonderful brunch entrée.

>   1 purchased Chinese roast duck
>   1 cup finely shredded radicchio
>   or purple cabbage
>   ½ cup julienned Chinese water
>   chestnuts, preferably fresh,
>   or jicama
>   3 green onions, finely slivered
>   ½ cup slivered almonds, toasted
>   1 cup fresh orange segments
>   or 1 can (11 oz) mandarin
>   orange segments, drained
>   and chilled
>   1 small bunch fresh coriander
>   2 tablespoons black sesame
>   seed, toasted
>   2 cups crumbled Deep-fried Rice
>   Stick Noodles (see page 38),
>   for garnish

Plum-Orange Vinaigrette

>   ¼ cup freshly squeezed
>   orange juice
>   ¼ cup roast duck juices, if
>   available
>   2 slices fresh ginger, squeezed
>   through a garlic press
>   1 tablespoon Chinese plum sauce
>   1 tablespoon Chinese-style dry
>   mustard blended with
>   1 tablespoon water
>   2 teaspoons soy sauce
>   2 teaspoons Asian sesame oil

1. Bone duck, reserving juices from cavity. Cut meat, including skin, into ¼-inch-thick strips.

2. In a large bowl combine duck, radicchio, water chestnuts, green onion, almonds, and half each of the orange segments, coriander, and sesame seed. Toss with two thirds of the Plum-Orange Vinaigrette.

3. Line a serving platter with crumbled rice stick noodles. Arrange duck mixture on top and garnish with remaining orange segments, coriander, and sesame seed. Pour remaining vinaigrette on top.

Serves 6.

Plum-Orange Vinaigrette In a medium bowl whisk together all ingredients.

Makes about ¾ cup.

SZECHUAN GARLIC-EGGPLANT SOUP WITH SCALLOP NOODLES

The delicate texture and scallop flavor of these dried ramen-style noodles work well with slightly pungent Szechuan eggplant. If scallop noodles are not available, substitute any flat egg noodle.

>   5 tablespoons peanut or corn
>   oil, or as needed
>   1 teaspoon salt
>   4 Asian eggplants or ¾ domestic
>   eggplant, cut lengthwise
>   into strips ½ inch wide by
>   2 inches long
>   6 coils dried Chinese scallop
>   noodles
>   1 tablespoon minced fresh
>   ginger
>   1 tablespoon minced garlic
>   2 tablespoons hot bean sauce or
>   ¼ teaspoon hot-pepper flakes
>   3 green onions, chopped
>   2 tablespoons dark soy sauce
>   2 tablespoons sugar
>   3 cups chicken stock
>   1 tablespoon cornstarch mixed
>   with 1 tablespoon water
>   3 tablespoons red wine vinegar
>   1 tablespoon Asian sesame oil
>   1 tablespoon minced fresh
>   coriander, for garnish

1. Preheat wok over medium-high heat until hot. Pour in 3 tablespoons of the peanut oil and add salt. When oil is hot add eggplant in batches and fry until golden brown (3 to 5 minutes), adding more oil if needed. Drain on paper towels.

2. Meanwhile, bring a large pot of salted water to a boil over high heat. Add noodles and cook until al dente (about 2 minutes). Remove and let drain. Divide noodles among 6 small soup bowls.

3. Reheat wok over medium heat until hot. Pour in remaining 2 tablespoons peanut oil, and add ginger, garlic, and bean sauce. Sauté until oil is fragrant (about 15 seconds). Add green onion, soy sauce, sugar, and stock. Increase heat to high; bring to a boil. Reduce and simmer for 10 minutes. Increase to medium-high; stir in cornstarch mixture and cook until thickened. Blend in vinegar and sesame oil. Ladle soup over noodles, top with reserved eggplant, and garnish with coriander.

Makes 3 cups, serves 6.

Variation Top the soup with Grilled Asian Eggplant (see page 116) instead of the stir-fried eggplant and eliminate step 1.

ICED LEMONGRASS TEA

Lemongrass, a common ingredient in the cuisine of Southeast Asia, has found new admirers in the West. This refreshing drink is modeled after the novel treatment of this grass at the fashionable Lemon Grass restaurant in Bangkok.

>   8 stalks fresh lemongrass
>   1 quart water
>   2 tablespoons sugar, or to taste

Rinse lemongrass and cut stalks into thirds. Crush stalks with side of cleaver and place in a saucepan with the water. Bring to a boil over high heat, reduce heat, and simmer 30 minutes. Add sugar and let dissolve. Let cool, strain, and serve over ice.

Serves 6.

The citrus-duck salad cools the spicy Szechuan soup. Complete this summer brunch with crab imperial rolls and dipping sauce, and Iced Lemongrass Tea.

*Dungeness crab, mussels, clams,
and prawns are among the
shellfish used in the imaginative
seafood preparations of
Asian chefs.*

Seafood & Poultry Entrées

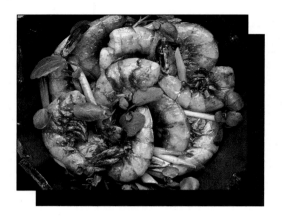

Few cuisines in the world can rival Asia's imaginative flair for fish, shellfish, and poultry. The recipes in this chapter include dishes from which to learn basic techniques, such as Classic Chinese Steamed Whole Fish (see page 78); recipes that work as well in a wok as in a pan (if not even better), such as old-fashioned Fried Chicken and Cream Gravy (see page 88); and unusual offerings for dinner guests, such as Mussels and Pasta With Saffron-Ginger Cream Sauce (see page 77). You will discover quick and easy recipes for two people, for casual entertaining, or simply for experimenting.

FISH AND SHELLFISH

To the Chinese cook seafood that is fresh means seafood that is live and wiggling. Chinese restaurants throughout Asia proudly display individual large tanks of swimming fish and crawling crabs and lobsters. Customers are invited to choose their seafood; within seconds the chosen animal is killed and cooked to one's liking. In Hong Kong live shrimp are brought to the table, and rice wine is liberally poured over them to create the classic and festive Chinese dish called Drunken Shrimp.

Asians consume fish and seafood with great gusto. As a reflection of their love for seafood, they have developed a host of recipes. Some of the recipes require the freshest of seafood; you will be rewarded for the extra effort required to find it fresh and not frozen.

SOUTHEAST ASIAN–STYLE SOFT-SHELL CRAB

In this recipe piquant seasonings of Southeast Asia—Thai fish sauce, fresh coriander, garlic, ginger, and lime—are used to sauce crispy panfried soft-shell crabs.

 8 small soft-shell crabs
 ¼ cup cornstarch
 5 tablespoons peanut or corn oil
 ½ teaspoon salt
 4 slices fresh ginger, minced
 2 cloves garlic, chopped
 3 green onions, cut into
   1-inch lengths
 3 tablespoons dry vermouth
 2 teaspoons Thai fish sauce
 1 teaspoon soy sauce
 2 tablespoons chicken stock
 ½ teaspoon sugar
 2 teaspoons minced lime zest
 2 tablespoons lime juice
 ½ cup toasted slivered almonds,
   for garnish
   Chopped fresh coriander,
   for garnish
   Cooked white long-grain rice,
   for accompaniment

1. If crabs need cleaning, lift up apron on underside of each and snap off. Brush and rinse exposed area.

Fold back shell at points of back; scrape and clean out spongy fingers. Rinse crabs and pat dry. Lightly coat crabs with cornstarch.

2. Preheat wok over medium heat until hot, then pour in 4 tablespoons of the oil. When hot add crabs in batches and sauté until crabs are brown and crisp (3 to 4 minutes per side). Remove to a serving plate and keep warm. Pour off oil from wok, wipe clean with a paper towel, and return wok to medium heat.

3. Add remaining 1 tablespoon oil, salt, ginger, garlic, and green onion; sauté until oil is fragrant (about 30 seconds). Increase heat to high; add vermouth, fish sauce, soy sauce, stock, and sugar. Stir until mixture is slightly thickened. Add lime zest and juice, stir once, remove from heat, and spoon over warm crabs. Garnish with toasted almonds and coriander. Serve immediately with rice.

Serves 4 with other dishes.

FRIED CATFISH WITH CHINESE HOT BEAN SAUCE

Frying catfish with the skin on creates a crisp crust. The sauce, a complex seasoning of spicy, sweet, sour, and savory flavors, complements the delicate sweetness of the catfish.

 4 whole catfish (about 8 oz
   each), gutted and heads
   and fins removed
 1 teaspoon salt
   Cornstarch, for dusting
 4 tablespoons peanut or corn oil
 1 tablespoon hot bean sauce
 1 tablespoon chopped fresh
   ginger
 1 tablespoon chopped garlic
 2 green onions, chopped
 1 tablespoon sugar
 1½ tablespoons dry vermouth
   or rice wine
 1½ tablespoons soy sauce
 ½ cup chicken stock or water
 2 tablespoon red wine vinegar
 1 tablespoons Asian sesame oil
   Cooked white long-grain rice,
   for accompaniment

1. Clean fish thoroughly. Make 3 diagonal slashes almost to the bone about 2 inches apart on both sides of fish. Rinse and pat dry. Salt fish and coat lightly with cornstarch, dusting slashes as well.

2. Preheat wok over medium-high heat until hot, then pour in peanut oil. When oil is hot, add fish and fry until golden brown (about 5 minutes per side). Remove fish to a serving plate and keep warm. Pour off all but 1 tablespoon oil from wok.

3. Reduce heat to medium. Add bean sauce, ginger, garlic, half the green onion, and sugar. Sauté until oil is fragrant (about 30 seconds). Add vermouth, soy sauce, and stock; increase heat to high and bring mixture to a boil. Lower heat to medium and reduce mixture to consistency of light cream (about 3 minutes). Stir in vinegar, sesame oil, and remaining chopped green onion. Spoon mixture over warm fish and serve with rice.

Serves 4 to 6 with other dishes.

OYSTERS, BELL PEPPERS, ONIONS, AND BACON

Although this recipe uses Western ingredients, it reflects the Chinese emphasis on a variety of flavors, textures, and colors. It is simple and quick to prepare and is delicious over egg noodles.

 3 strips thickly sliced bacon,
   each cut into fourths
 1 pound small shucked oysters,
   drained, or 1 jar (10 oz)
   small oysters, drained
 3 tablespoons flour, for coating
 1 teaspoon salt
   Freshly ground pepper, to taste
 2 tablespoons olive oil, or more
   as needed
 2 cloves garlic, chopped
 1 medium onion, coarsely
   chopped
 1 green bell pepper, seeds and
   ribs removed, cut into ½-inch
   squares
 1 large tomato, peeled, seeded,
   and coarsely chopped
   Cooked egg noodles, for
   accompaniment

1. Preheat ungreased wok over medium heat until hot. Fry bacon until cooked but not crisp (about 1 minute). Drain on paper towel. Pour off and reserve all but 2 teaspoons drippings, and return wok to heat.

2. Lightly flour oysters; add to wok in batches and cook until crisp and brown (1 to 2 minutes per side). Season with salt and ground pepper,

remove, and keep warm. Repeat with remaining oysters, adding more reserved drippings or oil as needed.

3. Add the 2 tablespoons oil to wok. When hot add garlic and onion and sauté until onion is soft. Increase heat to medium-high; add bell pepper and toss 1 minute. Add tomato and toss a few seconds; add reserved oysters and bacon and gently toss together. Serve hot over egg noodles.

Serves 4 to 6 with other dishes.

This Southeast Asian–style version of soft-shell crab is flavored with Thai fish sauce, garlic, and lime juice. Frying the crabs in a wok gives their edible shells a nicely browned crust and makes an easy and impressive entrée.

Mussels and Pasta With Saffron-Ginger Cream Sauce makes a perfect light Sunday supper. Serve it with green salad, a crusty loaf of French bread, and wine. A wok is perfectly shaped for steaming cumbersome ingredients such as mussels and other shellfish cooked in their shells.

OYSTERS WITH EGGS AND GARLIC CHIVES

You might call this dish Chinese-style hangtown fry. In a home-style Chinese dinner, it is served as one of many entrées. For a Western meal, mound the oysters and eggs on individual slices of toasted baguette or stuff them in a vol-au-vent pastry shell. Serve as a first course or a light luncheon dish.

   4 tablespoons peanut or corn oil
   1 slice fresh ginger, bruised
      Flour, for coating
   1 pound small shucked oysters, drained, or 1 jar (10 oz) small oysters, drained
      Pinch each salt and white pepper, or to taste
   ½ onion, cut lengthwise into ¼-inch-wide strips
   2 cloves garlic, finely minced
   1 cup chopped chives (2-in. pieces), preferably Chinese garlic chives
   5 large eggs, slightly beaten
   1 tablespoon oyster sauce, for drizzling (optional)

1. Preheat wok over medium-high heat until hot, then pour in 2 tablespoons of the oil. Add ginger. Meanwhile, lightly flour oysters. When oil is fragrant, add floured oysters and fry until golden brown (about 1 minute per side). Add salt and pepper. Remove to a plate and keep warm.

2. If food bits are stuck in wok, rinse with hot water and wipe dry with a paper towel. Preheat wok over high heat until hot; then pour in remaining 2 tablespoons oil. When hot add onion and stir-fry 15 seconds. Add garlic and chives; toss until chives begin to wilt (about 10 seconds). Add eggs and toss (do not stir) gently with greens until eggs are loosely scrambled; cook until set but not dry (about 1 minute). Fold in reserved oysters. Transfer to a serving platter and drizzle with oyster sauce, if used, or mound individual portions over slices of toasted baguette.

Serves 6 with other dishes.

MUSSELS AND PASTA WITH SAFFRON-GINGER CREAM SAUCE

In this recipe mussels are steamed with typical Asian seasonings, then combined with vermouth and cream and served over pasta. French bread is a perfect accompaniment.

    2   pounds mussels (about 24
        mussels), scrubbed and
        debearded
    4   slices fresh ginger, plus
        2 tablespoons finely shredded
        fresh ginger
    2   shallots, finely chopped
    2   cloves garlic, finely chopped
    ½   cup dry vermouth or
        white wine
    ½   teaspoon saffron threads
    ½   pound tagliarini pasta,
        cooked al dente in salted
        water
    1½ tablespoons virgin olive oil
    1½ tablespoons unsalted butter
    ½   pound medium shrimp,
        shelled and deveined
    ½   pound small bay scallops
    ½   cup heavy cream
    1   to 2 teaspoons freshly
        squeezed lemon juice
    ½   teaspoon salt
        Freshly ground pepper, to taste
        Fresh watercress or other bitter
        greens, for garnish

1. Place mussels in a shallow heat-resistant bowl that will fit comfortably in a covered bamboo steaming basket. Scatter ginger slices, shallot, and half the garlic on top and sprinkle with vermouth.

2. Prepare wok for steaming (see page 86). Place bowl of mussels in steaming basket and place basket in wok. Cover and steam over medium-high heat until mussels open (about 5 minutes). Pick out ginger slices and discard. Remove mussels and reserve; pour juices, including garlic and shallot, into a small saucepan. Wipe wok dry.

3. In a small bowl dissolve saffron in 1 tablespoon hot mussel juice mixture; add liquid to saucepan with rest of mussel juice mixture. Cook liquid over high heat until reduced to ½ cup. Set aside.

4. Drain pasta and place on a warmed platter or in individual pasta bowls; keep warm. Preheat wok over medium heat; when hot pour in oil, then add butter. When butter foam subsides add remaining garlic and shredded ginger and sauté until soft (about 30 seconds). Increase heat to medium-high; add shrimp and sauté until they just begin to turn pink (about 1 minute). Add scallops and toss together a few seconds. Add reserved reduced juices and cream; cook until sauce is reduced to a creamy consistency (1 minute). Add reserved mussels, lemon juice, salt, and pepper. Spoon over hot pasta. Garnish with watercress.

Serves 6 with other dishes.

Flat-leaved Chinese garlic chives are so good, it is worth searching Asian grocery stores to find them. They add a subtle, delicate garlic flavor to this oyster-egg stir-fry.

CLASSIC CHINESE STEAMED WHOLE FISH

To many culinary experts, Chinese steamed whole fish is perfection. The Cantonese, who have mastered its preparation, believe that only a few ingredients should be used, in order to enhance and not mask the sweet natural flavor of the fresh fish. It is essential never to overcook the fish. Carefully ladling sizzling hot oil over the cooked fish is the secret touch to accentuate the delicate flavor.

> 1 very fresh whole fish (about 2 lb), such as rock cod, red snapper, sea bass, or striped bass or 2 small whole trout (1 lb each)
> 2 teaspoons salt
> 2 green onions, bruised and cut into 2-inch lengths, plus 4 green onions, white part only, cut into 1½-inch-long shreds
> 2 tablespoons peeled, cut fresh ginger (1½-in.-long shreds), plus 1 slice fresh ginger
> 2 tablespoons soy sauce
> 2 tablespoons peanut oil
> Generous pinch white pepper
> Fresh coriander, for garnish
> Cooked white long-grain rice, for accompaniment

1. Clean and scale fish, leaving head and tail on; rinse and dry thoroughly. Make 3 diagonal slashes on each side. Rub fish with salt inside and out, including slashes.

2. Choose an oblong heat-resistant platter large enough to hold whole fish but small enough to fit in steamer with cover on. Scatter green onion lengths on platter and place fish on top. Scatter half of green onion shreds and 1 tablespoon of the ginger shreds on top of fish.

3. Prepare wok for steaming (see page 86). Position platter with fish on steaming rack, cover, and steam fish over medium-high heat until flesh is opaque and knife tip easily penetrates thickest part of fish (10 minutes per inch of thickness).

4. In a small saucepan over medium heat, warm soy sauce until fragrant (about 30 seconds). In another small saucepan over medium heat, slowly heat oil and ginger slice until hot and almost smoking.

5. Remove plate of fish from steamer. Pour off and discard half of accumulated juices from bottom of plate. Sprinkle with white pepper, pour warm soy sauce over fish, and scatter remaining green onion shreds and ginger shreds on top; then carefully ladle hot oil over entire fish. Oil should sizzle. Pick out and discard ginger slice, garnish fish with plenty of coriander, and serve immediately with rice.

Serves 6 with other dishes.

THAI FISH FILLETS WITH TAMARIND-GINGER SAUCE
Pla cien

Pla means *fish* in Thai. Tamarind, a popular Southeast Asian sour fruit, is used extensively in Asian cooking as a flavoring agent. Combining fresh ginger and palm sugar with tamarind makes a spicy sweet-and-sour sauce that is perfect for fish. This sauce may also be used as a dipping sauce for grilled shrimp or other shellfish.

> 1½ pounds fish fillets, such as sole, sea bass, snapper, cod, or catfish
> 1 teaspoon salt
> 3 tablespoons cornstarch
> ¼ cup peanut or corn oil
> 4 cloves garlic, crushed
> 6 green onions, bruised and cut into 2-inch lengths
> 2 tablespoons chopped fresh coriander, for garnish
> 2 fresh red chiles, slivered, for garnish
> 2 tablespoons fried shallot flakes (see Crisp Fried Garlic or Shallot Flakes, page 24), for garnish (optional)

Tamarind Sauce

> 6 tablespoons Tamarind Water (see page 24)
> 1 teaspoon grated fresh ginger
> 2 tablespoons palm sugar or firmly packed brown sugar
> 2 tablespoons soy sauce
> 1 tablespoon Thai fish sauce
> Freshly ground black pepper (about 6 twists)

1. Rinse fish and pat dry. Cut into 6-inch lengths; salt and coat lightly with cornstarch.

2. Preheat wok over medium-high heat until hot, then pour in oil. When hot add fish in batches and fry until golden brown (4 to 5 minutes per side). Drain fish on paper towels, transfer to a platter, and keep warm.

3. Pour off all but 2 tablespoons oil from wok. Reduce heat to medium. Add garlic; sauté until golden brown. Stir in Tamarind Sauce and cook until mixture is reduced to consistency of light cream (about 1 minute). Add green onion and simmer 1 minute. Spoon mixture over reserved fish; garnish with coriander, chiles, and shallot flakes (if used).

Serves 4 to 6 with other dishes.

Tamarind Sauce In a medium bowl combine all ingredients.

Makes about ½ cup.

Variation In Thailand fish is fried whole until the skin is very crisp. To prepare a whole fried fish, have the fishmonger scale, clean, and gut a 2-pound fish, leaving head and tail intact. Make deep diagonal slashes almost to the bone about 2 inches apart on both sides of fish. Rinse and pat dry, and dust with flour or cornstarch. Fill wok with enough oil to cover whole fish and fry at 375° F until skin and cuts are golden brown and crisp. Then continue with step 3.

Serves 4 to 6 with other dishes.

The tamarind sauce for these
Thai fish fillets is enhanced by the
buttery caramel-like flavor of
palm sugar; if necessary, brown
sugar can be substituted.

When dry-frying prawns in the shell, let them sit in the hot peanut oil without tossing or stirring so that the shells can form a browned crust. Adding the wine when the wok is hot quickly burns off the alcohol and reduces the wine to a glaze that coats the prawns.

KUNG PAO SHRIMP WITH CASHEWS

In this variation of the classic Szechuan *kung pao* chicken, jumbo cashews are used in place of the traditional peanuts, and shrimp are substituted for the chicken. When charring the chiles, be sure your exhaust fan is on and avoid breathing the strong chile fumes.

   1 *cup jumbo raw cashews*
1½ *tablespoons dark soy sauce*
   2 *tablespoons red wine vinegar*
   2 *teaspoons sugar*
   1 *teaspoon Asian sesame oil*
   2 *tablespoons peanut or corn oil*
  ½ *teaspoon salt*
   8 *small dried red chiles*
   2 *teaspoons minced fresh ginger*
   2 *cloves garlic, minced*
   1 *green or red bell pepper, seeds and ribs removed, cut into 1-inch squares*
   1 *pound medium shrimp, shelled, deveined, and patted dry*

1. Preheat oven to 325° F. In a flat pan spread cashews in a single layer; roast until golden brown (about 10 minutes), stirring occasionally. Remove and set aside.

2. In a small bowl combine soy sauce, vinegar, sugar, and sesame oil; set aside.

3. Preheat wok over medium heat until hot, then pour in peanut oil. Add salt and chiles; cook until chiles are charred (about 15 seconds). Add ginger and garlic; stir-fry until fragrant and lightly browned (about 30 seconds).

4. Increase heat to high; add bell pepper and stir-fry until pepper is seared (30 seconds). Add shrimp a handful at a time and stir-fry until shrimp are pink and feel firm to the touch (about 2 minutes total). Add reserved sauce mixture; toss and stir until sauce thickens to a glaze (about 30 seconds). Remove wok from heat. Gently stir in reserved roasted cashews. Serve hot.

Serves 4 to 6 with other dishes.

DRY-FRIED PRAWNS IN THE SHELL

Many chefs believe that much of the flavor of a prawn is in its shell. In this recipe the prawns are dry-fried with the shells on. When eating the prawns, bite off a small piece with the shell and chew, savoring the crunchy texture and intense flavor. You may then discard the shell. This dish serves equally well as an appetizer or an entrée.

   1 pound large prawns in the shell (about 15 prawns), heads removed
   3 tablespoons peanut or corn oil
   ½ teaspoon salt
   3 slices fresh ginger, bruised
   3 cloves garlic, bruised
   4 green onions, cut into 2-inch lengths
   Pinch each white pepper and sugar
   2 tablespoons dry vermouth or rice wine
   2 teaspoons dark soy sauce
   1 bunch fresh watercress, rinsed, large stems removed, for serving

1. Leave shells on prawns; devein if you wish. Rinse and pat dry.

2. Preheat wok over medium-high heat until hot, then pour in oil. Add salt, ginger, and garlic; crush against sides of wok to squeeze out juices. Remove and discard.

3. Add prawns to wok in batches and fry each side without stirring until prawns are browned and crusty (about 1 minute per side). Remove each batch and keep warm while frying remaining prawns. Increase heat to high. Return all prawns to wok; add green onion, pepper, and sugar and toss. Add vermouth and, seconds later, soy sauce; toss until mixture is reduced to a glaze that coats prawns (about 30 seconds). Serve hot over watercress.

Serves 6 with other dishes.

CLAMS IN CHILE-GARLIC BLACK BEAN SAUCE

In this recipe cherrystone clams are so quickly stir-fried in their shells that you can serve this entrée 10 minutes after starting it, but begin cooking the rice at least 20 minutes before stir-frying the clams.

   1 tablespoon salted black beans, soaked in water 5 minutes, rinsed well, and drained
   2 cloves garlic, chopped
   1 piece (1 in.) fresh ginger, minced
   2 tablespoons peanut or corn oil
   ½ teaspoon salt
   2 or 3 fresh green chiles serranos or other fresh hot chiles, coarsely chopped
   2 green onions, coarsely chopped
   2 pounds small cherrystone clams (about 24 clams), scrubbed
   1 teaspoon sugar
   White pepper, to taste
   2 tablespoons dry vermouth or rice wine
   1 tablespoon dark soy sauce
   ¼ cup chicken stock
   1 teaspoon cornstarch mixed with 1 tablespoon water
   1 teaspoon Asian hot chile oil
   Fresh coriander, for garnish
   Cooked white long-grain rice, for accompaniment

1. In a small bowl mash to a coarse paste black beans, garlic, and ginger. Preheat wok over high heat until hot, then pour in peanut oil. Add salt, black bean mixture, chiles, and green onion; stir-fry until oil is fragrant (about 15 seconds). Add clams and stir-fry 1 minute. Season with sugar and white pepper. Add vermouth and toss a few seconds. Add soy sauce and stock, cover, reduce heat to medium-high, and cook until clams open (about 5 minutes).

2. Remove cover from wok and stir cornstarch mixture into center of wok, stirring constantly until sauce thickens to a light glaze. Pour in chile oil and mix together. Garnish with coriander and serve with rice.

Serves 6 with other dishes.

Tips

...FOR STEAMING

☐ Think of the steamer as an oven. It needs preheating, just as an oven does. This means that the water must be boiling before you place food in the steamer and that the cooking time begins when the steamer is covered.

☐ Each time the lid is removed, steam is released and cooking time must be increased slightly.

☐ Check water level frequently and replenish only with boiling water.

☐ When steaming food such as dumplings placed directly on latticework of a bamboo steamer, brush the latticework with oil or set the food on top of bok choy leaves, spinach, or other greens. This helps prevent the food from sticking to the steamer.

☐ When steaming fish, allow 10 minutes per inch of thickness of fish.

☐ When steaming food in a metal steamer, allow less cooking time than for a bamboo steamer—generally 5 minutes less for every 25 minutes of steaming.

☐ When steaming with multiple tiers, place items that require less time on the top level so that all the tiers are done at the same time.

☐ When removing the steamer cover, always remember to open it away from your face. In addition, always allow the billowing steam to dissipate before you reach into the steamer.

THE TECHNIQUE OF STEAMING

The age-old Chinese technique of steaming food is still a popular every-day cooking method. In the Asian home kitchen, steaming is given at least as much attention as stir-frying and other cooking techniques. It is practical, efficient, and one of the most nutritious ways of cooking: Fewer vitamins are lost from food during steaming than during other cooking methods.

The highly touted Classic Chinese Steamed Whole Fish (see page 78) is an excellent example of the steaming technique. One of the finest methods of preparing fresh fish, steaming is a simple, pure technique that accentuates rather than alters the fresh, sweet flavor of the fish. This delicate steamed fish, seasoned with thin slivers of ginger, green onion, salt, and white pepper, is outstanding.

Steaming is fuel efficient; as many as three tiers containing different entrées may be stacked over a single heat source and steamed together. Steaming is also labor efficient; it requires little advance preparation, and you can relax once the steaming begins. During the steaming process, the marinated food gently simmers and bastes itself in its own juices, creating a luscious, rich sauce. The food emerges moist, light, and delicate and the sauces pure and honest.

A multicourse menu demands good planning. To entertain guests without being a slave to the kitchen, focus on a balanced menu of steamed dishes supplemented by one or two stir-fried entrées.

EQUIPMENT FOR STEAMING

The Chinese steamer is the Eastern equivalent of the Western oven. While Westerners cook or roast with dry heat in an oven, Asians steam-cook with moist heat on top of the stove

in a steamer. Dishes cooked in a "moist oven" are served piping hot straight from the steaming basket.

Electric woks are excellent for steaming; their finish is not harmed by boiling water, whereas the patina of a cast-iron or carbon spun-steel wok is eventually stripped by frequent and prolonged steaming. An electric wok also may be set away from the stove, thus freeing a burner to cook another dish.

Many types of steamers are available in cookware shops and Asian hardware stores. Bamboo steaming baskets, designed to sit firmly in a wok, lend an informal, homey feeling to the food that is served in them. Bamboo steaming baskets for home use range in diameter from 5 inches for dumplings and small individual servings to 12 inches for multiple servings of meat, seafood, poultry, and casseroles. The baskets should be 1 to 2 inches smaller than the wok in which they will sit. It is wise to select 12-inch baskets for the all-purpose 14-inch wok; three tiers and one tight-fitting cover will suffice. While one or two baskets of main entrées are being steamed, the top layer may be used for warming Mandarin pancakes or reheating cold rice. Bamboo baskets are also excellent for steaming breads and dim sum appetizers.

Another advantage of the bamboo steamer is that it absorbs the condensation built up during steaming, leaving the food moist and fluffy. Steam that condenses onto food can make it soggy.

Before using a new bamboo steamer, clean it well with a soft brush and water (avoid soap); then set it, covered, in a wok and steam for 15 minutes. After cooking in a steamer, clean it by thoroughly rinsing with water and air-drying.

Unless otherwise specified, all recipes in this book are designed

for 12-inch bamboo steaming baskets set in a 14-inch wok, preferably with a flat bottom. Bear in mind that the times given for steaming are estimates and are affected by the variables discussed in Tips for Steaming on page 81.

An aluminum multi-tier steamer fitted with a base pan is less cumbersome than a bamboo steamer atop a wok. The base pan holds more water, which is useful for long steaming. Metal steamers cook faster than their bamboo counterparts and do not retain odors. Condensation accumulates on the inside of their lids, however. To prevent the condensation from dripping onto the food, drape a dish towel over the steamer before putting on the lid, taking care that the towel is not so close to the heat source that it can catch on fire. The towel will absorb the excess moisture.

Steaming trays, racks, and trivets are often packaged with woks. A steaming tray is a thin, round metal plate with perforations; a steaming rack is similar to a 12-inch round cake-cooling rack; and a steaming trivet is merely a three-legged metal stand to support and elevate a plate above the boiling water. All work well for steaming items too large to fit in a 12-inch bamboo basket but not too large for a 14-inch wok. Often this is true for a small whole fish, which fits better on an oval plate than on a round one. In that case, simply set the steaming tray, rack, or trivet into the wok. Set the fish on its plate on top and cover with the dome-shaped lid of the wok. When food is steamed in this manner—directly in the wok—it cooks much more rapidly than in a steaming basket or aluminum steamer.

If you do not have a steamer, you can easily improvise one using the pans in the kitchen. A large Dutch oven, turkey roaster, or electric skillet works well in place of a wok to steam whole chicken, duck, or fish. Two shallow cans, such as tuna fish cans, with both ends removed can be used in place of a trivet to support a plate containing the food. Another alternative for steaming a large whole fish is to use two rectangular roasting pans long enough to accommodate the fish. Position one roasting pan across two adjacent burners; use two shallow cans with the ends removed, one at each end of the pan, to support the plate of fish above the water level. Invert the other pan over it as a cover. Or you can use aluminum foil as a cover instead.

Glass or ceramic pie plates make excellent containers for steaming foods. They must be heat resistant. For casserole-style dishes to be steamed in a 12-inch basket, the plate ideally should be 1½ to 2 inches deep and 9 inches wide. Although tradition favors slant-sided plates, ceramic quiche plates with straight fluted sides work well and add a decorative touch.

Whichever method of steaming you choose, the heat-resistant plate used to hold the food must have at least a 1-inch clearance from the inside perimeter of the bamboo basket, aluminum steamer, or wok in which it is set. The clearance permits the steam to rise and circulate freely. The level of the water in the steamer should be no closer than 1 inch from the bottom of the steaming plate, basket, tray, or trivet. During steaming, frequently check the water level and replenish with boiling water.

A special three-pronged hot plate retriever allows you to reach into a deep pot or basket and remove the steaming plate without having to touch the hot sides of the steamer. If the plate is heavy, before you assemble the steamer, make a sling of double-mesh cheesecloth long enough to run under the plate and drape up over the side of the pot. Do not let the cloth hang over the side, however; secure it on the lid to prevent it from catching on fire.

POULTRY

Poultry occupies a very special position in the cuisines of Asia. Chicken is prized for its versatility, and it cooks beautifully in a wok.

Whereas chicken is consumed daily and seafood is consumed nearly as often, duck and squab are special foods, generally left to master chefs and considered banquet and entertainment fare. Duck entrées are still regarded as one of China's great contributions to the international culinary arts. Peking duck, the pièce de résistance of the Chinese banquet, reflects imperial China's haute cuisine and continues to survive the changing fashions of centuries.

On the rare occasions that duck is served at home, it is usually purchased from a local delicatessen or restaurant. This chapter contains some of the great duck classics and some unusual salads and stir-fried entrées using fruit and purchased roast duck.

WALNUT CHICKEN WITH PEKING SAUCE

Peking sauce is the American term for what the Chinese refer to as *Chinese capital sauce*. It consists of a popular brown bean condiment that is used sparingly to impart a savory flavor base. Sweet and spicy hoisin sauce is often added to balance the strong flavor.

1½ cups walnuts, blanched in boiling water 3 minutes and drained
3 tablespoons peanut or corn oil
1 pound chicken meat, cut into ½-inch cubes
6 teaspoons sugar
2 tablespoons dry vermouth or rice wine
2 teaspoons cornstarch
1½ teaspoons Asian sesame oil
1½ tablespoons brown bean sauce or ground brown bean sauce
1 tablespoon hoisin sauce
2 teaspoons dark soy sauce
¼ cup chicken stock
1 teaspoon minced fresh ginger
4 green onions, cut into 2-inch lengths

1. Preheat oven to 325° F. Pat walnuts dry and mix with 1 tablespoon of the peanut oil. In a flat pan arrange walnuts in a single layer and roast until golden brown (about 15 minutes). Set aside.

2. In a medium bowl combine chicken, ½ teaspoon of the sugar, vermouth, cornstarch, and ½ teaspoon of the sesame oil. Set aside 15 minutes, or cover and refrigerate overnight.

3. In a small bowl combine remaining 5½ teaspoons sugar, bean sauce, hoisin sauce, soy sauce, and stock; set aside.

4. Preheat wok over medium-high heat until hot. Pour in remaining 2 tablespoons peanut oil and add ginger; cook until oil is fragrant (about 30 seconds). Increase heat to high; add marinated chicken in handfuls, seconds apart, and cook until chicken feels firm to the touch (about 2 minutes). Add green onion and reserved bean sauce mixture; stir-fry until sauce is fragrant and reduced to a light glaze (about 30 seconds). Add reserved walnuts and stir to combine. Blend in remaining 1 teaspoon sesame oil.

Serves 4 to 6 with other dishes.

An update of a popular 1950s duck-pineapple dish, this makes an exciting but easy dinner when served with hot cooked rice and a vegetable.

STIR-FRIED CANTONESE ROAST DUCK WITH PINEAPPLE

Do as the Chinese do—purchase a fully cooked Cantonese roast duck from your local Chinese delicatessen or restaurant and use it to prepare this recipe. If the duck juices are not available, the recipe can be prepared without them.

> 1 Cantonese roast duck, left whole
> ¼ cup duck juice (optional)
> 1 or 2 teaspoons grated fresh ginger
> 2 tablespoons firmly packed brown sugar
> 2 tablespoons red wine vinegar
> 1 tablespoon dark soy sauce
> 1 tablespoon peanut or corn oil
> ½ teaspoon salt
> 1 onion, cut into 1-inch cubes
> 1 red bell pepper, cut into 1-inch squares
> 1 cup cubed (1-in. cubes) fresh pineapple

1. Untruss duck and catch juices in a small bowl; set juices aside. Chop duck in half down the center; remove bones and save for another use. Cut meat with skin into 2-inch by ¾-inch strips; set aside.

2. Strain duck juice into a medium bowl. Add ginger, brown sugar, vinegar, and soy sauce. Set aside.

3. Preheat wok over high heat until hot. Pour in oil and add salt. When hot add onion and bell pepper; stir-fry until pepper is bright red (about 1 minute). Add duck juice mixture and toss together until well mixed (about 15 seconds). Toss in reserved duck strips; stir-fry until hot (about 15 seconds). Toss in pineapple and stir-fry to heat through (about 10 seconds).

Serves 4 to 6 with other dishes.

STEAMED CHICKEN WITH STRAW MUSHROOMS AND CHINESE SAUSAGE

A popular Chinese home-style dish is chicken chopped into bite-sized pieces with the skin, meat, and bone; tossed with a marinade and topped with one or two garnishes; then steamed. This version, for entertaining, uses boned chicken breasts topped with mushrooms, lily buds, and Chinese sausage. If the lily buds, mushrooms, or sausage are not available, the steamed marinated chicken is delicious solo. For an alternate serving suggestion, see Note.

> 4 medium Chinese dried black mushrooms
> 8 Chinese dried straw mushrooms
> ¼ cup dried lily buds
> 2 large whole chicken breasts, skinned, boned, and cut into ½-inch cubes
> 2 slices peeled fresh ginger, slivered
> 1 green onion, minced
> 1½ tablespoons dark soy sauce
> 2 tablespoons dry vermouth or rice wine
> ½ teaspoon sugar
> ½ teaspoon salt
> 1 tablespoon cornstarch
> 1 teaspoon Asian sesame oil
> 2 Chinese sausage links, sliced diagonally into ¼-inch pieces
>   Cooked white long-grain rice, for accompaniment

1. In 3 medium bowls filled with water, soak separately both kinds of mushrooms and lily buds until soft and pliable (20 to 30 minutes). Squeeze excess water from each. Cut off and discard black mushroom stems; cut caps into ¼-inch-wide strips. Snip off and discard hard ends of lily buds; tie each bud into a knot.

2. In a large bowl combine chicken, ginger, green onion, soaked mushrooms, and lily bud knots. Arrange chicken mixture on a wide, shallow heat-resistant plate that will fit comfortably in a bamboo steaming basket or on a steaming tray.

3. In a medium bowl blend together soy sauce, vermouth, sugar, salt, cornstarch, and sesame oil. Spread soy sauce mixture over chicken. Scatter sausage on top.

4. Steam chicken following the Step-by-Step on page 86. Take basket directly from wok to dinner table. Carefully remove cover of basket, stir chicken mixture, and serve hot with rice.

Serves 4 to 6 with other dishes.

<u>Note</u>   For a dinner party, divide and arrange chicken mixture equally among 4 individual plates. Steam as directed in the Step-by-Step on page 86; however, you may need to use 2 to 4 stacked steaming baskets to accommodate 4 plates (top 2 baskets will require 5 minutes extra steaming). For a steaming tray you may set 2 plates side by side on tray, lay 2 chopsticks across plates, and set next 2 plates on top of chopsticks. Cover and steam as directed.

As Steamed Chicken With Straw Mushrooms and Chinese Sausage cooks, a juice accumulates in the steaming plate that is a delicious blend of the flavors of earthy mushrooms, subtly sweet Chinese sausage, and grassy lily buds. To serve, spoon the meat, vegetables, and the delicious juice over hot rice.

STEAMING IN A WOK

Steaming is a popular Asian home cooking technique. The steamer, usually a wok, works as a "wet" oven, and has the same functions as a Western "dry" oven. To preserve the well-seasoned surface of a stir-frying wok, have a special wok just for steaming. If you have an electric wok, use it for steaming as illustrated here with Steamed Chicken With Straw Mushrooms and Chinese Sausage (see page 85). For general guidelines on steaming equipment and tips on steaming other foods, see pages 81 and 82.

The recipes in this book were designed to be steamed in a 14-inch wok, which is roomy enough to accommodate small poultry. For larger foods use a deep-sided roasting pan, inverting another roasting pan to serve as a cover or creating a tent with aluminum foil. This setup holds more water than a wok, which is important for long steaming. To support the steaming plates, use one or two tuna fish cans with the ends removed.

1. Prepare chicken for steaming as directed in recipe on page 85. Arrange chicken mixture on a wide, shallow, heat-resistant plate that will fit comfortably in a bamboo steaming basket. Spread soy sauce mixture over chicken and scatter sausage on top as directed in step 3 of recipe.

2. Set plate with chicken into steaming basket; cover.

3. Pour boiling water into wok. Set covered steaming basket in wok, being careful that water is at least 1 inch from the basket. Steam over medium-high heat 20 minutes.

4. Remove covered steaming basket from wok and transfer to dining table. Take off cover carefully to prevent steam burns. Serve chicken directly from basket.

TEA-SMOKED DUCK

Traditionally, the Chinese cook duck and other poultry whole with head and feet attached, although you may prefer to remove them, as specified in this recipe. The Chinese smoke poultry to add flavor. In this dish the duck is marinated, steamed to cook it and render its fat, and then smoked over black tea leaves, Szechuan peppercorns, and other aromatic ingredients. For a crispier skin, the smoked duck can be roasted in a 425° F oven for 5 to 10 minutes. For convenience, chop the duck in half lengthwise through its back before marinating. You may substitute chicken or Cornish hens for the duck in this recipe.

> 1 whole duck, rinsed
>   and patted dry
> 2 tablespoons Szechuan
>   peppercorns
> 2 tablespoons kosher salt
> 2 tablespoons sugar
> 2 green onions, bruised and
>   cut into 2-inch lengths
> 4 slices fresh ginger, shredded
> 4 tablespoons dry vermouth
>   or rice wine
>   Watercress, for garnish
>   Mandarin Pancakes (see page
>   115), for accompaniment
>   Hoisin Sauce Dip (see page
>   24), for dipping

Tea-Smoking Mixture

> 2 cinnamon sticks (3 in. each)
> 4 star anise
> ¼ cup Szechuan peppercorns
> ½ cup uncooked white
>   long-grain rice
> ½ cup dried black tea leaves
> ½ cup firmly packed dark
>   brown sugar

1. Remove and discard head, neck, and feet of duck. Chop body in half lengthwise through back if desired. Lay duck breast side up on countertop. With the palm of your hand, press down on breast to snap bone so breast lies flat. Prick skin all over with a fork. Set duck aside.

2. In an ungreased wok over medium heat, toast peppercorns and salt until fragrant (about 5 minutes), shaking and stirring occasionally. Transfer to a spice grinder, mortar, or food processor; grind to a powder. Transfer powder to a large bowl and add sugar, green onion, ginger, and vermouth. Add reserved duck and rub it inside and out with mixture. Cover bowl and let duck marinate at least 4 hours at room temperature, or overnight in the refrigerator.

3. Select a nonmetallic, heat-resistant pie or quiche plate that will fit comfortably in a steamer. Drain duck and arrange breast side up on plate. If duck was refrigerated, allow it to come to room temperature before steaming.

4. Prepare wok for steaming (see page 86). Set plate with duck on steaming rack. Cover and steam over medium-high heat until done (about 1 hour), occasionally checking water level and adding boiling water if needed. Allow duck to cool; then remove it to a cooling rack and reserve juices on plate for another use. Carefully scrape off and discard peppercorns, green onion, and ginger. Blot duck dry; then allow to dry completely in a cool, airy place at least 2 hours, or overnight, uncovered, in the refrigerator. Pour water from wok and wipe dry.

5. Line a wok with heavy-duty aluminum foil. Arrange Tea-Smoking Mixture on foil. Set a 10- to 12-inch round cake rack in wok. Place duck on rack over smoking mixture; set over medium-high heat. When mixture begins to burn, cover wok with a dome-shaped lid or enclose with aluminum foil. Smoke until duck takes on a rich, deep color (15 to 20 minutes). Remove wok from heat and allow to sit with lid on at least 5 minutes. Uncover and transfer duck to a chopping board. Discard foil containing smoking material.

6. Remove bones from the meat (leave skin on) and cut meat into ¼-inch-thick slices. Or chop duck, including skin, meat, and bones, crosswise into ½-inch-wide pieces.

Arrange on a platter lined with fresh watercress. Serve with Mandarin Pancakes and Hoisin Sauce Dip.

Serves 4 to 6 with other dishes.

Tea-Smoking Mixture Break cinnamon sticks and star anise into pieces in a small bowl. Add peppercorns, rice, tea leaves, and brown sugar and mix well.

Makes 2 cups.

CLASSIC CASHEW CHICKEN

Cashew chicken remains a popular Cantonese classic for Westerners as well as for the Chinese. Unfortunately, many restaurants serve it with lumpy cornstarch sauce and cut costs by using excessive amounts of fillers such as celery and onion. This recipe creates a perfect stir-fried entrée—one that reflects a variety of tastes, textures, and colors without the lumpy sauce.

1 *cup raw jumbo cashews*
1 *large whole chicken breast, skinned, boned, and cut into ¾-inch cubes*
1 *teaspoon sugar*
2 *tablespoons light soy sauce*
1 *tablespoon dry vermouth*
1 *teaspoon cornstarch*
2 *teaspoons Asian sesame oil*
3 *tablespoons peanut or corn oil*
1 *teaspoon salt*
2 *slices fresh ginger, bruised*
2 *cloves garlic, bruised*
4 *green onions, bruised and cut into 2-inch lengths*
1 *can (15 oz) whole straw mushrooms, rinsed and drained*
¼ *pound Chinese water chestnuts, preferably fresh, peeled, rinsed, and sliced*
¼ *pound snow peas, stems and strings removed*
  Pinch white pepper
¼ *cup chicken stock*
1 *teaspoon oyster sauce*
  Cooked white long-grain rice, for accompaniment

1. Preheat oven to 325° F. In a flat pan roast cashews until golden brown (about 10 minutes), stirring once or twice. Set aside.

2. In a medium bowl combine chicken, ½ teaspoon of the sugar, 1 tablespoon of the soy sauce, vermouth, cornstarch, and 1 teaspoon of the sesame oil; set aside at least 15 minutes but no longer than 1 hour.

3. Preheat wok over medium-high heat until hot, then pour in 2 tablespoons of the peanut oil, ½ teaspoon of the salt, ginger, and garlic; cook until oil is fragrant (about 30 seconds). Add marinated chicken in handfuls, seconds apart, and cook until it feels firm to the touch (about 2 minutes), tossing continuously. Add green onion and toss together 10 seconds. Remove chicken and set aside; leave ginger and garlic in wok.

4. Increase heat to high. Pour in remaining 1 tablespoon peanut oil and then add remaining ½ teaspoon salt. When oil is hot add in batches, seconds apart, mushrooms, water chestnuts, and snow peas; stir-fry until snow peas turn bright green (about 30 seconds). Sprinkle in remaining ½ teaspoon sugar, white pepper, and remaining 1 tablespoon soy sauce; toss. Add stock and oyster sauce; toss and cook until sauce mixture is reduced to a glaze (about 30 seconds). Add reserved chicken mixture, reserved cashews, and remaining 1 teaspoon sesame oil; gently stir together. Pick out garlic and ginger and discard. Serve hot over rice.

Serves 6 with other dishes.

FRIED CHICKEN AND CREAM GRAVY

Frying chicken in a wok is easy and minimizes the mess. The efficient design of a wok allows a greater frying surface than that of a skillet, diminishes the likelihood of over-crowding, and reduces the amount of oil needed for deep-frying. In this mouth-watering recipe, soaking the chicken in buttermilk produces plump, moist flesh and imparts a slightly sour flavor that contrasts nicely with the rich crust. Serve the chicken with mashed potatoes and baking powder biscuits.

> 1 frying chicken, cut into serving pieces, rinsed, and blotted dry
> 2 cups buttermilk, or more if needed
> Peanut oil, for deep-frying
> ¾ cup flour
> 2 teaspoons salt
> 1 teaspoon freshly ground pepper
> 1 teaspoon paprika

Cream Gravy

> 2 tablespoons flour
> ¾ cup chicken stock
> ¾ cup light cream
> Salt and freshly ground pepper, to taste

1. In a shallow dish arrange chicken pieces snugly in 1 layer. Cover with buttermilk; cover dish and soak chicken at least 1 hour, or overnight in the refrigerator.

2. Preheat wok over medium-high heat until hot. Pour in oil to a depth of 2 inches; heat to 360° F.

3. In a medium bowl combine flour, salt, pepper, and paprika. Remove chicken from buttermilk and roll in seasoned flour. Arrange dark chicken pieces in wok, followed 5 minutes later by white-meat pieces, and deep-fry until nicely browned (about 20 minutes), turning chicken with tongs and being careful not to crowd. Remove chicken, drain, and keep warm while preparing Cream Gravy.

Serves 4.

Cream Gravy With a ladle remove all but 2 tablespoons oil from wok, leaving behind small, crisp bits of crust. Place wok over low heat; stir in flour and blend, cooking until mixture is lightly browned (about 4 minutes). Gradually stir in stock and cream. Increase heat to medium and continue stirring until gravy thickens (about 5 minutes). Season with salt and pepper.

Makes 1½ cups.

PASTA WITH TEA-SMOKED DUCK, GRILLED MUSHROOMS, AND ARUGULA

This cross-cultural dish utilizes Japanese, Chinese, and Italian flavoring and cooking techniques, including grilling, tea-smoking, and pasta preparation. If you should be so lucky as to have leftover slivers of Tea-Smoked Duck (see page 86), this recipe makes use of them. Chinese dried black mushrooms are braised in soy sauce, sugar, and rice wine and then "grilled" in a dry wok. Tea-Smoked Duck combined with grilled mushrooms need be enhanced only with the fruity flavor of extravirgin olive oil.

> 6 ounces dry fettuccine or angel hair pasta
> 3 tablespoons extravirgin olive oil
> 2 cloves garlic, chopped
> 1 tablespoon chopped shallot
> ½ teaspoon salt
> Freshly ground pepper, to taste
> 3 tablespoons raspberry vinegar or other light, sweet vinegar
> ¼ pound arugula, dandelion, or other bitter greens
> ¼ cup toasted pine nuts
> ½ Tea-Smoked Duck breast (see page 86), cut into long, thin slivers

Grilled Sweet Soy Mushrooms

> 8 medium Chinese dried black mushrooms (about 2 in. across)
> 1 cup hot water
> 1 cup chicken stock
> 2 tablespoons dark soy sauce
> 1 tablespoons sugar
> 1 tablespoon rice wine or dry vermouth

1. Prepare Grilled Sweet Soy Mushrooms 1 hour ahead.

2. In a large pot of boiling salted water, cook pasta until al dente (8 to 10 minutes). Drain thoroughly.

3. Meanwhile, preheat wok over medium heat until hot, then pour in olive oil. When hot add garlic and shallot and gently sauté until soft but not browned (about 30 seconds). Add salt, pepper, and vinegar; toss. Add drained pasta, arugula, and Grilled Sweet Soy Mushrooms; toss. Transfer to individual plates; top with toasted pine nuts and smoked duck slivers.

Serves 4 as a first course.

Grilled Sweet Soy Mushrooms

1. In a medium bowl soak mushrooms in the hot water until soft and pliable (about 30 minutes). Remove mushrooms and reserve liquid. Cut and discard stems from base of mushrooms; reserve caps. Strain ½ cup of the mushroom soaking liquid into a small saucepan. Add stock, soy sauce, sugar, and rice wine. Over medium-high heat bring to a boil. Add mushroom caps and simmer 15 minutes. Allow to cool. Remove mushrooms; with your hands squeeze out excess liquid, then flatten with a rolling pin.

2. Preheat an ungreased wok over medium heat. When hot place mushrooms flat on bottom of wok. Grill 1 minute. With a spatula press down to squeeze out mushroom juices, turn over, grill about 1 minute, and press again so that mushrooms are rather dry. Remove and cut into ¼-inch-wide julienne strips.

Makes 8 mushrooms, serves 4.

East meets West in an unexpected combination of cooking techniques in Pasta With Tea-Smoked Duck, Grilled Mushrooms, and Arugula.

1. Preheat wok over medium-high heat until hot, then pour in oil. Add garlic and cook until lightly browned (about 45 seconds). Add chicken in batches and stir-fry until it feels firm to the touch (about 1 minute). Add chiles, green onion, sugar, fish sauce, oyster sauce, and stock; stir-fry until sauce thickens (about 45 seconds).

2. Add basil and cook just until leaves are wilted (about 10 seconds). Serve hot over rice.

Serves 4 to 6 with other dishes.

BASIC CHINESE STEAMED CHICKEN

Chicken steams best whole, but parts may be used. Leftover steamed chicken works well in cold salads and noodle entrées or stir-fried with vegetables.

> 1 chicken, whole or cut up
> 2 tablespoons rice wine
>   or dry vermouth
> 1 teaspoon salt
> 3 slices peeled fresh ginger
> 2 green onions, halved
>   lengthwise
> ½ cup chicken stock or water
>   Fresh coriander, for garnish
>   Oil-Seared Ginger Sauce
>   (see page 24)

1. Rub chicken inside and out with rice wine and salt. Insert ginger and green onion in cavity. Place chicken breast side up in a heat-resistant bowl that fits comfortably on a steaming tray in wok when cover is on. Pour stock over chicken.

2. Prepare wok for steaming (see page 86). Cover steamer and steam chicken over medium-high heat 40 minutes. Allow chicken to cool; then remove it to a cutting board. Carve whole chicken into thin slices; if cut-up chicken is used, with a cleaver chop chicken, including skin, meat, and bones, into 1¼-inch by 2-inch pieces. Garnish with coriander and serve with Oil-Seared Ginger Sauce.

Serves 4 to 6 with other dishes.

Adjust the hotness of this typical Thai stir-fried chicken dish by varying the number of chiles. You can use anise-flavored basil or mint if you can't find the purple-stemmed Thai basil. Better substitutes than dried basil, they are both easily grown in the garden or on a windowsill.

THAI STIR-FRIED CHICKEN WITH BASIL

Fresh Thai basil, or *bai horabha* (*Ocimum basilicum*), is similar to but has a more pronounced anise flavor than its American and European counterparts. In Thai cooking it is used not only as a seasoning herb but also sautéed as a leafy vegetable.

> 2 tablespoons peanut or corn oil
> 5 cloves garlic, chopped
> 1 pound chicken meat,
>   preferably dark meat,
>   cut into 1-inch
>   by ½-inch pieces
> 6 small fresh chiles serranos,
>   cut in half lengthwise
> 3 green onions, cut into
>   2-inch lengths
> 1 teaspoon sugar
> 1 tablespoon Thai fish sauce,
>   or to taste
> 2 teaspoons oyster sauce,
>   or to taste
> 2 tablespoons chicken stock
> 1 cup fresh basil leaves
>   Cooked white long-grain rice,
>   for accompaniment

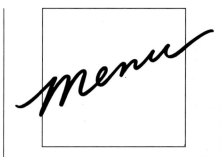

LIGHT SUNDAY BUFFET

Hunan Eggplant Salad
(see page 66)

Seafood With Corn, Okra,
and Tomatoes

Curry Crab-Noodle Cakes

Tandoori Chicken With Pappadams

Mexican Sopaipillas With Ice Cream

Beer and Tropical Fruit Juice

This international menu, which combines foods from the Far East, the Middle East, Europe, and the New World, reflects much creativity and flair. The menu includes dishes that can be made in advance and served at room temperature, kept hot on a warming tray, or briefly reheated. If you prepare the sopaipillas—Mexican fried bread—in advance, reheat them briefly in a 300°F oven.

SEAFOOD WITH CORN, OKRA, AND TOMATOES

Stir-frying in a wok can stretch your food dollars by using only minimal amounts of meat, fish, and poultry. In this recipe 1 pound of seafood serves 6 people.

- ½ pound salmon fillets, skin removed
- 4 tablespoons olive oil
  Salt and freshly ground pepper, to taste
- ½ pound large prawns, shelled and deveined
- 2 tablespoons unsalted butter
- 2 shallots, finely chopped
- ½ pound okra, tips and stems trimmed, cut into ¼-inch-thick slices
- 2 cups fresh corn (about 4 large ears corn, husked and scraped)
- 1 red bell pepper, seeded and diced
- 4 small tomatoes, peeled and diced
- 1 teaspoon sugar
  Hot-pepper sauce, to taste
  Corn bread, for accompaniment

1. Rinse fillets and blot dry. Cut into ½-inch by 2-inch strips.

2. Preheat wok over medium-high heat until hot, then pour in 2 tablespoons of the oil. When hot add salmon strips and cook until salmon is browned and feels firm to the touch (about 3 minutes), turning occasionally. Season with salt and ground pepper and remove to a medium bowl.

3. Add 1 more tablespoon of the oil to wok. When hot add prawns and stir-fry until they turn pink and feel firm to the touch (about 1 minute). Season with salt and ground pepper and add to reserved salmon.

4. Reduce heat to medium and add remaining 1 tablespoon oil and butter. When oil mixture is moderately hot, add shallot and okra; sauté 5 minutes, stirring occasionally. Add corn, bell pepper, tomato, sugar, and hot-pepper sauce; simmer until vegetables are tender (10 minutes). Add salmon mixture, season with salt and ground pepper, and toss together gently. Serve hot with corn bread.

Serves 8 with other dishes.

CURRY CRAB-NOODLE CAKES

These crab cakes should be crisp and delightfully crunchy on the outside and smooth and moist on the inside.

- 2 cups cooked fresh crabmeat (about ½ lb), picked clean of shells and cartilage
- ¼ pound cooked Chinese thin egg noodles (see page 36), well drained and cut into 1-inch lengths
- 1 large shallot, finely chopped
- 3 tablespoons julienned roasted red bell pepper
- 1 teaspoon salt
- ½ teaspoon freshly ground pepper
- 2 teaspoons curry powder
- 1 large egg, beaten
- 4 tablespoons chopped fresh coriander
- 6 to 8 tablespoons ghee or clarified unsalted butter, or as needed

1. In a large bowl combine crabmeat and noodles. Add shallot, bell pepper, salt, ground pepper, curry powder, egg, and coriander; blend well. Shape mixture into round cakes about 3 inches across by ½ inch thick; set aside 30 minutes on a waxed paper-lined pan.

2. Preheat a flat-bottomed wok over medium heat until hot. Pour in ghee to a depth of ¼ inch. When hot add cakes in batches and fry until brown and crusty (about 5 minutes total). Serve hot.

Makes 8 to 10 cakes.

TANDOORI CHICKEN WITH PAPPADAMS

Orchestrating a meal of more than two stir-fried entrées can be difficult. Tandoori chicken, an Indian dish traditionally cooked in a clay pit oven but also delicious cooked on a charcoal grill or in a very hot conventional oven, is perfect in a buffet of stir-fried dishes. It can be marinated days in advance, and while it is roasting, your wok is free for other uses. The crisp lentil *pappadam* wafers, available in specialty food stores, can be fried ahead in the wok and served at room temperature with the chicken.

> 2 very small broilers, skinned and quartered
> 4 tablespoons freshly squeezed lemon juice
> 1 teaspoon cumin seed
> 2 teaspoons coriander seed
> 1 piece (1 in.) peeled fresh ginger
> 4 cloves garlic
> 2 teaspoons salt
> ½ teaspoon cayenne pepper
> ½ teaspoon freshly ground black pepper
> 1 tablespoon paprika
> ½ teaspoon ground turmeric
> 1 teaspoon annatto, for coloring (optional)
> 2 tablespoons coarsely chopped fresh coriander
> 2 tablespoons coarsely chopped fresh mint
> 3 tablespoons unflavored yogurt
> 4 tablespoons ghee or clarified unsalted butter
> 2 lemons, cut into 4 wedges each, for accompaniment
> Indian Raita (see page 25)

Pappadams

> Peanut or corn oil, for deep-frying
> 16 pappadam wafers

1. Remove skin from chicken. Make deep diagonal slashes almost to the bone 1 to 2 inches apart across breast, thigh, and leg. Place in a large glass or stainless steel bowl and rub surface and slashes with lemon juice. Cover and marinate 1 hour at room temperature.

2. In an ungreased wok over low heat, toast cumin and coriander seed until aromatic (about 2 minutes). Transfer to a mortar or spice mill and grind to a powder; set aside.

3. In a food processor fitted with a steel blade, finely mince ginger. With processor running drop garlic and salt through feed tube and process to a fine mince. Add cayenne, black pepper, paprika, turmeric, annatto (if used), and cumin-coriander powder; process to a fine powder. Add fresh coriander, mint, and yogurt; process to a smooth paste.

4. Thoroughly coat marinated chicken with yogurt mixture. Cover and let stand at least 4 hours at room temperature, or refrigerate overnight, turning pieces occasionally. Allow chicken to come to room temperature before roasting.

5. Preheat oven to 500° F. Set a large wire rack over a slightly smaller roasting pan so chicken will be elevated above top edge of roasting pan. In a small saucepan melt ghee. Brush chicken pieces with melted ghee and place chicken on wire rack. Roast 15 minutes; turn chicken over, brush with ghee, and roast until done (about 10 minutes more). Serve chicken hot with lemon wedges, Pappadams, and raita.

Serves 8.

Pappadams   Preheat wok over medium-high heat until hot. Pour in oil to a depth of 1 inch and heat to 375° F. Add 1 wafer to oil; wafer will sizzle and begin to expand and curl around edges. With a spatula, press on top of wafer and push under oil 5 seconds. Remove wafer as soon as it turns crisp and slightly golden on both sides (5 to 10 seconds total); drain on paper towel. Repeat with remaining wafers.

Makes 16 wafers, serves 8.

MEXICAN SOPAIPILLAS WITH ICE CREAM

Mexican-cooking teacher Marge Poore fries these *sopaipillas* in a wok and serves them dripping with warm honey butter and with ice cream on the side.

> 2 cups unsifted flour
> 2 teaspoons baking powder
> ½ teaspoon salt
> 2 tablespoons vegetable shortening, cut into bits
> ¾ cup lukewarm water
> 2 cups peanut or corn oil, for deep-frying
> Ice cream, for accompaniment

Honey Butter

> 3 tablespoons unsalted butter
> 6 tablespoons honey

1. *To prepare in a food processor:* In the work bowl of a food processor fitted with a steel blade, place flour, baking powder, and salt; pulse once or twice to mix. Add shortening; pulse to consistency of cornmeal (about 10 seconds). With machine running pour the water through feed tube; process into a ball (about 10 seconds). *To prepare by hand:* In a large bowl combine flour, baking powder, and salt. Add shortening and blend to consistency of cornmeal. Add the water and mix dough to a rough ball.

2. Turn dough onto a lightly floured board; knead until dough is soft but no longer sticky (about 8 minutes). Place dough in a medium bowl, cover, and let stand 15 to 20 minutes.

3. Preheat wok over medium-high heat until hot, then pour in oil and heat to 375° F. Meanwhile, roll dough to a thickness of ⅛ inch. Cut into triangles 3 inches on each side. Add triangles to hot oil in batches and fry until puffed and golden (about 10 seconds per side). Remove and drain. Drip with Honey Butter and serve with ice cream on the side.

Makes about 24 triangles.

Honey Butter   In a small saucepan combine butter and honey; heat until they are warm.

Makes about ½ cup.

Counterclockwise from left, crab-noodle cakes, tandoori chicken, pappadams, sopaipillas with ice cream, and guava juice make a perfect light buffet.

Do as the Chinese do—purchase pork spareribs and barbecued pork from a local Chinese delicatessen or restaurant for part of a lunch or dinner menu.

Meat Entrées

The minimal use of meat is a distinctive and widely respected feature of Asian cooking. In stir-frying, meat is an accent for a medley of vegetables. As a main course meat is traditionally reserved as a special entrée for company. In this chapter are spectacular dishes, such as Sizzling Mongolian Lamb (see page 106), that will impress your special dinner guests, as well as simple, homespun fare such as Steamed Chinese Country Pâté (see page 96).

PORK

Pork is the main meat of China and most of Southeast Asia, except among Muslims, for whom pork is restricted for religious reasons.

TAIWAN FRIED PORK CHOP NOODLES

How do you eat a Chinese-style pork chop? With chopsticks. Lift the chop to your mouth, take a bite, and put the chop back on top of the soup noodles. The porcelain soup spoon in your other hand helps balance the pork chop. The crisp, seasoned chops teamed with soft boiled noodles in broth make a hearty lunch.

  6 center-cut bone-in pork chops
     (no more than ⅜ in. thick)
  1 pound Chinese egg noodles
     (see page 36), cooked, rinsed,
     and drained
  3 green onions, chopped
  2 cups peanut oil
  1 egg yolk, beaten
  3 tablespoons cornstarch
  ⅓ cup Szechuan preserved
     mustard greens
  1 tablespoon chopped garlic
  2 teaspoons sugar
  4 cups chicken stock
  1 teaspoon Asian sesame oil
     Chopped fresh coriander,
     for garnish

Pork Chop Marinade

  1   teaspoon minced fresh ginger
  1½ tablespoons soy sauce
  2   teaspoons dry vermouth
  2   teaspoons red wine vinegar
  ¼   teaspoon freshly ground
      pepper
  1   teaspoon sugar
  1   teaspoon Asian hot chile oil

1. With blunt edge of cleaver, lightly pound pork chops to tenderize. Add pounded chops to Pork Chop Marinade. Allow to marinate 1 hour.

2. Divide noodles among 6 large soup bowls and scatter each with green onion; set aside.

3. Meanwhile, preheat wok over medium-high heat until hot. Then pour in peanut oil and heat to 375° F. While oil is heating, drain

chops, reserving marinade. Add egg to chops and mix well. Dip chops into cornstarch and thoroughly coat both sides. Add pork chops to hot oil and fry until deep golden brown and crusty (5 to 7 minutes total), turning once. Drain chops on paper towels and place 1 chop on each bowl of noodles (see Note). Remove all but a thin film of oil from wok.

4. Reheat wok over medium heat until moderately hot. Sauté mustard greens and garlic. Add sugar, stock, sesame oil, and reserved marinade; simmer 5 minutes. Ladle soup over chops. Garnish with coriander.

Serves 6 with other dishes.

Pork Chop Marinade   In a large bowl combine all ingredients.

Makes about 4 tablespoons.

<u>Note</u>   Chops can also be cut into strips and arranged on noodles.

STEAMED PORK SPARERIBS WITH TOASTED RICE CRUMBS

This assertive yet delicately seasoned dish calls for a toasted rice crumb coating, a Szechuan specialty, over marinated spareribs. Have your butcher chop the rib bones into 1-inch-long strips. You may also use sliced pork or beef.

  1½ pounds pork spareribs,
      chopped into 1-inch-long strips
  1   teaspoon minced fresh ginger
  1   teaspoon minced garlic
  ¼   teaspoon salt
  1   teaspoon sugar
  2   tablespoons soy sauce
  1   tablespoon rice wine or
      dry vermouth
  2   teaspoons hot bean sauce
  ½   teaspoon five-spice powder
  1   teaspoon Asian sesame oil
  3   tablespoons glutinous rice
      Cooked white long-grain rice,
      for accompaniment

1. Cut between ribs to form 1-inch squares. Place in a large bowl and add ginger, garlic, salt, sugar, soy sauce, wine, bean sauce, five-spice powder, and sesame oil. Mix well; set aside.

2. In an ungreased wok over low heat, toast glutinous rice until lightly browned (6 to 8 minutes), stirring occasionally. Remove from heat and let cool. Transfer glutinous rice to a mortar or food processor and grind to consistency of cornmeal. Pour rice crumbs over reserved marinated ribs and toss lightly to coat.

3. Prepare wok for steaming (see page 86). Arrange no more than 2 layers of coated ribs on a shallow heat-resistant plate. Cover and steam over medium-high heat 45 minutes. Serve hot with cooked rice.

Serves 6 with other dishes.

STEAMED CHINESE COUNTRY PÂTÉ

When the Chinese think of home cooking, images come to mind of steamed juice-filled meat patties, such as this slightly coarse pâté, topped with seasonings such as preserved cabbage and preserved mustard greens (see variations).

  4   medium Chinese dried black
      mushrooms
  ¾   pound coarsely minced pork
      butt, including some fat
  1   green onion, white part only,
      minced, plus green section,
      chopped, for garnish
  1   teaspoon salt
  ½   teaspoon sugar
  1   tablespoon soy sauce
  1   tablespoon rice wine or
      dry vermouth
  1   teaspoon cornstarch
  3   tablespoons chicken stock
  1   teaspoon Asian sesame oil
  8   Chinese water chestnuts,
      preferably fresh, peeled
      and chopped
      Cooked white long-grain rice,
      for accompaniment

1. In a small bowl soak mushrooms in enough warm water to cover until soft and pliable (about 30 minutes). Cut off and discard tough stems at base of caps; coarsely chop caps and set aside.

2. In a medium bowl combine pork, minced green onion, salt, sugar, soy sauce, rice wine, and cornstarch; mix well. Add stock and sesame oil to

pork mixture and blend well. Mix in reserved mushrooms and water chestnuts. Transfer to an 8-inch quiche-type heat-resistant dish. Lightly pat mixture to a patty not more than ½ inch thick. Top with chopped green onion.

3. Prepare wok for steaming (see page 86). Place the dish with meat in steamer, cover, and steam over medium-high heat 20 minutes. Remove dish from steamer and bring directly to table. With a fork break up patty. Onto each of 6 individual servings of rice, spoon a small portion of pâté with juices from steaming dish and serve.

Serve 6 with other dishes.

Country Pâté and Sausage For a subtle sweet flavor, cut 1 Chinese sausage into ¼-inch pieces and add to pork mixture with mushrooms in step 2.

Country Pâté and Preserved Mustard Greens Substitute Szechuan preserved mustard greens for mushrooms and water chestnuts. Rinse ½ cup greens with warm water and coarsely chop. Scatter on top of pâté with green onion in step 2.

Country Pâté and Preserved Cabbage Substitute preserved Tientsin cabbage for mushrooms and water chestnuts. Rinse cabbage with warm water, drain well, and mix with pork or scatter on top of pâté with green onion in step 2.

For a colorful presentation, arrange steamed marinated pork spareribs on half a squash. The ribs can also be steamed on ½-inch slices of squash instead of on a plate.

The Lemon-Gin Sauce used in this pork dish is a complementary balance of sweetness and tartness— it isn't cloyingly sweet like typical sweet-and-sour sauce. A bit of salt brings out the best of both tastes.

CHINESE SAUSAGE

Chinese sausage is made of chopped fresh pork, honey, and a strong liquor. It has a sweet, delicate taste and a slightly coarse, hard texture like that of dry salami. Three types of sausage are available: pork, with small bits of fat; lean pork, without the fat; and duck liver–pork, in which small bits of cured duck liver are mixed with the pork. These delicacies come in links and need to be steamed before serving. In a Chinese meal they are served as a main course or stir-fried with vegetables, or they are used as a seasoning ingredient in casseroles. They also work well as an appetizer for a Western-style cocktail party.

4 Chinese pork sausage links

1. Remove string from sausages; rinse links with cold water and place on a shallow heat-resistant plate.

2. Prepare wok for steaming (see page 86). Set plate with sausages in steamer, cover, and steam over medium-high heat until fat in sausage looks translucent (about 15 minutes). Let cool, cut sausage diagonally into thin slices, and arrange on a serving plate. Serve at room temperature.

Serves 8 with other dishes.

Variation Sausages may also be steamed in a rice pot. Place sausages on a plate small enough to fit in pot. Or to flavor rice with sausage, cook rice; when all the water has boiled off and pits form on surface of rice, place sausages directly on top of rice. In either case, cover pot, reduce heat to low, and simmer 20 minutes.

LEMON PORK WITH GIN AND BLACK SESAME SEED

This recipe is also delicious with chicken or shrimp. If water chestnut flour is available, use it to coat the pork; it makes an exceptionally crisp, light crust.

> 1 pound pork tenderloin
> 1 teaspoon salt
> 1 teaspoon grated fresh ginger
> 1 tablespoon soy sauce
> 1 tablespoon gin
> 1 large egg, beaten until frothy
> 1 tablespoon water chestnut flour or all-purpose flour
> 1 tablespoon cornstarch
> 1 tablespoon sesame seed, preferably black
> 2 cups peanut or corn oil
> Zest of 1 lemon, julienned, for garnish

Lemon-Gin Sauce

> ¼ cup fresh lemon juice (about 2 lemons)
> ½ teaspoon salt
> 2 tablespoons sugar
> ¼ cup chicken stock
> 2 tablespoons gin
> 1 teaspoon grated fresh ginger
> Zest of 1 lemon, grated
> 1 teaspoon water chestnut flour or cornstarch, mixed with 1 tablespoon water

1. Cut pork crosswise into ½-inch-thick slices. With flat side of cleaver, pound pork to a thickness of ¼ inch. Place in a medium bowl. Add ½ teaspoon of the salt, ginger, soy sauce, and gin; marinate 30 minutes.

2. Drain pork, reserving marinade. Add beaten egg to pork; toss together. In a small bowl mix together flour, cornstarch, sesame seed, and remaining ½ teaspoon salt. Lightly dust pork with flour mixture; shake off excess.

3. Preheat wok over medium-high heat until hot. Pour in peanut oil and heat to 350° F. Add pork in small batches and deep-fry until golden brown and crisp (about 3 minutes). Remove, drain, and keep warm on a serving platter.

4. Add reserved marinade to Lemon-Gin Sauce. Pour over warm pork. Garnish with lemon zest and serve.

Serves 6 with other dishes.

Lemon-Gin Sauce In a medium saucepan over medium heat, combine all ingredients; bring to a boil, stirring constantly.

Makes about ½ cup.

TWICE-COOKED PORK WITH BRUSSELS SPROUTS

Twice-cooked pork is traditionally made with fresh bacon, which Chinese cooks call five-flower pork because of its alternating layers of fat and meat. When cooked properly, the rendered fatty layers become deliciously soft and succulent. Pork loin or butt can be substituted for fresh bacon, as in this recipe.

> 1½ pounds boneless pork loin or butt (see Note)
> 1 piece (1 in.) fresh ginger, bruised, plus 2 slices fresh ginger
> 3 cloves garlic, bruised
> 1 green onion, bruised
> 2 tablespoons peanut or corn oil
> 1 large leek, split lengthwise, then cut into 2-inch lengths
> ¼ pound Brussels sprouts, each sprout cut into 4 wedges, then blanched until tender (about 5 minutes)
> ½ teaspoon salt
> 1 teaspoon Asian sesame oil
> Cooked white long-grain rice, for accompaniment

Twice-Cooked Seasonings

> ½ teaspoon salt
> 1 tablespoon hot bean sauce
> 1 tablespoon hoisin sauce or sweet bean paste
> 2 teaspoons sugar
> 1 tablespoon dark soy sauce
> 1 tablespoon rice wine or dry vermouth

1. Trim pork of fat, place in wok, and add enough cold water to cover pork by 1 inch. Add piece of ginger, 2 cloves of the garlic, and green onion. Bring to a boil and skim froth that rises to top. Simmer, uncovered, 30 minutes. Drain pork, pat dry, and allow to cool. Cut lengthwise into 2-inch-wide strips, then crosswise into ⅛-inch-thick slices. Set aside.

2. Preheat wok over medium heat until hot, then pour in 1 tablespoon of the peanut oil. When hot add leek and Brussels sprouts. Stir-fry vegetables until leek begins to wilt (about 30 seconds). Remove vegetables and set aside.

3. Into wok pour remaining 1 tablespoon peanut oil and add ginger slices, remaining 1 clove garlic, and salt; cook until oil is fragrant (about 30 seconds). Increase heat to high; when oil is hot add reserved pork and stir-fry until meat becomes firm and browned (about 3 minutes). Push pork up sides of wok and add Twice-Cooked Seasonings to center of wok; stir-fry together until sauce thickens into syrupy glaze. Add reserved leek and Brussels sprouts, swirl in sesame oil, and toss once or twice to mix. Pick out and discard ginger and garlic. Serve hot with rice.

Serves 6 with other dishes.

Twice-Cooked Seasonings In a small bowl combine all ingredients; whisk to blend.

Makes about 5 tablespoons.

<u>Note</u> To use fresh bacon instead of pork, in step 1 cover wok and simmer bacon 1 hour. Let cool; then cut meat crosswise into ⅛-inch-thick slices.

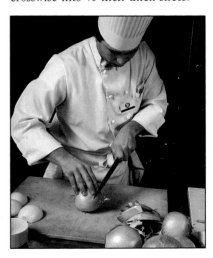

Ants Climbing a Tree, a traditional Szechuan dish, uses bits of pork and translucent bean thread noodles. Make sure you have the right noodles (also known as glass or cellophane noodles), which are made with mung beans. They are easily confused with rice stick noodles, which are made with rice.

ANTS CLIMBING A TREE

In this Szechuan recipe the chopped pork mingled with the bean thread noodles gives the appearance of ants (the pork bits) climbing a tree (the noodles, which resemble branches of a tree).

- 2 tablespoons small dried shrimp
- 4 ounces bean thread noodles
- 6 ounces pork butt, minced
- 1½ tablespoons peanut or corn oil
- 1 teaspoon salt
- 2 teaspoons minced fresh ginger
- 2 green onions, minced, plus 1 green onion, cut into 2-inch slivers
- 2 dried red chiles, coarsely chopped
- 1 teaspoon sugar
- 1 tablespoon hot bean sauce
- 1 tablespoon dry vermouth
- 1½ tablespoons dark soy sauce
- 1¾ cups chicken stock
- 1 teaspoon Asian sesame oil

Pork Marinade

- ¼ teaspoon sugar
- 2 teaspoons soy sauce
- 1 teaspoon dry vermouth or rice wine
- 1 teaspoon cornstarch

1. In a small bowl cover shrimp with warm water and soak 30 minutes. Drain and set aside. In a large bowl cover noodles with warm water and soak until soft and pliable (about 30 minutes); drain and set aside.

2. In a medium bowl toss pork with Pork Marinade, mixing thoroughly; set aside.

3. Preheat wok over medium-high heat until hot. Pour in peanut oil and add salt. When oil is hot add marinated pork and stir-fry until pork turns gray (about 1 minute). Remove and set aside. In hot wok place reserved shrimp, ginger, minced green onion, chiles, sugar, and bean sauce; stir-fry until fragrant (about 30 seconds). Add vermouth, soy sauce, stock, and reserved noodles; bring to a boil, reduce heat to low, and simmer until liquid is absorbed and noodles are plump and transparent (about 5 minutes), stirring occasionally. Add reserved pork mixture, stir to combine, and simmer 1 minute more. Drizzle with sesame oil. Adjust seasoning, garnish with green onion slivers, and serve hot.

Serves 6 with other dishes.

Pork Marinade In a small bowl whisk together all ingredients.

Makes about 1½ tablespoons.

BEEF AND LAMB

The predominant meats of the Mongolians, beef and lamb, worked their way south into the Chinese diet. More lamb and beef recipes are found in northern China, however; the southern Chinese still prefer pork, perhaps as a holdover from when cows were more commonly used as work animals than as a food source.

DRY-FRIED SPICY SHREDDED BEEF

Dry-frying, a stir-fry variation, produces a highly seasoned dry glaze. In this recipe the beef is cooked until slightly chewy, like jerky.

> ¾ *pound beef rump or flank steak, cut into 2-inch-long matchsticks*
> 3 *tablespoons peanut oil*
> 1 *slice fresh ginger, bruised*
> 1 *stalk celery, cut into 2-inch-long matchsticks*
> 1 *carrot, cut into 2-inch-long matchsticks*
> ½ *teaspoon salt*
> 4 *dried red chiles, stems removed*
> 1 *teaspoon minced garlic*
> 1 *tablespoon hot bean sauce*
> 1 *tablespoon sugar*
> 2 *green onions, shredded*
> 1 *teaspoon Asian sesame oil Deep-fried Rice Stick Noodles (see page 38), for accompaniment*

Spicy Beef Marinade

> 1 *teaspoon minced fresh ginger*
> 2 *teaspoons sugar*
> 1 *tablespoon dark soy sauce*
> 1 *tablespoon rice wine or dry sherry*
> 2 *teaspoons cornstarch*
> 1 *teaspoon Asian sesame oil*

1. Add beef to Spicy Beef Marinade; set aside at least 15 minutes.

2. Preheat wok over medium-high heat until hot. Pour in 1 tablespoon of the peanut oil and add ginger; cook until oil is fragrant (about 30 seconds). Add celery and carrot; stir-fry until vegetables are tender (about 45 seconds). Remove vegetables and set aside; discard ginger.

3. Increase heat to high. Pour in remaining 2 tablespoons peanut oil and add salt. When oil is hot add marinated beef in batches, seconds apart, stirring beef strips constantly. Spread strips across bottom of wok and allow to sit until all liquid is reduced (about 8 minutes), tossing and stirring a few times. Beef should appear dry and seared.

4. Push beef up sides of wok and add chiles, garlic, and bean sauce to center of wok. Cook until garlic is browned (about 30 seconds), then toss with beef. Add sugar and toss until sugar glazes beef. Immediately add reserved celery and carrots; mix well. Add green onion and sesame oil. Serve over rice stick noodles.

Serves 6 with other dishes.

Spicy Beef Marinade In a medium bowl whisk together all ingredients.

Makes about 3 tablespoons.

Serve Dry-Fried Spicy Shredded Beef as a first course to stimulate the palate. Its jerkylike texture and twiglike appearance are intriguing and its slightly sweet, peppery flavor is tantalizing.

Lamb chops are wrapped in their long tails and browned in a wok, then coated with Mustard-Rosemary Marinade, which reduces to a light glaze.

BEEF AND BITTER MELON IN BLACK BEAN SAUCE

The distinctive flavor of bitter melon produces a pleasant cooling effect like that of arugula, dandelion, or chicory. In this recipe the bitter flavor is balanced with a little sugar. If bitter melon is not to your liking, you may substitute fresh asparagus, cut diagonally and blanched briefly. Do not salt the asparagus.

  ¾ *pound flank steak*
  ¾ *pound bitter melon*
  1½ *teaspoons salt*
  1 *tablespoon salted black beans, soaked in water 5 minutes and rinsed well*
  1 *teaspoon minced garlic*
  1 *teaspoon minced fresh ginger, plus 1 slice peeled fresh ginger*
  3 *tablespoons peanut or corn oil*
  1 *onion, cut into ¼-inch-wide slices*
  1 *teaspoon sugar*
  2 *teaspoons dark soy sauce*
  ¼ *cup chicken stock or water*
  1 *tablespoon oyster sauce Cooked white long-grain rice, for accompaniment*

Beef Marinade

  1 *tablespoon soy sauce*
  1 *tablespoon dry vermouth or rice wine*
  ½ *teaspoon sugar*
  1 *tablespoon cornstarch*
  1 *teaspoon Asian sesame oil*

1. Cut meat lengthwise into 2-inch-wide strips, then crosswise into ⅛-inch-thick slices. Toss meat slices with Beef Marinade. Let stand 30 minutes.

2. Cut bitter melon in half lengthwise. Scrape out seeds and white pith. Cut crosswise into ¼-inch-thick slices. In a medium bowl combine melon and 1 teaspoon of the salt; let stand 15 minutes. Plunge slices into a medium saucepan full of boiling water; let stand 3 minutes. Drain, rinse with cold water, and gently squeeze out excess water. Set aside.

3. In a small bowl mash together black beans, garlic, and minced ginger; set aside.

4. Preheat wok over high heat until hot, then pour in 2 tablespoons of the oil. Add ginger slice; cook until oil is fragrant (about 30 seconds). Add reserved marinated beef in batches and sear both sides until beef is medium-rare (30 seconds per batch); remove and set aside while cooking remaining beef.

5. Pour remaining 1 tablespoon oil into hot wok and add remaining ½ teaspoon salt. When hot add reserved black bean mixture; sauté until fragrant (about 15 seconds). Add onion and stir-fry until onion glistens (about 30 seconds). Add reserved bitter melon and stir-fry until melon is seared and tender (about 1 minute). Add sugar and soy sauce; stir once or twice. Add stock and oyster sauce; stir and cook until sauce thickens to a glaze. Add reserved beef and mix together. Serve hot over rice.

Serves 6 with other dishes.

Beef Marinade   In a medium bowl combine all ingredients.

Makes about 3½ tablespoons.

ROLLED LAMB CHOPS WITH MUSTARD-ROSEMARY SAUCE

This recipe works best with a flat-bottomed steel wok and no wok collar or stand. The flat bottom of the wok offers a greater browning area and more direct contact with the burner than does a round-bottomed wok on a collar.

  6 *lamb loin chops (1½ in. thick), well trimmed, long tails on*
  1 *tablespoon olive oil, or as needed*
  2 *tablespoons unsalted butter, or as needed Salt and freshly ground pepper, to taste*
  3 *tablespoons minced shallot or green onion*
  ½ *cup dry white wine or dry vermouth*
  ½ *cup whipping cream Chopped chives, for garnish*

Mustard-Rosemary Marinade

  2 *tablespoons olive oil*
  ⅓ *cup Dijon mustard*
  1 *tablespoon fresh lemon juice*
  2 *cloves garlic, pressed*
  1 *teaspoon grated fresh ginger*
  1 *tablespoon fresh rosemary, crushed, or 1½ teaspoons dried rosemary*
  ½ *teaspoon freshly ground pepper*

1. In a large bowl rub Mustard-Rosemary Marinade over chops. Spiral tail around each chop; skewer with a toothpick and trim off excess toothpick. Marinate, covered, at least 2 hours.

2. Preheat ungreased wok over medium-high heat until hot. Reserve marinade clinging to chops. Stand chops with fat edge down in wok. Fry until fat is browned; then roll chops to brown all edges (3 minutes total).

3. Remove chops and spoon off all but a thin layer of fat from wok. Add oil and 1 tablespoon of the butter. When hot return chops to wok and sear until medium-rare (3 to 4 minutes total), turning once and adding more butter and oil if needed. Season with salt and pepper. Remove chops and keep warm. Pour off all fat from wok, leaving browned bits.

4. Reduce heat to medium and add remaining 1 tablespoon butter to wok. Add shallot and sauté until soft (about 1 minute). Add reserved marinade and wine; increase heat to medium-high and bring mixture to a boil while scraping loose the browned bits of food. Reduce to a light glaze (about 2 minutes). Add cream and stir, boiling slowly until thickened (2 minutes more).

5. Remove toothpicks from chops. Spoon sauce over chops, garnish with chives, and serve immediately.

Serves 6 with other dishes.

Mustard-Rosemary Marinade
In a small bowl whisk together all ingredients.

Makes about ½ cup.

BEEF WITH THAI RED CURRY PEANUT SAUCE
Panaeng nuea

A variety of Thai curry pastes (see page 28) can be prepared in advance and frozen in ice cube trays. With two cubes of red curry paste, this dish can be prepared in less than 30 minutes.

> 1 can (14 oz) unsweetened coconut milk (see page 8)
> 3 tablespoons vegetable oil
> 1½ pounds beef rump or sirloin, cut into slices ¼ inch thick by 1 inch wide by 2 inches long
> 10 small fresh red chiles, stems removed, sliced diagonally
> 2 tablespoons Thai Red Curry Paste (see page 28)
> 4 tablespoons roasted ground peanuts or peanut butter
> 2 tablespoons Thai fish sauce
> 1½ tablespoons palm sugar or firmly packed brown sugar
> 7 whole fresh Kaffir lime leaves or fresh citrus leaves
> 1 cup packed fresh basil leaves
> Fresh mint leaves or basil leaves, for garnish
> Cooked white long-grain rice, for accompaniment

1. Without shaking can, pour coconut milk into tall glass container and set aside until coconut cream rises to top (1 to 2 hours). Skim off ½ cup cream, pour into separate container, and set both containers aside.

2. Preheat wok over medium-high heat until hot, then pour in 2 tablespoons of the oil. When hot add beef in batches and stir-fry until browned (about 3 minutes total), removing beef as it is browned. Add chiles to last batch; remove and set aside.

3. Reduce heat to medium, add reserved coconut cream, and cook until oil separates from cream (at least 5 minutes), stirring continuously. Add curry paste and sauté 3 minutes, stirring constantly. Add peanuts and cook until sauce is thick and well blended (about 1 minute). Add fish sauce and sugar; stir and cook until fragrant (about 30 seconds). Add 1¼ cups coconut milk and lime simmer 3 minutes, stirring occasionally. Add basil and cook until leaves wilt.

4. Reduce heat to low. Add reserved beef and chiles and simmer until heated through (about 1 minute). Garnish with mint. Serve with rice.

Serves 6 with other dishes.

LAMB AND LEEKS WITH HOT BEAN SAUCE

Although the strong flavor of lamb is not usually appealing to the southern Chinese, this dish is popular throughout China. The garlic and leeks complement the lamb.

> 1 pound lean leg or shoulder of lamb
> 2 small leeks, including 2 inches of green leaves
> 1 small carrot
> 2 tablespoons dark soy sauce
> 2 teaspoons grated fresh ginger
> 4 teaspoons sugar
> 1 tablespoon rice wine or dry vermouth
> 2 teaspoons cornstarch
> 2 teaspoons Asian sesame oil
> 1 tablespoon red wine vinegar
> 2½ tablespoons peanut or corn oil
> ½ teaspoon salt
> 3 large cloves garlic, thinly sliced
> 2 teaspoons hot bean sauce
> Cooked white long-grain rice, for accompaniment

1. Cut lamb crosswise into slices ⅛ inch thick by 1 inch wide by 2 inches long. Trim leeks, halve lengthwise, and cut into 2-inch-long slivers. Cut carrot into ⅛-inch wide by 2-inch-long julienne; blanch briefly in boiling salted water and drain. Set vegetables aside.

2. In a medium bowl combine lamb slices, 1 tablespoon of the soy sauce, ginger, 1 teaspoon of the sugar, wine, cornstarch, and 1 teaspoon of the sesame oil. Marinate 30 minutes.

3. In a small bowl combine vinegar and the remaining 1 tablespoon soy sauce, 3 teaspoons sugar, and 1 teaspoon sesame oil; set aside.

4. Preheat wok over high heat until very hot, then pour in 2 tablespoons of the peanut oil. When hot add lamb in 3 batches, seconds apart, and stir-fry until meat is seared and no longer pink (about 30 seconds per batch), pushing meat up sides of wok and adding next batch in center. Remove meat and set aside.

5. Reduce heat to medium-high and pour in remaining 1½ teaspoons peanut oil; add salt and garlic. Stir-fry until garlic is lightly browned and fragrant (about 15 seconds). Add reserved leek and carrot; stir-fry 15 seconds. Push vegetables up sides of wok, add bean sauce in center, and sauté until sauce is fragrant (about 15 seconds). Add reserved vinegar mixture; cook and stir until it is reduced to a thick consistency. Add reserved cooked lamb, toss once or twice, and serve hot with rice.

Serves 6 with other dishes.

TOMATO BEEF WITH SHALLOW-FRIED NOODLE CAKES

This popular topping for Chinese noodles is made with ingredients commonly found in American kitchens. It may also be served over rice. Cook the beef in a very hot wok so it will be juicy inside and seared on the outside.

> ¾ pound beef flank steak
> 2 teaspoons dark soy sauce
> ½ teaspoon sugar
> 2 teaspoons dry vermouth or rice wine
> 2 teaspoons cornstarch
> 1 teaspoon Asian sesame oil
> 3 tablespoons peanut oil
> 2 slices peeled fresh ginger, bruised
> 3 green onions, cut diagonally into 2-inch lengths
> 1 clove garlic, bruised
> ½ teaspoon salt
> 1 medium onion, cut into 1-inch cubes
> 1 bell pepper, seeded and cut into 1-inch squares
> 3 small firm tomatoes, quartered, then halved crosswise
> 4 warm Shallow-Fried Noodle Cakes (see page 47)

Sweet-and-Sour Tomato Sauce

1 teaspoon cornstarch
¼ cup chicken stock
1 tablespoon tomato paste
1 tablespoon sugar
1 teaspoon dark soy sauce
3 tablespoons red wine vinegar

1. Cut beef crosswise into strips 2 inches wide and ¼ inch thick. Marinate beef in soy sauce, sugar, vermouth, cornstarch, and sesame oil for 15 minutes.

2. Preheat wok over high heat until hot. Pour in 2 tablespoons of the peanut oil and add 1 slice of the ginger; cook until oil is fragrant. Add green onion and stir-fry 15 seconds. Add beef in batches; sear both sides until medium-rare (30 seconds per batch). Remove and set aside while cooking remaining beef.

3. Into hot wok pour remaining 1 tablespoon peanut oil and add remaining 1 slice ginger, garlic, and salt; cook until oil is fragrant (about 30 seconds). Add onion and pepper; stir-fry until onion is soft and pepper is bright in color (about 30 seconds). Add tomato and toss about 30 seconds (be careful not to crush). Gently push ingredients up sides of wok and add Sweet-and-Sour Tomato Sauce to center of wok. Stir and cook until sauce is thickened. Add reserved beef mixture and toss once or twice. Pour mixture over Shallow-Fried Noodle Cakes and serve.

Serves 4 with other dishes.

Sweet-and-Sour Tomato Sauce
In a small bowl combine cornstarch and stock; mix well. Add tomato paste, sugar, soy sauce, and vinegar and blend thoroughly.

Makes about ½ cup.

The tomato and beef topping on these shallow-fried noodle "pancakes" is a favorite with children. For a more traditional presentation, break the cakes into a loose net of noodles and toss with the topping.

SEARED BEEF WITH CHILE HOISIN SAUCE

Cutting beef at an angle allows it to cook faster and makes even tough cuts tender. And the wider surface allows more sauce to cling to the meat without penetrating it and disguising its natural flavor.

1½ pounds beef tenderloin, top round, or sirloin tip
1 teaspoon Szechuan peppercorns
1 teaspoon minced fresh ginger
½ teaspoon salt
2 teaspoons sugar
1½ tablespoons soy sauce
2 tablespoons hoisin sauce
1 tablespoon Worcestershire sauce
3 tablespoons peanut or corn oil
3 dried red chiles
3 green onions, including some of the green tops, cut into 2-inch lengths, bruised
1 bunch fresh watercress, large stems removed, for garnish
Cooked white long-grain rice, for accompaniment

1. Cut beef diagonally into slices ¼ inch thick by ¾ inch wide by 1¼ inches long; set aside.

2. Preheat ungreased wok over low heat until hot. Dry-roast peppercorns until fragrant (about 5 minutes), then grind roasted peppercorns into powder in an electric minichopper.

3. In a medium bowl combine powdered peppercorns, ginger, salt, sugar, soy sauce, hoisin sauce, and Worcestershire sauce. Remove ¼ cup of marinade and set aside. Toss reserved beef strips with remaining marinade and set aside no longer than 10 minutes.

4. Preheat wok over medium-high heat until hot, then pour in oil. When hot add chiles; cook until they are charred (10 to 15 seconds). Increase heat to high; add beef in batches and fry without stirring until seared (1 minute total), removing beef and keeping warm while frying remaining beef. Add green onion and stir-fry 10 seconds. Pour in reserved ¼ cup marinade and quickly sauté. Add beef and toss together 20 seconds to coat. Arrange over a bed of watercress. Serve hot with rice.

Serves 6 with other dishes.

SIZZLING MONGOLIAN LAMB

The origin of this dish can be traced to the shepherds of Mongolia. Briefly deep-frying the lamb makes it juicy and tender. For a spectacular presentation pour the stir-fried mixture on a sizzling cast-iron platter moments after the meat is finished cooking in the wok. Flank steak may be substituted for lamb in this recipe.

1 pound lean leg or shoulder of lamb
2 cups corn or peanut oil
½ teaspoon salt
1 teaspoon minced fresh ginger
1 teaspoon minced garlic
6 dried red chiles, stems removed
2 bunches green onions, cut into 2-inch lengths
2 tablespoons soy sauce
1 tablespoon dry vermouth
2 teaspoons sugar
1 teaspoon Asian sesame oil
Small handful Deep-fried Rice Stick Noodles (see page 38), for garnish

Mongolian Lamb Marinade

1 tablespoon dry vermouth
1 tablespoon soy sauce
⅛ teaspoon white pepper
2 teaspoons sugar
2 teaspoons cornstarch
1 teaspoon Asian sesame oil

1. Cut lamb lengthwise into 2-inch-wide strips, then crosswise into ¼-inch-thick slices. Toss with Mongolian Lamb Marinade; set aside 20 minutes.

2. Preheat wok over medium-high heat until hot, then pour in corn oil and heat to 375° F. Add lamb in 2 batches and deep-fry about 10 seconds per batch. Drain well and set aside. Remove all but a thin film of oil from wok and place wok over high heat.

3. On a separate burner preheat a cast-iron platter over high heat about 10 minutes. Sprinkle a few drops of water to test heat; water should bubble and dance.

4. Meanwhile, in hot wok place salt, ginger, garlic, chiles, and green onion; sauté until browned (15 seconds). Add soy sauce, vermouth, sugar, and sesame oil. Bring to a boil and cook until mixture is reduced to a creamy consistency; immediately add reserved lamb and toss together 10 seconds.

5. Place a heat-resistant trivet on dining table and position hot cast-iron platter on trivet. Immediately pour lamb and sauce onto hot platter. Garnish with rice stick noodles.

Serves 6 with other dishes.

Mongolian Lamb Marinade   In a medium bowl combine all ingredients; blend well.

Makes about 4 tablespoons.

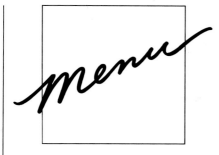

LIGHT THEATER SUPPER
FOR SIX

Pearl Balls With
Pine Nut–Spinach Filling

Aunt Carrie's Chinese
Pickled Vegetables

Szechuan Braised Beef Noodles
With Baby Bok Choy

Fresh Chilled Mango, Singapore Style

Warm Sake

In this menu humble Szechuan braised beef noodles are transformed into a light, comfortable meal before an evening at the theater. Begin the braised beef early in the day so that all you have to do at dinnertime is boil the noodles and ladle the reheated broth over them. The pearl balls can also be prepared ahead and then steamed 20 minutes before dinner is ready. Decant the purchased bottle of sake into the traditional porcelain container and heat it in a hot water bath. Serve the warm sake in small sake cups.

PEARL BALLS WITH PINE NUT–SPINACH FILLING

These rice-studded balls make a good first course as well as an attractive entrée on a buffet table.

- ¾ cup glutinous rice
- ¼ cup white long-grain rice
- 1 pound pork butt, ground
- ¼ pound shrimp, shelled, deveined, and coarsely chopped
- ¼ cup finely minced peeled Chinese water chestnuts, preferably fresh
- 2 green onions, white section only, minced
- 1 teaspoon grated fresh ginger
- ½ teaspoon salt
- ½ teaspoon sugar
- ⅛ teaspoon white pepper
- 1 tablespoon soy sauce, plus more for dipping
- 1 teaspoon Asian sesame oil, plus more for dipping
- 1 tablespoon dry vermouth or rice wine
- 1 egg, slightly beaten
- 1 tablespoon cornstarch
  Large spinach leaves, to line steaming baskets

Pine Nut–Spinach Filling

- ½ pound fresh spinach
- 1 teaspoon dark soy sauce
- ½ teaspoon sugar
- 1 teaspoon Asian sesame oil
- 2 tablespoons toasted pine nuts or coarsely chopped walnuts

1. Rinse both kinds of rice with cold water until water runs clear. Drain. Soak rice in enough water to cover for 4 hours or, preferably, overnight. Drain well.

2. In a medium bowl combine pork, shrimp, water chestnuts, green onion, ginger, salt, sugar, white pepper, soy sauce, sesame oil, and vermouth. Add egg and blend well. Sprinkle with cornstarch and mix together.

3. With moistened hands take a full tablespoon of pork mixture and flatten into a round pancake. Place ½ teaspoon Pine Nut–Spinach Filling in center of pork mixture and mold into a densely packed 1½-inch-diameter ball. Set aside.

4. Line each steaming basket with 1 layer of spinach leaves. Spoon reserved rice into a shallow dish. Roll pork balls in rice and pat gently to embed grains. Arrange balls at least ½ inch apart on spinach.

5. Prepare wok for steaming (see page 86). Cover balls and steam over medium-high heat 20 minutes. Serve with small dishes of soy sauce and sesame oil.

Serves 6 as a first course.

Pine Nut–Spinach Filling

Blanch spinach and squeeze out excess water; chop coarsely. Transfer to a small bowl and mix with soy sauce, sugar, sesame oil, and pine nuts.

AUNT CARRIE'S CHINESE PICKLED VEGETABLES

In traditional Chinese meals pickled vegetables are served communally and picked up with chopsticks. Cut vegetables in sizes you prefer.

- 1 small Chinese mustard cabbage
- 1 small green cabbage
- 1 red bell pepper, seeded
- 1 green bell pepper, seeded
- 3 cups water
- ¾ cup sugar
- ½ cup white vinegar
- 2 tablespoons salt
- 1 piece (1 in.) peeled fresh ginger
- 1 clove garlic, bruised
- 1 dried red chile

1. Cut mustard cabbage stems into 1-inch cubes and tear leaves into 1-inch pieces. Tear green cabbage and peppers into 1-inch pieces. Place vegetables in a large glass container.

2. In a 1½-quart saucepan combine the water, sugar, vinegar, salt, ginger, garlic, and chile; bring to a boil and cook until sugar and salt are dissolved. Pour hot liquid over cabbage mixture and stir. Let cool, cover, and refrigerate. Serve chilled.

Makes about 2 quarts.

SZECHUAN BRAISED BEEF NOODLES WITH BABY BOK CHOY

This noodle dish makes perfect winter lunch or dinner fare. Cutting the meat diagonally creates an interesting texture, reduces cooking time, and helps the meat absorb more flavor without getting too dry. As with other long-cooking dishes, you may prepare this dish in advance; it freezes well.

> 2 pounds stewing beef, trimmed
> 2 tablespoons dry vermouth
>   or rice wine
> 3 tablespoons peanut or corn oil
> 6 teaspoons sugar
> ¼ cup hot bean sauce
> 1 teaspoon Szechuan
>   peppercorns (optional)
> 6 cloves garlic, bruised
> 3 pieces (1 in. each) fresh
>   ginger, bruised
> 3 green onions, each tied into
>   a knot, plus 2 green onions,
>   coarsely chopped, for garnish
> 3 tablespoons soy sauce
> 1 pound Chinese egg noodles
>   (see page 36), cooked, rinsed,
>   and drained
> 6 stalks baby bok choy (about
>   4 in. long), cut in half
>   lengthwise, for garnish
> 2 tablespoons Asian hot chile
>   oil, or to taste

1. Cut beef diagonally into strips ⅜ inch thick by 1 inch wide by 2 inches long. In a large bowl toss beef with vermouth; allow to marinate at least 15 minutes.

2. Preheat wok over medium-high heat until hot, then pour in peanut oil. When hot add beef in 3 batches and sauté until browned (about 3 minutes per batch), sprinkling each with 2 teaspoons of the sugar, cooking together to caramelize sugar, and pushing meat up sides of wok when done. To center of wok add bean sauce, peppercorns (if used), garlic, ginger, and green onion knots; stir-fry with beef until well mixed (about 1 minute). Add soy sauce and toss together.

3. Add enough boiling water to just cover meat (about 5 cups); bring to a boil. Reduce heat to low, cover, and simmer until meat is tender (1 hour). Remove meat; strain stock and discard ginger, garlic, and green onion knots. Skim off fat from stock and set aside.

4. Boil noodles about 15 minutes before beef will be ready; divide among 6 soup bowls. On each bowl of noodles place several pieces of meat and 2 halved bok choy stalks; scatter chopped green onion on top. Ladle a generous helping of reserved hot stock on top of each. Sprinkle with chile oil.

Serves 6 with other dishes.

FRESH CHILLED MANGO, SINGAPORE STYLE

The sweet yet tart flavor of a mango makes it a refreshing finish for a highly seasoned meal. Select fully ripe fruit with smooth skin and a sweet fragrance.

> 3 fresh ripe mangoes
> 1 lime, cut into 6 wedges

Cut each mango in half lengthwise following the contour of the pit. Score the flesh in a diagonal criss-cross pattern just shy of the skin. Arrange 2 sections, pattern side up, on each plate with 1 lime wedge. Serve chilled.

Serves 6.

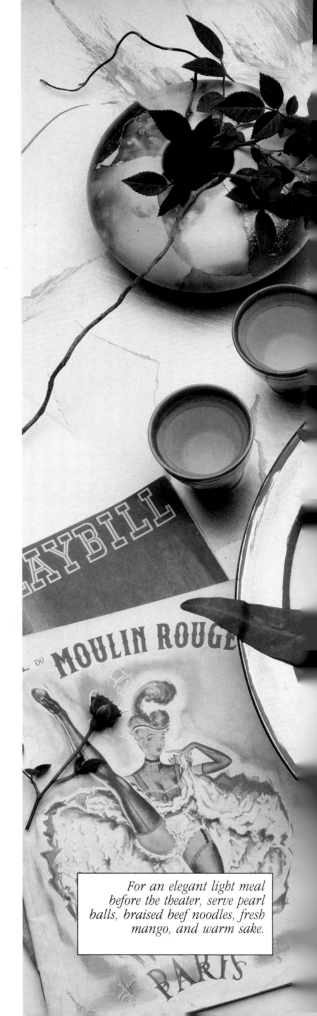

For an elegant light meal before the theater, serve pearl balls, braised beef noodles, fresh mango, and warm sake.

The exotic seeds and sweet snacks in this colorful still life are staples and garnishes for many Asian dishes.

Festive Foods

Entertaining at home is an art. Exotic international foods can create an exciting ambience and act as conversation openers. The recipes in this chapter are terrific for both formal and casual entertaining. Spicy Pork Shreds Stuffed in Sesame Pocket Bread (see page 112) is an exciting buffet entrée that rivals the delicious but more familiar Mu Shu Pork With Mandarin Pancakes (see page 115) as a casual party dish. The zesty pocket bread "sandwich" may be held in one hand and a drink in the other. The Minced Cornish Hen Wrapped in Lettuce Cups (see page 120) is dazzling banquet fare, but it also makes an impressive beginning for an informal dinner.

DISHES FOR ENTERTAINING

Parties centered around an open kitchen let you flaunt your cooking skills preparing mu shu pork (see page 115), for example, while your guests join in and fill their own Mandarin pancakes (see page 115). While guests converse, casually stir-fry Ginger–Green Onion Crab Baked in the Shell (see page 118); set the wok on the table flanked by simple fried rice, lots of napkins, and finger bowls, and let your guests dig in. Or for a formal occasion, dazzle guests with an impressive banquet menu including Eight-Jewel Chicken (see page 120). The recipe may seem intimidating, but actually it simply needs careful organization and preparation. The results are delicious and spectacular.

If multicourse meals are not compatible with your schedule, design a menu that spotlights one of these festive recipes and includes others from your repertoire of favorite dishes. For example, as a dramatic opener serve Sizzling Tangerine Scallops (see page 116) and follow it with grilled steaks, roasted bell peppers, and a tossed green salad.

SPICY PORK SHREDS STUFFED IN SESAME POCKET BREAD

This exciting entrée can be the star of a buffet table, yet both components are delicious individually. The spicy pork shreds can be served over noodles. The pocket bread, or *shao bing*, can be served for breakfast or as a snack or with a Mongolian fire pot and Mongolian barbecue. It can hold any of several stir-fried meats and vegetables and be eaten like a sandwich, or used like bread to soak up juices from other dishes. The pocket bread can be made well in advance and frozen (see Note).

1 pound boneless pork loin
2 tablespoons peanut or corn oil
1 teaspoon finely minced fresh ginger
2 teaspoons hot bean sauce
1 green onion, minced
½ cup finely shredded Szechuan preserved mustard greens

2 cups shredded cabbage
1 tablespoon firmly packed brown sugar
1 tablespoon soy sauce
2 tablespoons dry vermouth or rice wine
1 teaspoon Asian sesame oil

Pork Shred Marinade

2 teaspoons soy sauce
1 teaspoon sugar
1 tablespoon dry vermouth or rice wine
2 teaspoons cornstarch
1 teaspoon Asian sesame oil

Sesame Pocket Bread

¼ cup lard or peanut oil
3½ cups flour, plus more for dusting
1 teaspoon active dry yeast
1 tablespoon sugar
1 cup lukewarm water
1 teaspoon salt
1 tablespoon honey mixed with 1 tablespoon water
¼ cup sesame seed

1. Cut pork across grain into ⅛-inch-thick slices; then cut crosswise into ⅛-inch-thick by 2-inch-long shreds. Add to marinade; toss together. Set aside.

2. Preheat wok over medium-high heat until hot, then pour in peanut oil. When hot add ginger, bean sauce, and green onion; stir-fry 10 seconds. Add reserved pork shreds; stir-fry until shreds separate (about 30 seconds). Push meat up sides of wok and add mustard greens and cabbage to center; stir-fry a few seconds in center; then stir-fry with pork. Add brown sugar; toss 10 seconds. Add soy sauce and vermouth; toss 5 seconds. Fold in sesame oil. Transfer to a serving platter.

3. To serve, cut Sesame Pocket Bread in half crosswise. Stuff pocket with 2 to 3 tablespoons filling and eat like a sandwich.

Serves 6 with other dishes.

Pork Shred Marinade In a medium bowl combine all ingredients.

Makes about ½ cup.

Sesame Pocket Bread

1. Place lard in wok and heat over medium heat to 350° F. Add ½ cup of the flour and stir constantly with a wire whisk until roux turns caramel brown and fragrant. Let cool. Transfer roux to a heat-resistant bowl and chill until firm (about ½ hour).

2. In a small bowl combine yeast, sugar, and ¼ cup of the water. Let stand until yeast foams (about 5 minutes). In a large bowl combine remaining 3 cups flour and salt. Add yeast mixture and remaining ¾ cup water; mix into a rough dough. Gather dough into a ball; knead on floured work surface until dough is smooth and spongy. Transfer to a greased bowl, cover, and let rise in a warm place until double in bulk (about 1 hour).

3. Punch down dough and return to lightly floured surface; knead until no longer sticky. Roll dough into a 9- by 12-inch rectangle. Spread reserved roux evenly over rectangle, leaving a ½-inch border. Starting with long edge, roll up jelly-roll style; pinch ends to seal. Flatten roll slightly and cut crosswise into 12 pieces. Pinch open ends of each piece to seal. Cover with a damp cloth.

4. Roll 1 piece of dough into a 6-inch square. Fold opposite sides toward center, overlapping edges 1 inch. Pinch ends closed; then fold toward center, just overlapping edges to form a 3-inch square. Roll into a 3- by 6-inch rectangle.

5. Brush unseamed side with honey water; then dip dough into sesame seed and press seeds lightly in place. Place dough, sesame seed side down, on an ungreased baking sheet. Cover and let rise at least 30 minutes. Repeat with remaining dough.

6. Preheat oven to 375° F. Bake bread 8 minutes; turn over and bake until bread is browned and flaky (about 5 minutes more). Serve warm.

Makes 24 pocket breads.

<u>Note</u> To reheat frozen bread, thaw and place in 350° F oven 5 to 8 minutes.

Sesame Pocket Bread, traditionally eaten at breakfast, makes an appealing holder for spicy pork-shred filling. The pocket bread may be frozen and reheated.

MAKING STUFFINGS IN A WOK

A wok is ideal for making stuffings; they are easy to toss, and minimal oil is required.

EIGHT-JEWEL RICE STUFFING

Rather than using bread in stuffing, Asian cooks use glutinous rice.

- 1 cup glutinous rice
- 12 dried chestnuts
- ½ teaspoon baking soda
- 6 Chinese dried black mushrooms
- ¼ cup small dried shrimp (optional)
- 1¼ cups chicken stock
- 1 tablespoon soy sauce
- 2 teaspoons Asian sesame oil Large pinch white pepper
- 2 Chinese sausage links, cut into ¼-inch slices
- 1 tablespoon peanut or corn oil
- 6 Chinese water chestnuts, preferably fresh, peeled and diced
- 2 green onions, chopped
- 2 tablespoons coarsely chopped fresh coriander

1. Rinse rice in cold water until the water runs clear; drain thoroughly and set aside. In a small bowl combine dried chestnuts, baking soda, and 2 cups boiling water; soak 1 hour. Rinse and discard red skins. In a small saucepan bring to a boil 2 more cups water and soaked chestnuts. Reduce heat and simmer 1 hour. Cut chestnuts into quarters; set aside.

2. In separate bowls soak mushrooms and shrimp (if used) in warm water until soft (about 30 minutes). Remove and discard mushroom stems. Cut caps into ¼-inch dice and set aside. Drain shrimp well and set aside.

3. In a 1½-quart heat-resistant bowl, combine reserved rice, stock, soy sauce, sesame oil, pepper, and sausage. Set aside 1 hour or overnight.

4. Prepare wok for steaming (see page 86). Set bowl with rice in steamer, cover, and steam over medium-high heat 30 minutes. Remove cover and let rice stand 15 minutes. Dry wok and return to heat.

5. Into hot wok pour peanut oil, and add reserved mushrooms and shrimp, water chestnuts, reserved soaked chestnuts, and green onion; stir-fry 1 minute. Remove from heat; add reserved rice and coriander.

Makes about 3 cups.

ITALIAN SAUSAGE, MUSHROOM, AND BREAD STUFFING

This recipe makes enough stuffing to fill 1 chicken or 6 Cornish hens with extra stuffing on the side.

- ½ pound Italian sausage, crumbled
- 2 stalks celery, chopped
- 1 cup chopped onion
- ½ red bell pepper, chopped
- ½ green bell pepper, chopped
- 4 tablespoons unsalted butter
- ½ pound mushrooms, cubed
- 1 teaspoon dried sage, crumbled
- 1 teaspoon dried thyme
- 6 cups cubed stale bread
- 1 cup chicken stock, or more if needed
  Salt and freshly ground pepper, to taste

1. Preheat ungreased wok over medium-high heat until hot. Sauté sausage until lightly browned (about 5 minutes). Remove excess fat. Add celery, onion, and bell pepper; sauté until vegetables are soft (about 5 minutes). Remove and set aside.

2. Place butter in hot wok. When foam subsides add mushrooms; stir-fry until they squeak when pressed against wok (about 5 minutes). Add sage, thyme, and bread cubes; toss until bread cubes begin to soften. Add enough stock to moisten bread. Season with salt and pepper; stir-fry 3 minutes more.

Makes 6 cups.

SINGAPORE CHILE CRAB

One of Singapore's national dishes is chile crab—a mixture of Singapore and Malay cooking—with a piquant sauce made with prepared Singaporean or Malaysian chile sauce, which contains vinegar. Serve this spicy dish with a salad.

- 1 live crab (2 to 3 lb), preferably Dungeness
- 2 tablespoons peanut or corn oil
- 1 teaspoon salt
- 2 teaspoons minced fresh ginger
- 3 cloves garlic, coarsely chopped
- 2 fresh red chiles, seeded and chopped
- 2 shallots, minced
- 2 tablespoons Singaporean-style chile sauce or chile paste with garlic
- 1 tablespoon soy sauce
- 3 tablespoons tomato paste
- 1 tablespoon sugar
- 2 tablespoons red wine vinegar, or to taste
- ½ cup chicken stock or water
- 2 teaspoons cornstarch mixed with 1 tablespoon water
- 1 large egg, beaten

1. Plunge live crab into a large stockpot of boiling water for 1 minute. Remove crab. When cool enough to handle, remove claws, legs, and back, discarding gills and reserving tomalley for another use. Rinse and pat dry. Chop body in half; then cut crosswise into thirds. With a hammer or nutcracker, crack shells at each joint of legs and claws, leaving shells on.

2. Preheat wok over medium-high heat until hot. Pour in oil. When hot add crab in batches, seconds apart, first claws, then legs and body pieces; stir-fry until shells turn bright orange (about 1 minute per batch).

3. Reduce heat to medium, push crab up sides of wok, and add salt, ginger, garlic, chiles, and shallot to center of wok. Stir-fry seasonings in center of wok only until lightly browned.

4. Increase heat to high and add chile sauce, soy sauce, tomato paste, and sugar to center of wok; stir-fry 30 seconds. Add vinegar and stock; toss with crab. Stir in cornstarch mixture and cook until thickened (about 10 seconds).

5. Remove wok from heat. Pour beaten egg evenly over crab and let egg slide into sauce. Stir gently to blend. Serve hot.

Serves 4 to 6 with other dishes.

MU SHU PORK WITH MANDARIN PANCAKES

Mu shu pork, a regional specialty from northern China, is a mixture of stir-fried pork shreds, wood ear mushrooms, and vegetables tossed with scrambled egg morsels. It is served wrapped in a steamed Mandarin pancake, dressed with the popular tangy hoisin sauce condiment, and eaten like a burrito. It works beautifully as a buffet entrée and may be served hot or at room temperature. Mandarin pancakes are traditional accompaniments for mu shu pork and Peking duck. This dish uses only half the pancakes made in the recipe (allow 2 per person), but the extras, if well wrapped, will keep frozen up to 2 months (see Note).

> ½ *cup dried lily buds*
> 3 *large dried wood ear mushrooms*
> ½ *pound pork loin or butt*
> 3 *tablespoons peanut or corn oil*
> 3 *eggs, slightly beaten*
> ½ *teaspoon salt*
> 2 *cups shredded cabbage*
> ¼ *teaspoon white pepper*
> ½ *teaspoon sugar*
> 1 *tablespoon light soy sauce*
> 2 *tablespoons dry vermouth or dry sherry*
> 3 *green onions, slivered*
> 1 *teaspoon Asian sesame oil*
> *Hoisin Sauce Dip (see page 24), for topping*
> 1 *bunch fresh coriander, large stems removed*

Ginger Marinade

> 1 *teaspoon minced fresh ginger*
> 2 *teaspoons light soy sauce*
> ½ *teaspoon sugar*
> 1 *tablespoon dry vermouth or dry sherry*
> 2 *teaspoons cornstarch*
> 1 *teaspoon Asian sesame oil*

Mandarin Pancakes

> 2 *cups flour, plus more for dusting*
> *Pinch salt*
> 1 *cup boiling water*
> 3 *tablespoons Asian sesame oil, for brushing*

1. In 2 separate medium bowls, soak lily buds and wood ears with enough water to cover until soft and pliable (about 20 minutes). Drain and squeeze dry. Snip off and discard hard ends of lily buds. Remove and discard hard clusters in center of wood ears. Roll each wood ear into a tight roll and cut crosswise into thin slivers. Set aside.

2. Cut pork crosswise into slices ⅛ inch thick by 1½ inches long; then cut into julienne strips. Add to Ginger Marinade and let stand 30 minutes.

3. Meanwhile, preheat wok over medium-high heat until hot. Pour in 1 tablespoon of the peanut oil. When hot add egg and tilt wok so egg slides up along sides. Push egg in center up sides, allowing uncooked egg to slide down. Cook, tossing occasionally, until egg is set, light, and fluffy (about 30 seconds). Coarsely chop egg, remove immediately to a small dish, and set aside.

4. Add remaining 2 tablespoons peanut oil and the salt to wok. When oil is hot add marinated pork; stir-fry until pork separates into strands and is no longer pink (about 1 minute). Add cabbage, reserved lily buds, and wood ears in separate batches, tossing each item 10 seconds before adding the next. Sprinkle with pepper and sugar; toss together. Add soy sauce and vermouth and toss together 15 seconds. Add green onion, reserved egg morsels, and sesame oil; mix together.

5. To serve, spread 2 or 3 tablespoons of the pork mixture across middle of each pancake. Drizzle 1 teaspoon Hoisin Sauce Dip over meat, then top with a few coriander leaves. Fold in opposite edges of pancake to make a rectangular pocket.

Serves 6 with other dishes.

Ginger Marinade In a large bowl whisk together all ingredients.

Makes about 3 tablespoons.

Mandarin Pancakes

1. In a medium bowl combine flour and salt. Immediately after the water comes to a boil, add to flour mixture and blend well. Gather into a ball, turn onto a floured work surface, and knead until dough is no longer sticky (about 5 minutes). Cover with a damp towel and let stand 15 minutes.

2. Return dough to floured work surface and knead until dough is smooth. Divide dough in half. Roll half of dough into a ¼-inch-thick sheet. Cut out 24 rounds, each 2½ inches in diameter. Brush 1 round with sesame oil. Top with an unoiled round and roll into a 7-inch circle no more than ⅛ inch thick. Repeat with remaining rounds.

3. In an ungreased wok or skillet over medium-low heat, cook 1 pancake until it begins to puff and bottom becomes speckled (45 to 60 seconds). Turn over and cook 30 to 45 seconds more. Pancake should not cook too quickly (it will be dry) or too slowly (it will be tough). Remove pancake from pan; while hot, peel layers apart, making 2 pancakes. Repeat with remaining pancakes. Then repeat with remaining half of dough.

4. Prepare wok for steaming (see page 86). Arrange pancakes in 2 steamer baskets and steam over medium-high heat 2 minutes. Serve directly from bamboo steamers.

Makes 2 dozen 7-inch pancakes.

Note To prepare frozen pancakes, thaw and reheat in a 350° F oven 8 minutes, or steam 5 minutes.

THAI RED CURRY SHELLFISH WITH BASIL

This is a recipe for which having Thai Red Curry Paste on hand is a must. The grilled eggplant is a delicious accompaniment.

 1 can (14 oz) unsweetened coconut milk (see page 8)
 2 tablespoons vegetable oil
 ½ pound large prawns, shelled and deveined
 1 pound squid (including tentacles), cleaned, bodies cut into 1-inch-wide rings
 2 tablespoons Thai Red Curry Paste (see page 28)
 2 tablespoons Thai fish sauce
 2 teaspoons palm sugar or firmly packed brown sugar
 2 fresh red chiles, slivered
 18 mussels, debearded and scrubbed
 12 to 15 fresh Thai basil leaves
 2 tablespoons coarsely chopped fresh coriander leaves, for garnish
 1 tomato, peeled, seeded, and coarsely chopped, for garnish
 Cooked angel hair pasta, for accompaniment

Grilled Asian Eggplant

 4 Asian eggplants
 ⅓ cup red wine vinegar
 ¼ cup olive oil
 1 clove garlic, squeezed through a garlic press
 1 teaspoon grated ginger
 Salt and freshly ground pepper, to taste

1. Without shaking can, pour coconut milk into a tall glass container and set aside until coconut cream rises to the top (1 to 2 hours). Skim off ½ cup cream and pour into a small bowl; set aside. Reserve remaining milk in glass.

2. Preheat wok over medium-high heat until hot, then pour in oil. Add prawns and stir-fry until they begin to curl (about 1 minute). Add squid and stir-fry 1 minute. Remove seafood and set aside.

3. Pour reserved coconut cream into wok. Cook over medium-high heat until thick and oily (about 2 minutes), stirring constantly. Add curry paste and cook until aromatic (about 3 minutes), stirring continuously. Add fish sauce, sugar, chiles, and reserved coconut milk. Bring almost to a boil, reduce heat to medium, and simmer, uncovered, until sauce thickens to a creamy consistency (about 5 minutes), stirring often. Add mussels and simmer until they open (about 2 minutes). Add basil and reserved prawn mixture; cook only long enough to heat through (about 1 minute). Garnish with coriander leaves and tomato. Arrange in a bowl with a mound of pasta in the middle and grilled eggplant on the side.

Serves 8.

Grilled Asian Eggplant Prepare coals. Cut eggplants lengthwise, then crosswise into thirds. In a medium bowl combine vinegar, olive oil, garlic, ginger, salt, and pepper. Add eggplant and marinate until ready to grill (30 to 60 minutes). Grill over very hot coals 2 minutes per side.

Serves 8.

SIZZLING TANGERINE SCALLOPS

The peel of the sour tangerine of southern China is prized for its aromatic oil and pleasant, bitter flavor. Although orange and tangerine peel do not taste quite the same, you may use either as a substitute. Entertainer Danny Kaye shared this recipe with his friend Jim Nassikas, president of the Stanford Court Hotel in San Francisco. The recipe inspired from Mr. Nassikas's version includes sizzling the scallop mixture, an optional step, which not only adds a dramatic touch, but also sharpens the flavors and infuses them into the sauce.

 1 pound large sea scallops (about 30), well drained
 3 tablespoons peanut or corn oil
 ½ teaspoon salt
 1 slice fresh ginger, bruised, plus 2 teaspoons minced fresh ginger
 1 large zucchini, cut into ¼-inch-wide by 2-inch-long julienne strips
 2 cloves garlic, coarsely minced
 1 teaspoon Szechuan peppercorns (optional), toasted in an ungreased skillet over low heat 3 minutes, then finely ground
 2 dried red chiles, soaked in warm water until soft, then drained
 1 piece (1 in. square) dried tangerine peel, soaked in warm water until soft (about 30 minutes), then thinly julienned
 4 green onions, cut into 2-inch lengths
 1 teaspoon Asian sesame oil
 Cooked white long-grain rice, for accompaniment

Scallop Marinade

 1 teaspoon sugar
 1 teaspoon dry vermouth
 1 teaspoon cornstarch
 1 teaspoon Asian sesame oil

Tangerine Sauce

 2 teaspoons chile paste
    with garlic
 1 tablespoon hoisin sauce
 1 tablespoon dark soy sauce
 ¼ cup tangerine juice or
    orange juice
 2 teaspoons red wine vinegar
 1 teaspoon firmly packed
    brown sugar

1. Toss scallops with Scallop Marinade; set aside.

2. To sizzle the dish, set a cast-iron platter over high heat until a drop of water dances when sprinkled on it (about 10 minutes).

3. Preheat wok over medium-high heat until hot, then pour in 2 tablespoons of the peanut oil. Add salt and ginger slice. Cook until oil is fragrant (about 30 seconds). Add reserved scallops and stir-fry until they begin to feel firm (about 30 seconds). Remove to a medium bowl; set aside. Pick out and discard ginger.

4. Pour remaining 1 tablespoon peanut oil into hot wok. Add zucchini and stir-fry until it is almost cooked (about 1 minute). Add minced ginger, garlic, ground peppercorns (if used), chiles, tangerine peel, and green onion; stir-fry until mixture is aromatic (about 30 seconds). Increase heat to high, add Tangerine Sauce, and cook until sauce thickens (about 30 seconds). Stir in reserved scallops and sesame oil; remove scallop mixture to a serving plate.

5. Carefully transfer hot cast-iron platter to trivet on dining table. Immediately pour scallop mixture onto platter. Serve with rice.

Serves 6 with other dishes.

Scallop Marinade   In a medium bowl combine all ingredients.

Makes about 3 teaspoons.

Tangerine Sauce   In a small bowl combine all ingredients.

Makes about ½ cup.

In Hong Kong, sizzling seafood entrées, such as these citrus-flavored scallops, are extremely popular. Sizzling is more than a theatrical technique: It sharpens and fuses the flavors of a dish.

117

Arm yourself with a large bib and lots of napkins and dig in, savoring the juices clinging to this Ginger–Green Onion Crab Baked in the Shell. Use the pointed tips of the legs to pry out the sweet crabmeat from the rest of the body.

GINGER–GREEN ONION CRAB BAKED IN THE SHELL

Cantonese seafood restaurant menus say baked when in fact this dish is braised for a short time. The key to success is to use a very hot wok and to reduce the sauce quickly. Serve with hot rice and a soup or stir-fried green beans.

> 1 live crab (2 to 3 lb), preferably Dungeness, scrubbed
> 3 tablespoons peanut oil
> 1 teaspoon salt
> 8 pieces (½ in. each) fresh ginger, bruised
> 4 cloves garlic, bruised
> 1 teaspoon sugar
> ¼ teaspoon white pepper
> 6 green onions, cut into 2-inch lengths
> 1 tablespoon dark soy sauce
> ¼ cup dry vermouth or sherry
> ¼ cup chicken stock
> 1 teaspoon cornstarch mixed with 1 tablespoon water
> 1 teaspoon Asian sesame oil
>   Cooked white long-grain rice, for accompaniment

1. Plunge live crab into a large stockpot of boiling water for 1 minute. Remove crab. When cool enough to handle, remove claws, legs, and back, discarding gills and reserving tomalley for another use. Rinse and pat dry. Chop body in half; then cut crosswise into thirds. With a hammer or nutcracker, crack shells at each joint of legs and claws, leaving shells on.

2. Preheat wok over medium heat until hot, then pour in peanut oil. Add salt, ginger, and garlic; stir-fry slowly until oil is fragrant (about 2 minutes).

3. Increase heat to high. Add claws and legs; stir-fry until shells turn orange (about 1 minute). Add body pieces; stir-fry 2 minutes longer. Add sugar, pepper, and green onion and toss; then add soy sauce. Deglaze sides of wok with vermouth and stock, cover, and cook about 5 minutes, shaking occasionally. Remove cover, add cornstarch mixture to center of wok, and stir until thickened (about 10 seconds). Fold in sesame oil. Remove crab to a platter and serve with rice.

Serves 4.

BONING A WHOLE CHICKEN

These photographs illustrate how to bone a whole chicken, keeping the meat and skin intact. Turn the skin inside out to expose the area you're working on. When finished, pull the skin back over meat. You will have a boned chicken with lower leg and lower wing bones attached. The chicken is then ready to be stuffed and reshaped into a bird, as in the recipe for Eight-Jewel Chicken (see page 120).

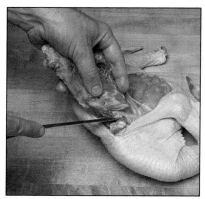

1. Massage chicken to loosen flesh. Pull neck skin over to expose neck and wing region. Bend each wing backward to crack joint connecting it to body; without cutting through skin, cut joint to detach wing.

2. With a sharp boning knife, make short cuts around base of neck. Cut around wishbone, tracing inside and outside lines of bone; lift bone and snap to remove. Roll skin back as much as possible to expose breast

meat. Slip knife tip between breast meat and ribs. Keep cutting edge of knife against ribs and use ribs as a guide to cut 1 to 2 inches at a time down length of breastbone until all meat is freed from bone.

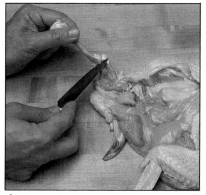

3. Turn chicken over. Fillet back in same manner, cutting only 1 to 2 inches at a time down back so thin skin does not tear. Alternate between back and breast, circling around body until meat is freed. Bend each thigh backward to crack joint connecting it to body; without cutting through skin, carefully cut joint to detach thigh.

4. Pull skin over cavity to expose tail. Cut through bone, freeing meat but leaving tail attached. Remove and discard skeleton.

5. On each thigh turn skin inside out to expose joint. Cut and scrape meat to expose leg joint. Snap joint backward. Cut through joint separating thigh from leg; discard thigh bone and leave drumstick bone attached to thigh meat.

6. On each wing pull skin over joint. Beginning at large joint, cut and scrape meat, working toward and exposing second joint. Snap joint backward. Cut upper from lower wing bone; discard upper wing bone and leave lower wing bone attached to meat.

7. Pull skin back over chicken. It is now ready to be stuffed.

EIGHT-JEWEL CHICKEN

Shanghai chefs prefer steaming the whole boned, stuffed chicken for this classic dish to achieve a juicy, delicate texture, whereas the Cantonese elect roasting for a strong, dry taste. Both methods are used in this recipe to combine the best characteristics of each.

> 1 chicken (3 to 4 lb)
> Eight-Jewel Rice Stuffing (see page 114)
> 2 tablespoons soy sauce
> 1 tablespoon Asian sesame oil
> 2 teaspoons honey
> ¼ cup vermouth

1. Bone chicken following the Step-by-Step on page 119.

2. Lay boned chicken breast side down. Fill wings with stuffing. Cover neck opening with neck skin; stitch closed. Fill legs with stuffing. Reposition breast meat in its proper place. Fill body with stuffing, but do not overstuff; stitch cavity closed. Reshape into a bird.

3. In a small bowl mix together soy sauce and sesame oil; rub all over chicken, reserving unused portion. Place chicken breast side down in a wide heat-resistant bowl that will fit in steaming basket.

4. Prepare wok for steaming (see page 86). Cover and steam chicken over medium-high heat 45 minutes. Let cool; then transfer chicken, breast side up, to a roasting rack. Reserve steaming juices in a small saucepan.

5. Preheat oven to 425° F. Add honey to reserved soy sauce mixture; brush over chicken. Roast chicken until skin is crisp (10 to 15 minutes). Remove to a serving platter. Deglaze roasting pan with reserved steaming juices and vermouth. Pour mixture back into saucepan and, over high heat, reduce to a thin cream.

6. To serve Western style, quarter chicken and serve 1 piece per person. To serve Chinese style, slice whole chicken into 2-inch pieces and serve with other entrées.

Serves 4 Western style or 8 Chinese style with other dishes.

AN ELEGANT DINNER

Crisp Sugared Walnuts

Minced Cornish Hen Wrapped in Lettuce Cups

Hot-and-Sour Soup

"Squirrel Fish" With Szechuan Sweet-Sour Chile Sauce

Sweet Silver-Thread Rolls (see page 47)

Ginger-Peach Sorbet

Hot Tea

Successful orchestration of an Asian menu requires advance preparation. The Cornish hen and soup can both be cooked early in the day, quickly reheated in a microwave oven or on top of the stove, and assembled moments before serving. The sugared walnuts can also be prepared in advance. They will keep several weeks in an airtight container. Slip away from your guests for 8 to 10 minutes to deep-fry the prepared "squirrel fish" and, while the fish is cooking, reheat the sauce. Serve the fish with the freshly steamed silver-thread rolls in their steaming basket.

CRISP SUGARED WALNUTS

This traditional Asian dish—perfect snack food for cocktail parties—can be made in a wok as directed, or the nuts can be baked in a preheated 325° F oven for 10 minutes.

> 2 cups boiling water
> 2 cups walnut or pecan halves
> 6 tablespoons sugar
> Pinch of salt
> 2 cups peanut oil

1. In a medium bowl combine the boiling water and walnuts; soak 3 minutes. Drain and pat dry. While nuts are hot, toss with sugar and salt to coat. Spread on waxed paper and let stand until dry (at least 1 hour).

2. Preheat wok over medium-high heat until hot, then pour in oil and heat to 325° F. Add nuts and deep-fry until they glisten and begin to caramelize (about 5 minutes). Remove, drain, and let cool on waxed paper, separating nuts so that they harden.

Makes 2 cups.

MINCED CORNISH HEN WRAPPED IN LETTUCE CUPS

Squab is traditionally used in this famous recipe. But the more economical Cornish hen, with its light, gamy flavor, makes a good substitute.

> 6 small dried oysters or 6 smoked oysters packed in oil, drained
> 6 Chinese dried black mushrooms
> 1 teaspoon cornstarch
> 2 teaspoons oyster sauce
> 1 Cornish hen or 2 chicken thighs, skinned, boned, and finely minced
> 2 tablespoons peanut or corn oil, or as needed
> ½ teaspoon salt
> 2 teaspoons finely minced fresh ginger
> 3 green onions, finely chopped
> 8 Chinese water chestnuts, preferably fresh, peeled and finely minced
> ½ cup finely minced bamboo shoots
> ¼ teaspoon sugar
> Large pinch white pepper

2 teaspoons soy sauce
1 teaspoon Asian sesame oil
2 cups crushed Deep-fried Rice
  Stick Noodles (see page 38),
  for garnish (optional)
12 chilled lettuce cups, preferably
  iceberg lettuce, for
  accompaniment (see Note)
⅓ cup Hoisin Sauce Dip
  (see page 24)

Cornish Hen Marinade

1 teaspoon dry vermouth
1 teaspoon soy sauce
¼ teaspoon sugar
1 teaspoon cornstarch
1 teaspoon Asian sesame oil

1. If using dried oysters, cover with warm water and soak until soft (at least 2 hours, or overnight). Rinse, pat dry, and finely mince; set aside. In a separate bowl cover mushrooms with water until soft (about 30 minutes). Squeeze out excess water, reserving soaking liquid. Discard stems; finely mince caps. Strain 2 tablespoons soaking liquid into a small bowl; add cornstarch and oyster sauce and blend well. Set aside.

2. Combine minced hen with Cornish Hen Marinade. Preheat wok over medium-high heat until hot, then pour in oil. Add salt, ginger, half the green onion, and Cornish hen mixture; stir-fry until meat becomes opaque (about 2 minutes). Add reserved oysters and mushrooms, water chestnuts, and bamboo shoots in batches, seconds apart, and stir-fry about 2 minutes total, adding more oil if necessary. Season with sugar, pepper, and soy sauce; toss mixture 10 seconds. Stir in reserved cornstarch mixture; cook until mixture holds together (about 10 seconds). Fold in sesame oil. Transfer to a platter. Garnish with ¼ cup of the rice stick noodles, if used, and with remaining green onion. Arrange lettuce cups on a separate platter.

3. To serve, place 2 tablespoons rice stick noodles (if used) in center of each lettuce cup. Top with 2 tablespoons Cornish hen mixture and 1 teaspoon Hoisin Sauce Dip.

Serves 6 with other dishes.

Cornish Hen Marinade   In a medium bowl thoroughly blend all ingredients.

Makes about 4 teaspoons.

Note   To make lettuce cups core lettuce and discard heart. Submerge head in water to loosen leaves. With scissors trim each leaf into a 3-inch circle; then wrap circles in towel and refrigerate until well chilled.

HOT-AND-SOUR SOUP

The three essential ingredients of this family-style soup are dried lily buds, Chinese dried black mushrooms, and dried wood ear mushrooms. Each imparts a distinctive musky flavor and contributes an intriguing chewy texture.

6 Chinese dried black
  mushrooms
3 large dried wood ear
  mushrooms
3 dozen dried lily buds
1 half chicken breast, skinned,
  boned, and cut into
  matchstick-sized strips
1 tablespoon peanut or corn oil
1 teaspoon salt
1 slice peeled fresh ginger,
  bruised
1 tablespoon soy sauce
2 tablespoons dry vermouth
  or sherry
4 cups chicken stock
2 tablespoons water chestnut
  flour or cornstarch mixed
  with 4 tablespoons water
1 egg, slightly beaten with
  1 teaspoon oil
¼ pound firm fresh tofu cut into
  ¼-inch-thick by 1½-inch-long
  strips (optional)
1 green onion, shredded

Chicken Strip Marinade

1 teaspoon light soy sauce
1 teaspoon dry vermouth
  or sherry
¼ teaspoon sugar
1 teaspoon cornstarch
1 teaspoon Asian sesame oil

Hot-and-Sour Seasoning

2 tablespoons red wine vinegar
1 tablespoon light soy sauce
1 teaspoon white pepper
2 teaspoons Asian hot chile oil,
  or to taste
1 tablespoon Asian sesame oil

1. In separate bowls soak black mushrooms, wood ears, and lily buds in water until soft. Squeeze out excess water. Remove and discard stems from black mushrooms; julienne. Remove and discard hard centers of wood ears. Tightly curl each wood ear; cut crosswise into thin strips. Remove and discard hard ends of lily buds. Set aside.

2. Toss chicken with Chicken Strip Marinade. Let marinate briefly.

3. Preheat wok over medium-high heat until hot, then pour in oil. Add salt, ginger, and chicken mixture; stir-fry until chicken turns opaque; remove and set aside.

4. Increase heat to high. Add reserved black mushrooms, wood ears, and lily buds, separately and seconds apart; stir-fry until fragrant (about 1 minute total). Add soy sauce and vermouth; toss 5 seconds. Add stock, bring to a boil, reduce heat to low, and simmer 20 minutes.

5. Increase heat to high and return mixture to a boil. Add water chestnut flour mixture; stir continuously until thickened (about 30 seconds). Remove wok from heat. Slowly pour egg mixture into soup in a circular motion while stirring slowly with chopsticks. Add tofu and reserved chicken.

6. Pour half of Hot-and-Sour Seasoning into a shallow soup tureen. Ladle soup on top. Scatter with green onion; then float remaining Hot-and-Sour Seasoning on top. Stir gently.

Serves 6 with other dishes.

Chicken Strip Marinade   In a medium bowl mix all ingredients.

Makes about 4 teaspoons.

Hot-and-Sour Seasoning   In a small bowl combine all ingredients; stir once or twice. Do not overmix.

Makes about 5 tablespoons.

"SQUIRREL FISH" WITH SZECHUAN SWEET-SOUR CHILE SAUCE

"Squirrel fish" is a Shanghai style of preparing a whole fish. The flesh is scored with a diamond pattern, and frying accentuates the pattern, simulating fluffy puffs of squirrel fur. This impressive presentation is reserved for festive occasions. Fillets are perfectly suitable substitutes for a whole fish.

   1 whole red snapper, rock cod, or sea bass (2½ to 3 lb), scaled and gutted, tail attached
      Peanut oil, for deep-frying
      Salt, for sprinkling
      Cornstarch, for coating
   1 egg, beaten
      Flour, for coating
   1 green onion, minced, for garnish
   1 cucumber, peeled, seeded, and cubed, for garnish

Szechuan Sweet-Sour Chile Sauce

    1 tablespoon peanut oil
    1 tablespoon minced fresh ginger
    1 tablespoon minced garlic
    3 tablespoons chile paste with garlic
  1½ tablespoons tomato paste
    3 tablespoons sugar
  1½ tablespoons soy sauce
   ¼ cup dry vermouth or rice wine
   ⅓ cup chicken stock
    3 tablespoons red wine vinegar
    1 tablespoon Asian sesame oil

1. Remove head of fish and flatten with side of cleaver; set aside. Cut fillets free from backbone but leave fillets joined at tail. Discard backbone. Lay fillets skin side down and score each with a 1-inch diamond pattern almost to skin but taking care not to cut through it.

2. Fill wok half full of water; bring to a boil over high heat. Hold fillets skin sides together by tail; lower into boiling water and scald until diamond pattern becomes pronounced (about 5 seconds). Remove fish and thoroughly pat dry. Dry wok and return to medium-high heat.

3. Place platter in oven and preheat oven to 250° F. Fill hot wok half full of peanut oil and heat to 375° F. Sprinkle fish head and body with salt, including scored crevices. Lightly coat with cornstarch; then brush with beaten egg. Lightly coat with flour. Add fish head to hot oil; deep-fry until browned and crisp (about 3 minutes). Gently remove, drain, and set on hot platter in oven. With fillets skin sides together, slide 2 spatulas under fish and carefully lower fish into hot oil. Fry until brown and crisp (about 5 minutes). To remove fish, slide 2 spatulas under fish and lift out of oil, drain, and arrange on hot platter patterned side facing out with fish head at top of body. Spoon warm Szechuan Sweet-Sour Chile Sauce over fish. Top with green onion. Scatter cubed cucumber around fish. Serve hot.

Serves 6 with other dishes.

Szechuan Sweet-Sour Chile Sauce In a small saucepan over medium heat, combine peanut oil, ginger, and garlic; sauté until oil is fragrant (about 30 seconds). Increase heat to medium-high. Blend in chile paste, tomato paste, and sugar; cook until mixture becomes a thick, sticky glaze (3 to 5 minutes). Immediately add soy sauce, vermouth, and stock; cook 1 minute. When ready to serve fish, reheat sauce and stir in vinegar and sesame oil.

Makes 1 cup.

GINGER-PEACH SORBET

In Asia fresh fruit is often served for dessert. This sensational sorbet nicely complements highly seasoned foods. It also adds a refreshing touch as a palate cleanser between courses or as a finale, topped with a plain cookie. Sweet stem ginger, also called candied ginger, comes in jars and is available through specialty food suppliers.

   2 quarts water
   2 tablespoons baking soda
   4 medium-sized fresh freestone peaches
   2 tablespoons sugar
   2 tablespoons fresh lime juice
   1 egg white, beaten until stiff
   5 pieces sweet stem ginger in syrup, chopped
      Lemon or lime zest, for garnish

1. In a large pot over high heat, bring the water and baking soda to a boil. Add peaches and poach 2 minutes. Remove and let cool. Remove and discard skin and seed. Cut fruit into small chunks.

2. In the work bowl of a food processor fitted with steel blade, purée peaches, sugar, and lime juice. Pour mixture into an 8- or 9-inch cake pan; freeze until edges of mixture are firm but top is soft to the touch (about 2 hours).

3. Return purée to work bowl; pulse until frothy. Add egg white and ginger; pulse just enough to blend. Transfer mixture to an airtight container and freeze until firm but not solid (1 to 2 hours). Serve garnished with zest.

Makes about 3 cups.

Impress your guests with an elegant meal of Cornish hen in lettuce cups (bottom), "squirrel fish," sugared walnuts, and Ginger-Peach Sorbet.

INDEX

Note: Page numbers in italics refer to photographs separated from recipe text.

A

Agar-agar, 10, *13*
Anchovy-Caper Rémoulade, Deep-Fried Mushrooms With, 16
Ants Climbing a Tree, 100
Appetizers, 15–33
  See also Dips and dipping sauces
  Brad Borel's Cajun Popcorn, *30–31,* 32
  Chinese Sausage, 98
  Classic Shrimp Toast, 19
  Crisp Fried Wontons, 33
  Crisp Sugared Walnuts, 120, *123*
  Deep-fried Mushrooms With Anchovy-Caper Rémoulade, 16
  dim sum, 16
  Dry-Fried Prawns in the Shell, *80,* 81
  Egg Net Pillows, 20–21, *back cover*
  Gambas al Ajillo, 29
  Hawaiian Rice Stick Prawns, 25
  Indonesian Corn-Shrimp Fritters, 26, *27*
  Indonesian Potato and Beef Fritters, *30–31,* 33
  Kuo Teh, 26–27
  Minced Cornish Hen Wrapped in Lettuce Cups, 120–21, *123*
  Natalie's New Orleans Barbecued Shrimp, *18,* 19
  Pearl Balls With Pine Nut–Spinach Filling, 107, *109*
  Shrimp Mousse–Stuffed Roasted Peppers, 18–19
  Steamed Siu Mai, 32
  Suppli al Telefono, 29
  Tamales con Mole Verde de Pepitas, 30
  Tamarind Shrimp Dip With Sizzling Rice Cakes, 16–17
  Thai Angel Wings, 22–23
  Thai Galloping Horses, 29, *30–31*
  Vietnamese Crab Imperial Rolls, 69, *71*
Asparagus, Deep-fried, With Gazpacho Coulis, 58, *59*
Asparagus beans. *See* Long beans
Aunt Carrie's Chinese Pickled Vegetables, 107
Avocado, Corn, Roasted Peppers, and, 60

B

Bacon or *pancetta*
  Oysters, Bell Peppers, Onions, and, 74–75
  Stir-fried Brussels Sprouts, Pancetta, and Parmesan, 61
  Wilted Escarole Salad With Fried Polenta Sticks, 66–67
Barbecued Pork Buns, 40–41
Barbecued Pork and Shrimp Egg Fu Yung, 45
Basic Chicken Marinade, 57

Basic Chinese Steamed Chicken, 90
Basic Wontons, 42
Basil, 10
  in Beef With Thai Red Curry Peanut Sauce, 104
  Thai Red Curry Shellfish With, 116
  Thai Stir-fried Chicken With, 90
Bean curd. *See* Tofu
Beans. *See* Black beans; Green beans; Long beans
Bean sauce, black. *See* Black bean sauce
Bean sauce, brown, 10, *13*
Bean sauce, hot, 10
Bean sprouts, Lo Mein Noodles With Barbecued Pork and, 38–39
Bean thread noodles, *13, 34,* 36–37
  Ants Climbing a Tree, 100
  Bon Bon Chicken Salad, 66, *67*
  Vietnamese Crab Imperial Rolls, 69, *71*
Beef
  Beef and Bitter Melon in Black Bean Sauce, 103
  Beef With Thai Red Curry Peanut Sauce, 104
  Dry-Fried Spicy Shredded, 101
  Indonesian Potato and Beef Fritters, *30–31,* 33
  Seared Beef With Chile Hoisin Sauce, 106
  Szechuan Braised Beef Noodles With Baby Bok Choy, 108, *109*
  Tomato Beef With Shallow-Fried Noodle Cakes, 104–5
Beef Marinade, 103
  Spicy, 101
Beverages. *See* Teas
Bitter melon, *54,* 56
  Beef and, in Black Bean Sauce, 103
Blachan (shrimp paste), 12
Black bean sauce
  Beef and Bitter Melon in, 103
  Clams in Chile-Garlic, 81
Black beans, salted, 10
Blanching vegetables, 7
Boiling
  Basic Wontons, 42
  noodles, 36–37
  "Squirrel Fish" With Szechuan Sweet-Sour Chile Sauce, 122, *123*
Bok Choy, Baby, Szechuan Braised Beef Noodles With, 108, *109*
Bon Bon Chicken Salad, 66, *67*
Boning chicken wings, 22
Boning a whole chicken, 119
Brad Borel's Cajun Popcorn, *30–31,* 32
Breads
  Chinese Sweet Yeast Bread Dough, 47
  Crisp Green Onion Pancakes, 52, *53*
  Pappadams, 92, *93*
  Sesame Pocket, 112, *113*
  Sweet Silver-Thread Rolls, 47

Broccoli, Chinese. *See* Kale, Chinese
Brown bean sauce, 10, *13*
Brussels sprouts
  Stir-fried Brussels Sprouts, Pancetta, and Parmesan, 61
  Twice-Cooked Pork With, 99

C

Cabbage
  Aunt Carrie's Chinese Pickled Vegetables, 107
  Kuo Teh, 26–27
  Mandarin-Style Orange-Duck Salad, 70, *71*
  in Peking Burrito, 44, *45*
Cabbage, preserved Tientsin, 12, *13*
  Country Pâté and Preserved Cabbage, 97
Cajun Dirty Rice, 48
Cashews
  Classic Cashew Chicken, 87
  Kung Pao Shrimp With, *front cover,* 80
Cellophane noodles. *See* Bean thread noodles
Chicken
  Basic Chinese Steamed, 90
  Bon Bon Chicken Salad, 66, *67*
  boning chicken wings, 22
  boning whole, 119
  Chinese Asparagus Beans With, 57
  Classic Cashew, 87
  Eight-Jewel, 120
  Fried Chicken and Cream Gravy, 88
  gizzards and livers, in Cajun Dirty Rice, 48
  in Hot-and-Sour Soup, 121
  Italian Sausage, Mushroom, and Bread Stuffing for, 114
  in Shrimp and Barbecued Pork Fried Rice, 43
  Singapore Curry Rice Stick Noodles, 38, *39*
  Steamed Chicken With Straw Mushrooms and Chinese Sausage, 85
  Tamales con Mole Verde de Pepitas, 30
  in Tamarind Shrimp Dip With Sizzling Rice Cakes, 16–17
  Tandoori Chicken With Pappadams, 92, *93*
  Thai Angel Wings, 22–23
  Thai Stir-fried Chicken With Basil, 90
  in Thai Stir-fried Flat Rice Noodles, 48, *49*
  Walnut Chicken With Peking Sauce, 83
Chicken Marinade, Basic, 57
Chicken Strip Marinade, 121
Chile oil, Asian hot, 8
Chile paste with garlic, 10, *13*
Chiles, 11, *13*
  Ants Climbing a Tree, 100
  Beef With Thai Red Curry Peanut Sauce, 104
  charring, 80
  Clams in Chile-Garlic Black Bean Sauce, 81
  in Corn, Roasted Peppers, and Avocado, 60

Chiles *(continued)*
  in Dry-Fried Spicy Shredded Beef, 101
  Seared Beef With Chile Hoisin Sauce, 106
  Singapore Chile Crab, 114–115
  Tamales con Mole Verde de Pepitas, 30
  Thai Chile-Pork Omelet, *title page,* 43
Chile sauce, Sriracha, 10
Chilled Noodles in Peking Meat Sauce, 51, *53*
Chinese egg noodles. *See* Noodles
Chinese parsley. *See* Coriander
Chinese Sweet Yeast Bread Dough, 47
Chives, Garlic, Oysters With Eggs and, 76, *77*
Cilantro. *See* Coriander
Clams in Chile-Garlic Black Bean Sauce, 81
Classic Chinese Steamed Whole Fish, 78
Cleaning a wok, 6
Coating, Seasoned Corn Flour, 32
Coconut milk or cream, 8, *13*
  Beef With Thai Red Curry Peanut Sauce, 104
  Thai Red Curry Shellfish With Basil, 116
Coconut sugar (palm sugar), 11
Condiments, 8, *13*
  Crisp Fried Garlic or Shallot Flakes, 24
  Indian Raita, 25
  Peggy's Pineapple Salsa, 25
  Thai Sweet-and-Sour Cucumber Relish, 25
Cookies, Sugared Bow Ties, 52, *53*
Coriander, 11
  Mandarin-Style Orange-Duck Salad, 70, *71*
  Orange-Coriander Chile Sauce, 51
  Smoked Ham–Coriander Fried Wonton Soup, 68
Corn
  Corn, Roasted Peppers, and Avocado, 60
  Indonesian Corn-Shrimp Fritters, 26, *27*
  Seafood With Corn, Okra, and Tomatoes, 91
Corn Flour Coating, Seasoned, 32
Cornish Hen, Minced, Wrapped in Lettuce Cups, 120–121, *123*
Cornish Hen Marinade, 121
Cornstarch, 7, 8
Crab
  Curry Crab-Noodle Cakes, 91, *93*
  Ginger–Green Onion Crab Baked in the Shell, 118
  Singapore Chile, 114–115
  Southeast Asian–Style Soft-Shell, 74, *75*
  Vietnamese Crab Imperial Rolls, 69, *71*
Crayfish, Brad Borel's Cajun Popcorn, *30–31,* 32

Cream Gravy, Fried Chicken
    and, 88
Crêpes, Crispy Egg-Lace, 44
Crisp Fried Garlic or Shallot
    Flakes, 24
Crisp Fried Wontons, 33
Crisp Green Onion Pancakes,
    52, *53*
Crisp Sugared Walnuts, 120, *123*
Cucumber
    Indian Raita, 25
    Thai Sweet-and-Sour Cucumber
        Relish, 25
Curry
    Beef With Thai Red Curry
        Peanut Sauce, 104
    Curry Crab-Noodle Cakes,
        91, *93*
    Singapore Curry Rice Stick
        Noodles, 38, *39*
    Thai Red Curry Paste, 28
    Thai Red Curry Shellfish With
        Basil, 116

D
Dad's Whiskey Stir-fried Chinese
    Kale, 58
Deep-frying, 16
    Basic Wontons, 42
    Brad Borel's Cajun Popcorn,
        30-31, 32
    Classic Shrimp Toast, 19
    Crisp Fried Garlic or Shallot
        Flakes, 24
    Crisp Fried Wontons, 33
    Crisp Green Onion Pancakes,
        52, *53*
    Crisp Sugared Walnuts,
        120, *123*
    Curry Crab-Noodle Cakes,
        91, *93*
    Deep-fried Asparagus With
        Gazpacho Coulis, 58, *59*
    Deep-fried Mushrooms
        With Anchovy-Caper
        Rémoulade, 16
    Deep-fried Rice Stick
        Noodles, 38
    Fried Catfish With Chinese Hot
        Bean Sauce, 74
    Fried Chicken and Cream
        Gravy, 88
    Hawaiian Rice Stick Prawns, 25
    Indonesian Corn-Shrimp
        Fritters, 26, *27*
    Indonesian Potato and Beef
        Fritters, *30-31, 33*
    Kuo Teh, 26-27
    Lemon Pork With Gin and Black
        Sesame Seed, *98, 99*
    Mexican Sopaipillas With Ice
        Cream, 92, *93*
    Pappadams, 92, *93*
    Shrimp Mousse–Stuffed Roasted
        Peppers, 18-19
    Sizzling Mongolian Lamb, 106
    Sizzling Tangerine Scallops,
        116-117
    "Squirrel Fish" With Szechuan
        Sweet-Sour Chile Sauce,
        122, *123*
    Sugared Bow Ties, 52, *53*
    Suppli al Telefono, 29
    Taiwan Fried Pork Chop
        Noodles, 96

E
Egg Net Pillows, 20-21
Egg noodles, *34, 36*. *See also*
    Noodles
Eggplant, Asian, *54, 56*
    Eggplant Szechuan Style, *62, 63*
    Grilled, 116
    Hunan Eggplant Salad, 66
    Szechuan Garlic-Eggplant Soup
        With Scallop Noodles, 70, *71*
Eggs
    Barbecued Pork and Shrimp Egg
        Fu Yung, 45
    Coin Purse Eggs With Oyster
        Sauce, 46
    Crispy Egg-Lace Crêpes, 44
    Egg Net Pillows, 20-21,
        back cover
    Oysters With Eggs and Garlic
        Chives, 76, *77*
    Savory Steamed Shrimp Egg
        Custard, 64
    Thai Chile-Pork Omelet,
        title page, 43

Deep-frying *(continued)*
    Tamarind Shrimp Dip With
        Sizzling Rice Cakes, 16-17
    Thai Angel Wings, 22-23
    Thai Fish Fillets With Tamarind-
        Ginger Sauce, 78, *79*
    tofu, 55
    Vietnamese Crab Imperial Rolls,
        69, *71*
Desserts
    Fresh Chilled Mango, Singapore
        Style, 108, *109*
    Ginger-Peach Sorbet, 122, *123*
    Mexican Sopaipillas With Ice
        Cream, 92, *93*
    Sugared Bow Ties, 52, *53*
Dim sum, 16. *See also* Dumplings
Dips and dipping sauces, 10, *13*
    Hoisin Sauce Dip, 24
    Nuoc Cham Dipping Sauce,
        69, *71*
    Oil-Seared Ginger Sauce, 24
    Shaved Pineapple Sweet-and-
        Sour Sauce, 33
    Soy Vinegar Chile, 26, 27
    Tamarind Shrimp Dip With
        Sizzling Rice Cakes, 16-17
    Thai Hot Sauce (Nam Prik), 25
    Thai Sweet Garlic Dipping
        Sauce, 24
Dried ingredients, stir-frying, 8
Dry-frying, 101
    Dry-Fried Prawns in the Shell,
        80, 81
    Dry-Fried Spicy Shredded
        Beef, 101
    Szechuan Dry-Fried Green
        Beans, *64,* 65
Duck
    Mandarin-Style Orange-Duck
        Salad, 70, *71*
    Pasta With Tea-Smoked Duck,
        Grilled Mushrooms, and
        Arugula, 88, *89*
    Peking Burrito, 44, *45*
    Stir-fried Cantonese Roast Duck
        With Pineapple, 84
    Tea-Smoked, 86-87
Dumplings
    Barbecued Pork Buns, 40-41
    Kuo Teh, 26-27
    Steamed Siu Mai, 32

Eight-Jewel Chicken, 120
Eight-Jewel Rice Stuffing, 114
Entertaining, dishes for, 112-22
Equipment
    kadhai (Indian-style wok), 28
    for steaming, *4, 82-83*
    woks, 6
Escarole Salad, Wilted, With Fried
    Polenta Sticks, 66-67

F
Fillings
    See also Stuffings
    Basic Shrimp Mousse, 18-19
    Basic Wonton, 42
    Pine Nut–Spinach, 107
Fish
    Classic Chinese Steamed
        Whole, 78
    Fried Catfish With Chinese Hot
        Bean Sauce, 74
    Seafood With Corn, Okra, and
        Tomatoes, 91
    "Squirrel Fish" With Szechuan
        Sweet-Sour Chile Sauce,
        122, *123*
    Thai Fish Fillets With Tamarind-
        Ginger Sauce, 78, *79*
Fish sauce, Thai (*nam pla*), 10, *13*
Five-spice powder, 11
Flat rice noodles, *34,* 37
    Thai Stir-Fried (Pad Thai),
        48, *49*
Fresh Chilled Mango, Singapore
    Style, 108, *109*
Fried Catfish With Chinese Hot
    Bean Sauce, 74
Fritters
    Indonesian Corn-Shrimp, 26, *27*
    Indonesian Potato and Beef,
        30-31, 33

G
Galangal, 11
Garlic
    Crisp Fried Garlic or Shallot
        Flakes, 24
    Gambas al Ajillo, 29
    seasoning oil with, 7, 8
    Thai Sweet Garlic Dipping
        Sauce, 24
Garlic Chives, Oysters With Eggs
    and, 76, *77*
Garnishes
    Crisp Fried Garlic or Shallot
        Flakes, 24
    Crispy Egg-Lace Crêpes, 44
    Gazpacho Coulis, Deep-fried
        Asparagus With, 58, *59*
Ghee, 8
Ginger, *14,* 56
    Ginger–Green Onion Crab
        Baked in the Shell, 118
    Ginger Marinade, 115
    Ginger-Peach Sorbet, 122, *123*
    Oil-Seared Ginger Sauce, 24
    seasoning oil with, 7, 8
Ginger, Siamese (*galangal*), 11
Glass noodles. *See* Bean thread
    noodles
Glutinous rice, *34,* 96, 107, 114
Golden needles. *See* Lily buds,
    dried
Green beans, Szechuan Dry-Fried,
    64, 65

Green onion
    Crisp Green Onion Pancakes,
        52, *53*
    Oil-Seared Ginger Sauce, 24
    seasoning oil with, 7, 8
Grilled Asian Eggplant, 116
Grilled Sweet Soy Mushrooms, 88

H
Ham
    Singapore Curry Rice Stick
        Noodles, 38, *39*
    Smoked Ham–Coriander Fried
        Wonton Soup, 68
Hawaiian Rice Stick Prawns, 25
Hoisin sauce, 10
    Chile, Seared Beef With, 106
    Hoisin Sauce Dip, 24
Honey Butter, 92
Hot-and-Sour Seasoning, 121
Hot-and-Sour Soup, 121
Hot bean sauce, 10
    Lamb and Leeks With, 104
Hot chile oil, 8
Hunan Eggplant Salad, 66

I
Iced Lemongrass Tea, 70, *71*
Indian Raita, 25
Indonesian Corn-Shrimp Fritters,
    26, *27*
Indonesian Potato and Beef
    Fritters, *30-31, 33*
Ingredients, 8, 10-14
    noodles, *34, 36-37*
    rice paper wrappers, 37
    wonton wrappers, 37
Italian Sausage, Mushroom, and
    Bread Stuffing, 114

J, K
Jaggery (palm sugar), 11
Kaffir lime, 11
Kale, Chinese, 56
    Dad's Whiskey Stir-fried, 58
Kapi (shrimp paste), 12
Kha (galangal), 11
Kung Pao Shrimp With Cashews,
    front cover, 80
Kuo Teh, 26-27

L
Lamb
    Lamb and Leeks With Hot Bean
        Sauce, 104
    Rolled Lamb Chops With
        Mustard-Rosemary Sauce,
        102, 103
    Sizzling Mongolian, 106
Leeks, seasoning oil with, 8
Lemon-Gin Sauce, 99
Lemongrass, 11
    Iced Lemongrass Tea, 70, *71*
Lemon Pork With Gin and Black
    Sesame Seed, *98, 99*
Lettuce Cups, Minced Cornish Hen
    Wrapped in, 120-121, *123*
Lily buds, dried, 11
    in Hot-and-Sour Soup, 121
Lime, Kaffir, 11
Lo Mein Noodles With Barbecued
    Pork and Bean Sprouts, *front
    cover,* 38-39
Long beans, Chinese, *54, 56*
    Chinese Asparagus Beans With
        Chicken, 57
Lotus root, 54
    Mom's Stir-fried Fresh, 58-59

125

M

Mandarin Fried Rice, 39
Mandarin Pancakes, 115
  Peking Burrito, 44, *45*
Mandarin-Style Orange-Duck
  Salad, 70, *71*
Mango, Fresh Chilled, Singapore
  Style, 108, *109*
Marinades
  Basic Chicken, 57
  Beef, 103
  Chicken Strip, 121
  Cornish Hen, 121
  Ginger, 115
  Mongolian Lamb, 106
  Mustard-Rosemary, 103
  Pork, 100
  Pork Chop, 96
  Pork Strip, 58–59
  Scallop, 116–17
  Spicy Beef, 101
  techniques with, 7
Meats, 95–108
  See also specific kinds
  moistening, 7
  stir-frying techniques, 7, 8
Mee Krob, 44
Menu planning, 36
  for entertaining, 112
  soups and salads in, 65
  steaming in, 82
Menus
  Classic Chinese Lunch,
    51–52, *53*
  An Elegant Dinner,
    120–122, *123*
  International Cocktail Party,
    28–33, *31*
  Light Sunday Buffet, 91–92, *93*
  Light Theater Supper for Six,
    107–108, *109*
  A Refreshing Summer Brunch,
    69–70, *71*
Mexican Sopaipillas With Ice
  Cream, 92, *93*
Mirror noodles. *See* Bean
  thread noodles
Mo-er (wood ears), 12, *13*
Mole Verde de Pepitas, 30
Mongolian Lamb Marinade, 106
Muk-yee (wood ears), 12, *13*
Mung bean noodles. *See* Bean
  thread noodles
Mushrooms, 12, *13, 14*
  Deep-fried, With Anchovy-Caper
    Rémoulade, 16
  Grilled Sweet Soy, 88
  in Hot-and-Sour Soup, 121
  Italian Sausage, Mushroom, and
    Bread Stuffing, 114
  Pasta With Tea-Smoked Duck,
    Grilled Mushrooms, and
    Arugula, 88, *89*
  Sautéed Wild Mushrooms With
    Marsala, 62
  Steamed Chicken With Straw
    Mushrooms and Chinese
    Sausage, 85
  in Vietnamese Crab Imperial
    Rolls, 69, *71*
Mu Shu Pork With Mandarin
  Pancakes, 115
Mussels and Pasta With Saffron-
  Ginger Cream Sauce, *76, 77*
Mustard cabbage, Chinese, in Aunt
  Carrie's Chinese Pickled
  Vegetables, 107
Mustard greens, Szechuan
  preserved, 11

Mustard greens, Chinese. *See* Kale,
  Chinese
Mustard greens, Szechuan
  preserved, 11
  Country Pâté and Preserved
    Mustard Greens, 97
  in Taiwan Fried Pork Chop
    Noodles, 96
Mustard-Rosemary Marinade, 103

N

Nam pla (Thai fish sauce), 10, *13*
Nam Prik (Thai Hot Sauce), 25
Noodles, *34,* 36–37
  Basic Wontons, 42
  Bon Bon Chicken Salad, 66, *67*
  Chilled Noodles in Peking Meat
    Sauce, 51, *53*
  Curry Crab-Noodle Cakes,
    91, *93*
  Deep-fried Rice Stick
    Noodles, 38
  Lo Mein Noodles With
    Barbecued Pork and Bean
    Sprouts, *front cover,*
    38–39
  Mussels and Pasta With Saffron-
    Ginger Cream Sauce, *76, 77*
  Pasta With Tea-Smoked Duck,
    Grilled Mushrooms, and
    Arugula, 88, *89*
  Shallow-Fried Noodle Cakes, 47
  Singapore Curry Rice Stick
    Noodles, 38, *39*
  Szechuan Braised Beef Noodles
    With Baby Bok Choy,
    108, *109*
  Szechuan Garlic-Eggplant Soup
    With Scallop Noodles, 70, *71*
  Taiwan Fried Pork Chop
    Noodles, 96
  Thai Crisp-Fried Rice Noodles
    (Mee Krob), 44
  Thai Stir-Fried Flat Rice Noodles
    (Pad Thai), 48, *49*
  Tomato Beef With Shallow-Fried
    Noodle Cakes, 104–5
  types of, *13, 34,* 36–37
  Wonton Noodles With Orange-
    Coriander Chile Sauce,
    50, 51
Nuoc Cham Dipping Sauce, 69, *71*

O

Oils, 8, *13*
  stir-frying techniques, 7, 8
Oil-Seared Ginger Sauce, 24
Okra, Seafood With Corn, Okra,
  and Tomatoes, 91
Oranges
  Mandarin-Style Orange-Duck
    Salad, 70, *71*
  Orange-Coriander Chile
    Sauce, 51
  Thai Galloping Horses, 29,
    30–31
Oysters
  Oysters, Bell Peppers, Onions,
    and Bacon, 74–75
  Oysters With Eggs and Garlic
    Chives, 76, *77*
Oysters, dried, 11
  in Minced Cornish Hens
    Wrapped in Lettuce Cups,
    120–121, *123*
Oyster sauce, 10, *13*
  Sesame, 58

P

Pad Thai, 48, *49*
Palm sugar, 11
Panaeng Nuea, 104
Pancakes
  Crisp Green Onion, 52, *53*
  Crispy Egg-Lace Crêpes, 44
  Mandarin, 115
  Sylvia's Potato Latkes, 65
  Tomato Beef With Shallow-Fried
    Noodle Cakes, 104–5
Pancetta. See Bacon or *pancetta*
Panfrying
  Oysters, Bell Peppers, Onions,
    and Bacon, 74–75
  Oysters With Eggs and Garlic
    Chives, 76, *77*
  Shallow-Fried Noodle Cakes, 47
  Southeast Asian–Style Soft-
    Shell Crab, 74, *75*
Pappadams, 92, *93*
Parsley, Chinese. *See* Coriander
Pasta. *See* Noodles
Peaches, Ginger-Peach Sorbet,
  122, *123*
Peanut oil, 8, *13*
Peanut Sauce, Thai Red Curry,
  Beef With, 104
Pearl Balls With Pine Nut–Spinach
  Filling, 107, *109*
Pea starch noodles. *See* Bean
  thread noodles
Peggy's Pineapple Salsa, 25
Peking Burrito, 44, *45*
Peking Meat Sauce, Chilled
  Noodles in, 51, *53*
Peppercorns, Szechuan, 11–12
Peppers, chile. *See* Chiles
Peppers, red or green bell
  Aunt Carrie's Chinese Pickled
    Vegetables, 107
  Corn, Roasted Peppers, and
    Avocado, 60
  in Kung Pao Shrimp With
    Cashews, *front cover,* 80
  Oysters, Bell Peppers, Onions,
    and Bacon, 74–75
  Shrimp Mousse–Stuffed Roasted
    Peppers, 18–19
Pickled Vegetables, Aunt Carrie's
  Chinese, 107
Pineapple
  Peggy's Pineapple Salsa, 25
  Shaved Pineapple Sweet-and-
    Sour Sauce, 33
  Stir-fried Cantonese Roast
    Duck With, 84
Pine nuts, *13*
  Pine Nut–Spinach Filling, 107
  Snow Peas, Pine Nuts, and
    Chinese Sausage, *9,* 57
Pla Cien, 78, *79*
Plum-Orange Vinaigrette, 70
Plums, salted, *13*
Polenta Sticks, Fried, 67
Pommes de Terres Sautées, 61
Pork, 96–100
  See also Sausage, Chinese
  Ants Climbing a Tree, 100
  Barbecued Pork Buns, 40–41,
    back cover
  Barbecued Pork and Shrimp
    Egg Fu Yung, 45
  in Basic Wonton Filling, 42
  in Cajun Dirty Rice, 48
  Chilled Noodles in Peking Meat
    Sauce, 51, *53*
  Egg Net Pillows, 20–21,
    back cover

Pork *(continued)*
  Lemon Pork With Gin and Black
    Sesame Seed, *98,* 99
  Lo Mein Noodles With
    Barbecued Pork and Bean
    Sprouts, 38–39
  in Ma Pocked Tofu, 63
  Mom's Stir-Fried Fresh Lotus
    Root (Siu Chao), 58–59
  Mu Shu Pork With Mandarin
    Pancakes, 115
  Pearl Balls With Pine Nut–
    Spinach Filling, 107, *109*
  Shrimp and Barbecued Pork
    Fried Rice, 43
  Singapore Curry Rice Stick
    Noodles, 38, *39*
  Spicy Pork Shreds Stuffed in
    Sesame Pocket Bread,
    112, *113*
  Steamed Chinese Country
    Pâté, 96–97
  Steamed Pork Spareribs With
    Toasted Rice Crumbs, 96, *97*
  Steamed Siu Mai, 32
  in Szechuan Dry-Fried Green
    Beans, *64,* 65
  Taiwan Fried Pork Chop
    Noodles, 96
  Thai Chile-Pork Omelet, 43
  Thai Galloping Horses, 29,
    30–31
  Twice-Cooked Pork With
    Brussels Sprouts, 99
  in Vietnamese Crab Imperial
    Rolls, 69, *71*
  Watercress Wonton Soup,
    52, *53*
Pork Marinade, 100
Pork Strip Marinade, 58–59
Potatoes
  Indonesian Potato and Beef
    Fritters, *30–31,* 33
  Pommes de Terres Sautées, 61
  Sylvia's Potato Latkes, 65
Potstickers, Kuo Teh, 26–27
Potsticker Wrappers, 26, 27
Poultry, 83, 83–90
  See also Chicken; Duck
  Italian Sausage, Mushroom, and
    Bread Stuffing for, 114
  Minced Cornish Hen Wrapped in
    Lettuce Cups, 120–121, *123*
Pumpkin seed, Tamales con Mole
  Verde de Pepitas, 30

R

Radishes, preserved, 12
Raita, Indian, 25
Rice
  Cajun Dirty, 48
  Eight-Jewel Rice Stuffing, 114
  Mandarin Fried, 39
  Pearl Balls With Pine Nut–
    Spinach Filling, 107, *109*
  Perfect, 37
  Rice Pilaf With Parmesan
    Cream, *42,* 43
  Shrimp and Barbecued Pork
    Fried, 43
  Sizzling Rice Cakes, 68
  Sizzling Rice Soup, 68
  Steamed Pork Spareribs With
    Toasted Rice Crumbs, 96, *97*
  steaming Chinese sausage
    on, 98
  Suppli al Telefono, 29
Rice cakes, dried, *13, 14*

Rice noodles. *See* Flat rice noodles;
  Rice stick noodles
Rice paper wrappers, 37
Rice stick noodles, *34, 37*
  Deep-fried, 38
  Singapore Curry, 38, *39*
  Thai Crisp-Fried (Mee Krob), 44
Rice wine, Shaoxing, *13*
Rolled Lamb Chops With Mustard-
  Rosemary Sauce, *102,* 103

S
Saffron-Ginger Cream Sauce,
  Mussels and Pasta With,
  76, 77
Salad dressings
  Hunan Vinaigrette, 66
  Plum-Orange Vinaigrette, 70
  Toasted Sesame Paste
    Dressing, 66
Salads, 65
  Bon Bon Chicken, 66, *67*
  Hunan Eggplant, 66
  Mandarin-Style Orange-Duck,
    70, *71*
  Wilted Escarole Salad With Fried
    Polenta Sticks, 66–67
Salsa, Peggy's Pineapple, 25
Salt, seasoning oil with, 8
Salted black beans, 10
Sauces
  Cream Gravy, 88
  Egg Fu Yung, 45
  Lemon-Gin, 99
  Orange-Coriander Chile
    Sauce, 51
  Peggy's Pineapple Salsa, 25
  Sesame Oyster, 58
  Shaved Pineapple Sweet-
    and-Sour, 33
  Sweet-and-Sour Tomato, 105
  Szechuan Sweet-Sour Chile, 122
  Tamarind, 78, *79*
  Tangerine, 117
  thickening, 8
Sausage, Chinese, 98
  Country Pâté and Sausage, 97
  Snow Peas, Pine Nuts,
    and, *9, 57*
  Steamed Chicken With Straw
    Mushrooms and, 85
  steaming with rice, 63
  in Stir-fried Spinach, 63
Sausage, Italian, Mushroom,
    and Bread Stuffing, 114
Sautéing
  Fried Catfish With Chinese Hot
    Bean Sauce, 74
  Oysters, Bell Peppers, Onions,
    and Bacon, 74–75
  Pommes de Terres Sautées, 61
  Rice Pilaf With Parmesan
    Cream, *42,* 43
  Rolled Lamb Chops With
    Mustard-Rosemary
    Sauce, 103
  Sautéed Wild Mushrooms With
    Marsala, 62
  Southeast Asian–Style Soft-Shell
    Crab, 74, *75*
Scallop Marinade, 116–117
Scallops
  in Mussels and Pasta With
    Saffron-Ginger Cream Sauce,
    76, 77
  Sizzling Tangerine, 116–117

Seafood With Corn, Okra, and
    Tomatoes, 91
Seared Beef With Chile Hoisin
    Sauce, 106
Seasoned Corn Flour Coating, 32
Seasonings, 10–12, *13*
  stir-frying techniques, 7, 8
Seasoning a wok, 6
Seaweed, agar-agar, 10, *13*
Sesame oil, Asian, 8, *13*
Sesame Oyster Sauce, 58
Sesame paste, Chinese, 10, *13*
Sesame Pocket Bread, 112, *113*
Sesame Seed, Black, Lemon Pork
    With Gin and, *98, 99*
Shallot Flakes, Crisp Fried, 24
Shallow-Fried Noodle Cakes, 47
  Tomato Beef With, 104–5
Shaoxing rice wine, *13*
Shaved Pineapple Sweet-and-
    Sour Sauce, 33
Shellfish
  See also Crab; Oysters; Scallops;
    Shrimp or prawns
  Brad Borel's Cajun Popcorn,
    30–31, 32
  Clams in Chile-Garlic Black
    Bean Sauce, 81
  Mussels and Pasta With Saffron-
    Ginger Cream Sauce, *76, 77*
  Thai Red Curry Shellfish With
    Basil, 116
Shiitake mushrooms, 12, *14*
Shrimp, dried, 12, *13, 14*
  in Ants Climbing a Tree, 100
  in Szechuan Dry-Fried Green
    Beans, *64,* 65
  in Thai Stir-fried Flat Rice
    Noodles, 48, *49*
Shrimp paste, 12
Shrimp or prawns
  Barbecued Pork and Shrimp Egg
    Fu Yung, 45
  in Basic Wonton Filling, 42
  Classic Shrimp Toast, 19
  Dry-Fried Prawns in the Shell,
    80, 81
  Gambas al Ajillo, 29
  Hawaiian Rice Stick Prawns, 25
  Indonesian Corn-Shrimp
    Fritters, 26, *27*
  Kung Pao Shrimp With Cashews,
    front cover, 80
  in Mussels and Pasta With
    Saffron-Ginger Cream Sauce,
    76, 77
  Natalie's New Orleans
    Barbecued Shrimp, *18,* 19
  Pearl Balls With Pine Nut–
    Spinach Filling, 107, *109*
  Savory Steamed Shrimp Egg
    Custard, 64
  Seafood With Corn, Okra, and
    Tomatoes, 91
  Shrimp and Barbecued Pork
    Fried Rice, 43
  Shrimp Mousse–Stuffed Roasted
    Peppers, 18–19
  Singapore Curry Rice Stick
    Noodles, 38, *39*
  Steamed Siu Mai, 32
  Tamarind Shrimp Dip With
    Sizzling Rice Cakes, 16–17
  Thai Red Curry Shellfish With
    Basil, 116

Shrimp or Prawns *(continued)*
  in Thai Stir-fried Flat Rice
    Noodles, 48, *49*
  Singapore Chile Crab, 114–15
  Singapore Curry Rice Stick
    Noodles, 38, *39*
  Siu Chao, 58–59
  Sizzling Mongolian Lamb, 106
  Sizzling Rice Cakes, 68
  Sizzling Rice Soup, 68
  Sizzling Tangerine Scallops,
    116–17
Smoking, Tea-Smoked Duck,
    86–87
Snow peas, 54
  in Peking Burrito, 44, *45*
  Snow Peas, Pine Nuts, and
    Chinese Sausage, *9, 57,*
    back cover
Sopaipillas, Mexican, With Ice
    Cream, 92, *93*
Sorbet, Ginger-Peach, 122, *123*
Soups, 65
  Hot-and-Sour, 121
  Sizzling Rice, 68
  Smoked Ham–Coriander Fried
    Wonton, 68
  Szechuan Garlic-Eggplant Soup
    With Scallop Noodles, 70, *71*
  Watercress Wonton, 52, *53*
Southeast Asian–Style Soft-Shell
    Crab, 74–*75*
Soybean curd. *See* Tofu
Soy sauce, 10, *13*
Soy Vinegar Chile Dip, 26, *27*
Spicy Beef Marinade, 101
Spicy Pork Shreds Stuffed
    in Sesame Pocket Bread,
    112, *113*
Spinach
  Pearl Balls With Pine Nut–
    Spinach Filling, 107, *109*
  in Savory Steamed Shrimp Egg
    Custard, 64
  Stir-fried, 63
Spread, Honey Butter, 92
Spring rolls, Vietnamese Crab
    Imperial Rolls, 69, *71*
Squid, in Thai Red Curry Shellfish
    With Basil, 116
Star anise, 12
Steamers, *4,* 82–83
Steaming, 81–83
  Barbecued Pork Buns, 40–41
  Basic Chinese Steamed
    Chicken, 90
  Bon Bon Chicken Salad, 66, *67*
  Chinese sausage, 63, 98
  Classic Chinese Steamed Whole
    Fish, 78
  Eight-Jewel Chicken, 120
  Hunan Eggplant Salad, 66
  Mandarin Pancakes, 115
  Mussels and Pasta With Saffron-
    Ginger Cream Sauce, *76, 77*
  Savory Steamed Shrimp Egg
    Custard, 64
  Steamed Chicken With Straw
    Mushrooms and Chinese
    Sausage, 85
  Steamed Chinese Country Pâté,
    96–97
  Steamed Pork Spareribs With
    Toasted Rice Crumbs, 96, *97*
  Steamed Siu Mai, 32
  Sweet Silver-Thread Rolls, 47

Tamales con Mole Verde de
    Pepitas, 30
techniques, 81–83
Stir-frying
  Ants Climbing a Tree, 100
  Barbecued Pork and Shrimp Egg
    Fu Yung, 45
  Beef and Bitter Melon in Black
    Bean Sauce, 103
  Beef With Thai Red Curry
    Peanut Sauce, 104
  Cajun Dirty Rice, 48
  Chilled Noodles in Peking Meat
    Sauce, 51, *53*
  Chinese Asparagus Beans With
    Chicken, 57
  Classic Cashew Chicken, 87
  Coin Purse Eggs With Oyster
    Sauce, 46
  Corn, Roasted Peppers, and
    Avocado, 60
  Dad's Whiskey Stir-fried Chinese
    Kale, 58
  Egg Net Pillows, 20–21,
    back cover
  Eggplant Szechuan Style, *62,* 63
  Gambas al Ajillo, 29
  Ginger–Green Onion Crab
    Baked in the Shell, 118
  Lamb and Leeks With Hot Bean
    Sauce, 104
  Mandarin Fried Rice, 39
  Ma Pocked Tofu, 63
  Minced Cornish Hens Wrapped
    in Lettuce Cups,
    120–121, *123*
  Mom's Stir-fried Fresh Lotus
    Root (Siu Chao), 58–59
  Mu Shu Pork With Mandarin
    Pancakes, 115
  Natalie's New Orleans
    Barbecued Shrimp, *18,* 19
  Oysters With Eggs and Garlic
    Chives, 76, *77*
  Peking Burrito, 44, *45*
  Rice Pilaf With Parmesan
    Cream, *42,* 43
  Seafood With Corn, Okra,
    and Tomatoes, 91
  Seared Beef With Chile
    Hoisin Sauce, 106
  Shrimp and Barbecued Pork
    Fried Rice, 43
  Singapore Chile Crab, 114–15
  Singapore Curry Rice Stick
    Noodles, 38, *39*
  Snow Peas, Pine Nuts, and
    Chinese Sausage, *9, 57,*
    back cover
  Spicy Pork Shreds Stuffed
    in Sesame Pocket Bread,
    112, *113*
  Stir-fried Brussels Sprouts,
    Pancetta, and Parmesan, 61
  Stir-fried Cantonese Roast Duck
    With Pineapple, 84
  Stir-fried Spinach, 63
  techniques, 7–8
  Thai Chile-Pork Omelet, 43
  Thai Crisp-Fried Rice Noodles
    (Mee Krob), 44
  Thai Galloping Horses, 29,
    30–31
  Thai Red Curry Shellfish With
    Basil, 116

Stir-frying (continued)
  Thai Stir-fried Chicken With
    Basil, 90
  Thai Stir-fried Flat Rice Noodles
    (Pad Thai), 48, *49*
  Tomato Beef With Shallow-Fried
    Noodle Cakes, 104–5
  Walnut Chicken With Peking
    Sauce, 83
Stock, adding to stir-fry, 8
Straw mushrooms, 12, *13*
Stuffings
  See also Fillings
  Eight-Jewel Rice, 114
  Italian Sausage, Mushroom,
    and Bread, 114
  wok techniques, 114
Suppli al Telefono, 29
Sweet-and-Sour Tomato
  Sauce, 105
Sylvia's Potato Latkes, 65
Szechuan Garlic-Eggplant Soup
  With Scallop Noodles, 70, *71*
Szechuan peppercorns, 11–12
Szechuan preserved vegetables, 11
Szechuan Sweet-Sour Chile Sauce,
  "Squirrel Fish" With,
    122, *123*

T
Tamales con Mole Verde
  de Pepitas, 30
Tamarind, 12
  Tamarind Sauce, 78, *79*
  Tamarind Shrimp Dip With
    Sizzling Rice Cakes, 16–17
  Tamarind Water, 24

Tandoori Chicken With
  Pappadams, 92, *93*
Tangerine peel, dried, 12
Tangerine Sauce, 117
Tangerine Scallops, Sizzling,
  116–17
Tapas, Gambas al Ajillo, 29
Teas
  chrysanthemum petal and
    jasmine, 51
  Iced Lemongrass, 70, *71*
  Tea-Smoked Duck, 86–87
  Tea-Smoking Mixture, 86–87
Techniques
  blanching vegetables, 7
  boning chicken wings, 22
  boning a whole chicken, 119
  charring chiles, 80
  cleaning a wok, 6
  cooking noodles, 36–37
  deep-frying, 16
  making barbecued pork
    buns, 40
  making egg nets, 20
  making stuffings in a wok, 114
  Perfect Rice, 37
  seasoning a wok, 6
  smoking, 86–87
  steaming, 81–83, 86
  stir-frying, 7–8
Thai Angel Wings, 22–23
Thai Chile-Pork Omelet, 43
Thai Crisp-Fried Rice Noodles
  (Mee Krob), 44
Thai curry pastes, 28
Thai Fish Fillets With Tamarind-
  Ginger Sauce (Pla Cien),
    78, *79*
Thai fish sauce (*nam pla*), 10, *13*

Thai Galloping Horses, 29, *30–31*
Thai Hot Sauce (Nam Prik), 25
Thai Red Curry Paste, 28
  Beef With Thai Red Curry
    Peanut Sauce, 104
  Thai Red Curry Shellfish With
    Basil, 116
Thai Stir-fried Chicken With
  Basil, 90
Thai Stir-fried Flat Rice Noodles
  (Pad Thai), 48, *49*
Thai Sweet-and-Sour Cucumber
  Relish, 25
Thai Sweet Garlic Dipping
  Sauce, 24
Tientsin cabbage. *See* Cabbage,
  preserved Tientsin
Tiger lily. *See* Lily buds, dried
Toasted Sesame Paste Dressing, 66
Tofu, 55
  fermented, as condiment, 10
  in Hot-and-Sour Soup, 121
  Ma Pocked, 63
  in Stir-fried Spinach, 63
  in Thai Stir-fried Flat Rice
    Noodles, 48, *49*
Tomato Beef With Shallow-Fried
  Noodle Cakes, 104–5
Tomato Sauce, Sweet-and-
  Sour, 105
Tools. *See* Equipment
Topping, Honey Butter, 92
Transparent noodles. *See* Bean
  thread noodles
Trasi (shrimp paste), 12
Twice-Cooked Pork With Brussels
  Sprouts, 99
Twice-Cooked Seasonings, 99

V, W, X, Y, Z
Vegetables, 56–65
  See also specific kinds
  Aunt Carrie's Chinese
    Pickled, 107
  Walnut Chicken With Peking
    Sauce, 83
  pre-cooking, 7, 58
  stir-frying techniques, 7, 8
Vietnamese Crab Imperial Rolls,
  69, *71*
Walnuts, Crisp Sugared, 120, *123*
Water chestnuts, 55
Watercress Wonton Soup, 52, *53*
Wilted Escarole Salad With Fried
  Polenta Sticks, 66–67
Wok
  deep-frying in, 16
  making stuffings in, 114
  smoking in, 86–87
  steaming in, 81–83, 86
  stir-frying in, 7–8
Woks and accessories, 6
Wontons
  Basic, 42
  Crisp Fried, 33
  Shaved Pineapple Sweet-and-
    Sour Sauce for, 33
  Smoked Ham–Coriander Fried
    Wonton Soup, 68
  Watercress Wonton Soup,
    52, *53*
  Wonton Noodles With Orange-
    Coriander Chile Sauce,
      50, 51
Wonton wrappers, 37
  Sugared Bow Ties, 52, *53*
Wood ears, 12, *13*
Yogurt, Indian Raita, 25

U.S. MEASURE AND METRIC MEASURE CONVERSION CHART

		Formulas for Exact Measures			Rounded Measures for Quick Reference		
	Symbol	When you know:	Multiply by:	To find:			
Mass (Weight)	oz	ounces	28.35	grams	1 oz		= 30 g
	lb	pounds	0.45	kilograms	4 oz		= 115 g
	g	grams	0.035	ounces	8 oz		= 225 g
	kg	kilograms	2.2	pounds	16 oz	= 1 lb	= 450 g
					32 oz	= 2 lb	= 900 g
					36 oz	= 2¼ lb	= 1,000g (1 kg)
Volume	tsp	teaspoons	5.0	milliliters	¼ tsp	= ¹⁄₂₄ oz	= 1 ml
	tbsp	tablespoons	15.0	milliliters	½ tsp	= ¹⁄₁₂ oz	= 2 ml
	fl oz	fluid ounces	29.57	milliliters	1 tsp	= ⅙ oz	= 5 ml
	c	cups	0.24	liters	1 tbsp	= ½ oz	= 15 ml
	pt	pints	0.47	liters	1 c	= 8 oz	= 250 ml
	qt	quarts	0.95	liters	2 c (1 pt)	= 16 oz	= 500 ml
	gal	gallons	3.785	liters	4 c (1 qt)	= 32 oz	= 1 liter
	ml	milliliters	0.034	fluid ounces	4 qt (1 gal)	= 128 oz	= 3¾ liter
Length	in.	inches	2.54	centimeters	⅜ in.		= 1 cm
	ft	feet	30.48	centimeters	1 in.		= 2.5 cm
	yd	yards	0.9144	meters	2 in.		= 5 cm
	mi	miles	1.609	kilometers	2½ in.		= 6.5 cm
	km	kilometers	0.621	miles	12 in. (1 ft)		= 30 cm
	m	meters	1.094	yards	1 yd		= 90 cm
	cm	centimeters	0.39	inches	100 ft		= 30 m
					1 mi		= 1.6 km
Temperature	°F	Fahrenheit	⁵⁄₉ (after subtracting 32)	Celsius	32°F		= 0°C
					68°F		= 20°C
	°C	Celsius	⁹⁄₅ (then add 32)	Fahrenheit	212°F		= 100°C
Area	in.²	square inches	6.452	square centimeters	1 in.²		= 6.5 cm²
	ft²	square feet	929.0	square centimeters	1 ft²		= 930 cm²
	yd²	square yards	8361.0	square centimeters	1 yd²		= 8360 cm²
	a.	acres	0.4047	hectares	1 a.		= 4050 m²